THE
BICENTENNIAL
GUIDE TO
THE
AMERICAN
REVOLUTION

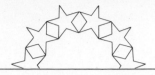

VOLUME TWO

THE BICENTENNIAL GUIDE TO THE AMERICAN REVOLUTION

THE MIDDLE COLONIES

Sol Stember

NEW YORK · 1974

SATURDAY REVIEW PRESS | E. P. DUTTON & CO., INC.

Maps by Ben Brown

Library of Congress Cataloging in Publication Data

Stember, Sol.
The bicentennial guide to the American Revolution.

Includes bibliographies.
CONTENTS: *v. 1. The war in the North.—v. 2. The middle Colonies.—
v. 3. The war in the South.*
1. United States—History—Revolution—Campaigns and battles.
2. United States—History—Revolution—Museums.
*3. United States—Description and travel—
1960–   —Guide-books. I. Title.*
E230.S74   973.3'3   73-23108

Published simultaneously in Canada by Clarke, Irwin & Company Limited, Toronto and Vancouver
ISBN: 0-8415-0314-1 (cloth)
ISBN: 0-8415-0316-8 (paper)
Designed by The Etheredges

To my wife, Rosaline,
who packed the bags, made the reservations,
helped with the research,
typed the manuscript, read the maps,
and shared the driving and walking all the way
from Lexington to Yorktown.

PUBLISHER'S NOTE: Much of the detailed factual information in this book has been and is subject to change. Visitors to historical sites are urged to check locally on times of opening and closing and on admission charges. They should also remember that highway route numbers may have changed since the book was compiled, especially for county and municipal routes. In addition, speed limits may have been altered in the attempt to conserve fuel. In some cases, continuing restoration on sites may have altered the sites from the way they are described here.

Boldface type has been used to designate major features on the sites—named structures and the like. *Boldface italics* point out smaller landmarks, mostly those without particular names.

CONTENTS

LIST OF MAPS   IX

ACKNOWLEDGMENTS   XI

PREFACE   XV

INTRODUCTION   3

I. WINTER OF HEARTBREAK AND VICTORY—
1776–77   9

THE JERSEY LANDING   9

WASHINGTON'S CROSSING: NEW JERSEY AND
PENNSYLVANIA   14

The Pennsylvania Encampment   16

Crossing the Delaware   21

THE BATTLES OF TRENTON: I   26

THE BATTLES OF TRENTON: II—ASSUNPINK CREEK   31

THE BATTLE OF PRINCETON   33

ROCKINGHAM: THE HOUSE AT ROCKY HILL   40

CAMPING OUT AT MORRISTOWN   43

Jockey Hollow   47

THE SPRINGFIELD RAID   52

II. BATTLE OF MONMOUTH   59

III. WAR IN THE OCEAN COUNTIES   74

IV. HOWE'S PHILADELPHIA CAMPAIGN—1777–78   85

COOCH'S BRIDGE   85
BATTLE OF THE BRANDYWINE   88
The Approaches   89
The Battle   96
PAOLI   110
VALLEY FORGE   115
THE PHILADELPHIA SITES   119
BATTLE OF GERMANTOWN   126
FORT MIFFLIN   132
FORT MERCER   138

V. SULLIVAN'S CAMPAIGN AGAINST THE IROQUOIS   142

SULLIVAN'S MARCH   143
Battle of Wyoming   149
NEWTOWN BATTLEFIELD   156
Sullivan's Advance   159

BIBLIOGRAPHY   163

INDEX   165

LIST OF MAPS

NEW JERSEY AND PENNSYLVANIA   4 – 5

PHILADELPHIA AND ENVIRONS   86

SULLIVAN'S MARCH   144 – 145

ACKNOWLEDGMENTS

(For all three volumes of the Guide)

No man is an island, particularly when he is trailblazing through territory new to him and most particularly when he attempts to produce a work of this extent. Space does not permit me to acknowledge all the help and advice I received from numerous historical societies and their members who were in touch with me at one time or another during the preparation and writing of this book. A few names, I confess, I either neglected to record or lost along the way. I am thinking particularly of the Francis Marion National Forest ranger who took us to the site of the Wambaw fight and the gentleman at the courthouse in Calhoun County, South Carolina, who finally put us on the right track to Fort Motte. To you and to others whom I may have neglected to mention, my sincere apologies. I am most grateful for your help and for the help of all those persons and organizations listed below by state or agency.

FEDERAL GOVERNMENT: John V. Vosburgh, Chief, Branch of Features, U.S. Department of the Interior, National Park Service. CANADA: David Lee, National Historic Sites Service; Sergeant F. C. Ouellette, College Militaire Royal, Saint-Jean, Quebec; Jacques Seguin, Regional Director, National and Historic Parks, Department of Indian Affairs and Northern Development. CONNECTICUT: Susan C. Finlay, Wethersfield; Preston R. Bassett, Ridgefield; Daniel M. McKeon, Ridgebury; Herbert Barbee, Connecticut Historical Commission. GEORGIA: James G. Bogle, Georgia Historical Commission; William Cox and Josephine Martin, Liberty County Historical Society; Carroll Hart, Director, Department of Arhives and History; Lilla M. Hawes, Director, Georgia Historical Society; Billy Townsend, Georgia Historical Commission; A. Ray Rowland,

Richmond County Historical Society; Dixon Hollingsworth, Sylvania; Mary Gregory Jewett, Director, Georgia Historical Commission; Savannah Chamber of Commerce. MAINE: John W. Briggs, State Park and Recreation Commission; White Nichols, President, Arnold Expedition Historical Society; Ellenore Doudiet, Curator, Wilson Museum, Castine. MASSACHUSETTS: John P. McMorrow, Boston Redevelopment Authority; Mary V. Darcy, Executive Secretary, Revolutionary War Bicentennial Commission; Bernard Wax, Director, American Jewish Historical Society; Bay State Historic League. NEW HAMPSHIRE: Dr. J. Duane Squires, Chairman, New Hampshire American Revolution Bicentennial Commission; Enzo Serafini, Chairman, New Hampshire Historical Commission; Ralph H. Morse, Department of Resources and Economic Development, Division of Economic Development. NEW JERSEY: Dirk Van Dommlan, Superintendent, Washington Crossing State Park; Frank Ender, Acting Superintendent, Monmouth Battlefield State Park; Milicent Feltus, Monmouth County Historical Association; Margaret M. Toolen, Fort Lee; Mary T. Hewitt, Hancock House, Hancock's Bridge; Isabelle Brooks, Office of Historic Sites, Department of Environmental Protection. NEW YORK: Willa Skinner, Fishkill Town Historian; May M. MacMorris, Argyle; Wallace F. Workmaster, Old Fort Ontario; Dole F. Watts, Thousand Islands State Park Commission; Jean Saunders, Curator and Mrs. Charles Franklin, Historian, Putnam County Historical Society; John H. Mead, Curator, New Windsor Cantonment; Marie C. Preston, County Historian, Livingston County; Raymond Safford, Historian, Staten Island; Virginia Moskowitz, Eastchester; William H. Seeger, Curator, Old Stone Fort, Schoharie; William Meuse, Superintendent, Saratoga National Historical Park; Albert Cerak, Miller House; Leon Dunn, Curator, Oriskany Battlefield; Frank Pabst, Plattsburgh; Dean Sinclair, Cherry Valley; Lieutenant Colonel Merle Sheffield (Ret.), West Point Military Academy; Lieutenant Colonel Patrick H. Dionne, Public Information Officer, West Point Military Academy; Mark Lawton, Director, New York State Historic Trust; Scott Robinson, White Plains; Josephine Gardner, Suffern; John Focht, Garrison; Mrs. Jankovsky, Middleburgh; New-York Historical Society. NORTH CAROLINA: Hugh B. Johnston, Jr., Wilson; Sharon Kuhne, Ruth Little, and Elizabeth Wilborn, Division of Historic Sites and Museums, Department of Archives and History; Edenton Chamber of Commerce; Duke Power Company (Cowan's Ford Hydroelectric Station); Catherine Hoskins, Summerfield; Tryon Palace Commission. PENNSYLVANIA: Mr. and Mrs. O. W. June, Paoli; Wilbur C. Kriebel, Administrative Director, Chester County American Independence Bicentennial Committee; Robert

I. Alotta, President, Schackamaxon Society, Inc.; William A. Hunter, Chief, Division of History, Pennsylvania Historical and Museum Commission; Edward Seladones, Department of Forest and Water, Pennsylvania Historical and Museum Commission. RHODE ISLAND: Albert T. Klyberg, Director, Rhode Island Historical Society; Richard Alan Dow, Rhode Island Development Council; Leonard J. Panaggio, Chief, Tourist Promotion Division of the Development Council. SOUTH CAROLINA: David V. Rosdahl, U.S. Department of Agriculture Forest Service, Columbia; Virginia Richard Sauls, Clarendon County Historical Commission; Dr. Thomas Marion Davis, Manning; Terry W. Libscomb, South Carolina Archives Department; W. Bruce Ezell, Ninety-six; J. Percival Petit, Isle of Palms; John Morall, Beaufort; Thomas Thornhill and Harrington Bissell, The Old Provost, Charleston; Charles Duell, Middleton Gardens; Helen McCormick, Gibbes Art Gallery, Charleston; Jean Ulmer, Calhoun County Library; Dr. and Mrs. P. Jenkins of James Island; Charleston Chamber of Commerce; Georgetown Chamber of Commerce; Camden Chamber of Commerce; Beaufort Chamber of Commerce. VIRGINIA: Howard A. MacCord, Sr., Archaeological Society of Virginia; Elie Weeks, President, Goochland County Historical Society; Charles E. Hatch, Jr., Yorktown Battlefield, Colonial National Historical Park; Mrs. Ashton W. Clark, Yorktown; J. R. Fishburne, Assistant Director and H. Peter Pudner, Virginia Historic Landmarks Commission; Rufus Easter, Executive Director, Charles Long, Program Director, and Mrs. S. Evans, Hampton Association for the Arts and Humanities; Colonel and Mrs. Boris Polanski, Hampton; Alf J. Mapp, Jr., Chairman, Portsmouth Revolutionary Bicentennial Commission; Robert F. Selden, Mathews County Historical Society; Edward A. Wyatt, Petersburg; Mr. and Mrs. John H. Wright, Goochland County; Mr. and Mrs. J. W. Seigfried, Point of Fork; Captain and Mrs. Igor Moravsky, Goochland County; Mabel Bellwood, Red Hill; Mary R. M. Goodwin, Williamsburg; Emily N. Spong, Portsmouth; Park Rouse, Director, Virginia Bicentennial Commission and Jamestown Foundation; Hampton Information Center.

I also wish to express my thanks to my publishers for staying with me all the way and especially to the editors without whose guidance and help I would never have finished: Steve Frimmer who got me started, Stephanie Erickson who pronounced the book acceptable, and Tom Davis who saw it through to the end. I have a particular word of thanks and admiration for Judy Bentley who cast an appraising, critical eye over the finished manuscript and guided me through a polishing process that improved the book immensely. I owe a special debt of gratitude to Joy

Meisels, Director of the New City Library, and to her staff for searching out and providing many of the books and other reference works upon which my research was based.

There is a bibliography in the usual place which lists most of the books, pamphlets, magazines, and other materials I consulted and read. Since my purpose was to produce a readable, practical history-travel guide, I was under no compulsion to uncover new, hitherto unknown or forgotten material or even to go to primary sources, which I did, nevertheless, when they were readily available. I found the standard works on the Revolution more than suitable for my purposes. I especially recommend to any reader who may want to go deeper into this fascinating period of American history Christopher Ward's *War of the Revolution,* the first two volumes of James Thomas Flexner's four-volume biography of *George Washington,* E. B. Greene's *The Revolutionary Generation,* John C. Miller's *Origins of the Revolution,* and Carl Van Doren's *Secret History of the Revolution.* The Arno Press reprint series of eyewitness accounts makes for wonderful reading. Mark Boatner's *Encyclopedia of the American Revolution* is the best ready reference book I have ever used and an excellent distillation of Revolutionary War fact and lore.

A word about maps. As much as possible, I tried to lay out routes and tours according to the standard road maps issued by the American Automobile Association and the oil companies. I found most of them adequate for generally finding my way, but naturally inadequate once we left the well-traveled, well-beaten paths. Surprisingly, some of these maps contradict each other in specific details such as the locations of certain towns and the routes followed by certain roads. Therefore, it is always a good idea to use more than one map. County maps were indispensable once state routes were left behind for the more remote, back-country areas in which many sites are located. They are cheap and can be obtained by writing to or visiting state highway and transportation departments in state capitals.

PREFACE

(To all three volumes of the Guide)

I fell in love with Clio, the Muse of history, the day I sat in George Washington's chair. At the time I was writing a series of children's educational television programs, and I had been assigned scripts on Washington, Lincoln, Benjamin Franklin, Columbus, Thanksgiving, and the Constitutional Convention of 1789.

The very first of these scripts to go on the air was the one about the Constitutional Convention. This was *live* television and I had obtained permission to use a number of props connected with the actual event, some of them of great historical value, including the chair Washington had sat in while he presided over the convention. It was that chair that stole my heart for the Muse. The chair was the focal point of the set and the script. I had traveled to Philadelphia to get it and had sworn to the authorities in charge that I would protect and defend it with my life, my fortune, and my sacred honor. It had come from Philadelphia by station wagon, carefully crated and heavily insured. It was then placed in my special care for twenty-four hours, no more.

When the show was over, I stood amid the cables and discarded scripts, looking at the chair. It had been left for last while the rest of the props were repacked and sent on their way to their rightful owners. For the moment, it was deserted and forgotten. The bright lights were dimmed now and the cameras were off, but briefly it had regained a measure of its former glory in the eyes of a far larger audience spread out across a nation far greater than anything the man who had made it famous could possibly have imagined or foreseen.

There is a design of the rayed sun carved into it, just above where

Washington's head must have touched when he sat in it, for though he was a tall man, this chair has a very high back. At the end of the convention, after all the wrangling and arguing and bad feelings had been resolved, and old and tired Franklin, who had worked so hard on the side of reason and compromise, rose to remark that all through the weary sessions he had been looking at that sun on the chairman's chair, wondering if it represented a rising or a setting sun. Now he knew, he said, that it was indeed a rising sun.

I too had been looking at the chair during the long hours of rehearsal and repetition and exasperation and frustration over the little but important mistakes and delays that made live television so alive, and then through the final, tension-filled half hour of the performance. What would it feel like, I thought, to sit in the chair that Washington sat in while he was making history? No one was paying any attention, and— what the hell!—it was my life, my fortune, and my sacred honor, right? I crossed the studio, stood in front of the chair for a moment, then turned and sat down.

I cannot pretend that during the few seconds I sat where Washington had sat I was transported back in time to 1789. I cannot say that I felt his eyes staring at me accusingly or felt a well-placed boot on my rear end as I got up and stepped away, which is what I really deserved. The prop men took the chair to its waiting crate, and a few minutes later it was on its way back to Philadelphia; I did not see it again—much less resume my seat—until I visited Philadelphia for this book. I do know that in that moment I felt a sense of continuity of Time and of Man.

I have had in my hands the letter Washington wrote from Valley Forge to Congress asking for money and supplies for his starving, freezing soldiers, the purse he left behind in Jumel Mansion, Lincoln's traveling desk on which he may have written the Gettysburg Address, an astrolabe used by a sixteenth-century Spanish navigator, a hand-illuminated Bible from the twelfth century, Ben Franklin's glass harmonium and a pair of his spectacles, Robert E. Lee's personal copy of Grant's surrender terms, Aaron Burr's dueling pistols, and a set of "running irons" used by rustlers in the 1880s. I have walked on the field where Pickett led his famous charge (in fact, I slept in a motel on that field), stood on Jefferson Rock and looked at much the same view of Harpers Ferry that Jefferson saw long before John Brown made the place famous, touched the stones of the Roman Forum, and felt the pavement of Pompeii under my feet while I listened with my eyes closed for the lost sound of chariot wheels. Still waiting for me are the ruins of Luxor, the fortress on Masada, the climb up the sacred hill to the oracle at Delphi, and the descent into the caves of Lascaux.

This book is for everyone who feels that same sense of continuity, in an American context. This book is an invitation to walk where Washington, Lafayette, Alexander Hamilton, Benedict Arnold, Daniel Morgan, Benjamin Franklin, Thomas Jefferson, Ethan Allen, and Molly Pitcher and all that host of men and women walked who fought and died long before we were born, but who still live in the stones and buildings and hills and fields they touched and held in their eyes. This book is a guide and a passport to a far country in a time past that is in a sense still with us. I have been there myself, visiting all the places I describe in this book. I invite you to follow.

VOLUME TWO

THE MIDDLE COLONIES

INTRODUCTION

New Jersey, the scene of two major campaigns and three decisive battles, not to mention a number of smaller and less crucial skirmishes, raids, and massacres, has been called by some historians "the cockpit of the Revolution." Strategically speaking, it was the site of some of the most important military maneuvering of the war, particularly during 1777–78. Both of the major campaigns centered around the control of Philadelphia, the political capital of the Revolution; the outcome of two of the battles determined the continued existence of the Continental Army and the Revolution itself.

It was in New Jersey that the revolutionary cause experienced its darkest hours; paradoxically, this was the period during which Washington redeemed himself as commander in chief by a display of brilliance unexpected and unprecedented. During those trying months he *was* the Revolution, and through the powers Congress invested in him he was also the government of the moment, to all intents and purposes. That he did not abuse those powers, but relinquished them willingly, indeed happily, and that he kept his faith in the American cause despite private misgivings, and continued to carry the fight forward almost alone is proof of the man's extraordinary strength and character.

After his defeat at Yorktown, Cornwallis is reported to have told Washington: "Fame will gather your brightest laurels from the banks of the Delaware rather than from the Chesapeake."

Between 1770 and 1780 New Jersey's population rose from 117,000 to 119,000. The western part of the state was home for a predominantly Quaker group who had become well-to-do land owners since the colony's

NEW JERSEY and PENNSYLVANIA

1 Alpine Landing
2 Ft. Lee Site
3 Washington's Crossing
4 Continental Camp
5 Coryell's Ferry Site
6 Bear Tavern
7 Battles of Trenton Sites
8 Princeton Battlefield
9 "Rockingham" Washington's Hq.
10 Jockey Hollow
11 Elizabeth Sites
12 Liberty Hall
13 Connecticut Farms
14 Caldwell Parsonage
15 Springfield Battle—Cannonball House
16 Tennent Church
17 Monmouth Battlefield
18 Englishtown Inn
19 Pulaski Massacre
20 Potter's Tavern
21 Greenwich Tea Party
22 Quinton Bridge
23 Hancock Massacre
24 Cooch's Bridgeton
25 British Campsites
26 British Army Divides
27 Anvil Tavern
28 Kennett Meeting House

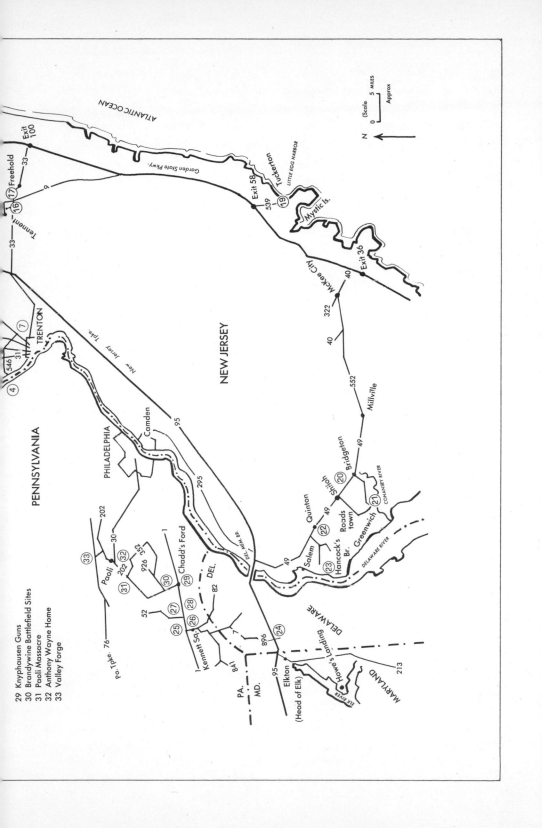

29 Knyphausen Guns
30 Brandywine Battlefield Sites
31 Paoli Massacre
32 Anthony Wayne Home
33 Valley Forge

founding in the seventeenth century. The eastern half had been settled largely by Calvinists from Scotland and New England, most of them small land-holders who were not enamored of the British king and his redcoats and mercenaries. Their anti-British sentiment was effectively offset by the Tory sentiments of the western half of the state; altogether New Jersey contributed six battalions of Loyalist militia to the forces. This was hardly a secure situation in which to maintain, maneuver, and train a revolutionary army.

Pennsylvania had a population of approximately 250,000; it was the second most populous state of the thirteen. (Virginia had the highest population—more than 450,000, almost half slave.) Its major city, Philadelphia, was the country's principal metropolis with a population of 34,000, and was then the second largest city in the British Empire. (London was the largest.) Like New Jersey, it had a Tory population that made itself painfully evident. Its Quakers and Germans were either neutral or Loyalist. Because of this, among the powers Congress gave Washington in 1777 was the right "to take, wherever he may be, whatever he may want for the use of the army, if the inhabitants will not sell it, allowing reasonable price for the same," a power he used to feed his ragged, starving troops while they camped and fought across these two predominantly food-producing regions.

Since Congress met regularly in Philadelphia and the administrative offices of the government were located there, the part of the state that surrounded the city and bordered the Delaware River became involved in the campaigns of 1777. As a result, you must expect to do some crossing and recrossing of the Pennsylvania–New Jersey state line as you follow the action up, down, and across the Delaware River region. As I did in New York, however, I have reorganized the war slightly to make your labors somewhat easier, but there will be some "jumping o'er times."

I have divided the sites in New Jersey into three. The first section takes you to those sites connected with the 1776–77 campaign, including Cornwallis's landing on the west side of the Hudson and the capture of Fort Lee, Washington's encampment on the Delaware River and his famous crossing, the battles of Trenton and Princeton, the encampments at Morristown, and Knyphausen's Springfield Raid. The second Jersey section is the Battle of Monmouth and the third, a swing through the ocean counties and central Jersey.

Pennsylvania is divided into two parcels as well. The first covers the Philadelphia campaign of 1777–78 when Howe defeated Washington at Brandywine, occupied Philadelphia, survived Washington's counterattack at Germantown, subdued the Delaware River forts, and then sat back comfortably in the Quaker City while Washington and his men froze out the winter at Valley Forge. The second Pennsylvania section takes you on a long trek up the Susquehanna River following General John Sullivan on his march into Iroquois country, as far north as the Finger Lake country in New York.

In both states, urbanization once more proves to be the blind, unrelenting enemy of the history buff and the historic conservationist. Some of the most important sites are changed beyond recognition, and the events that make them important can only be followed through historical markers. In industrialized and urbanized states such as New Jersey and Pennsylvania, this is not unexpected. What was unexpected, however, was finding one major site, the Battle of Monmouth, in pristine condition. This turned out to be a mixed blessing, as it is extremely difficult to find your way around such an area without at least some basic guide materials. Plans are afoot to correct this by the bicentennial.

Go back in time now to December, 1776. Turn your coat collar up, figuratively; bend your head to the wintry blasts and gusts of icy rain scudding across the Jersey marshlands and fields; and hurry to catch up with what is left of the American army on the west bank of the Hudson River.

WINTER OF HEARTBREAK AND VICTORY—1776-77

New York City was lost to the British after the fall of Fort Washington in November, 1776, and so was Manhattan Island and a good part of Westchester. Washington's command was now divided into three. One division of 7,000 men under General Charles Lee was based in North Castle, supposedly a reserve that could move to support Washington when he gave the word. General William Heath with the second division held the Hudson Highlands, keeping the vital river crossings open for the lines of supply and communication that connected the New England States with their Middle Atlantic and Southern sisters. Washington himself, with the few thousand men he had managed to get across the Hudson after the Battle of White Plains was now short of supplies and harried by Cornwallis, who would hound him mercilessly across New Jersey as he strove to set up line after line behind every river he came to until he could finally get his men behind the friendly Jersey hills and down to and across the Delaware River.

THE JERSEY LANDING

Having swallowed Fort Washington, General Howe proceeded to go after the other of the Hudson River twins, Fort Lee, which was then called Fort Constitution. Moving with what was for him great speed, Howe sent Cornwallis across the Hudson with about 6,000 troops on Wednesday, November 20. You can meet them as they come ashore by crossing the George Washington Bridge from New York City, bearing right as you come off on the Jersey side, then taking the Palisades Inter-state Parkway north to the Alpine exit.

Coming off the exit, follow the signs for the Palisades Park along a road that takes you in switchbacks down the face of the cliffs. At the bottom is a riverside park with a marina, picnic tables, rest rooms, re-freshment stands, and lots of parking space for a $1.00 fee. Leaving your car, follow the signs for the Shore Trail (you will be walking upstream with the Palisades on your left) past some log park maintenance build-ings until you come to a wide, grassy area fronting a two-story, white, frame and stone building nestled against the foot of the cliff with its door and windows opening onto the river view. A sign over the door identifies the building as **Cornwallis's Headquarters.** At the time of the British crossing this was a riverside inn at what was then known as Closter's Landing. The original building was half the size it is now; the frame addition did not appear until after the Revolution.

By the time General Charles Cornwallis came ashore at Closter's Landing, he was an old hand at amphibious landings. Two months before he had commanded the assault force that landed in Kips Bay, and just five weeks before that he had shared with Henry Clinton the command of the troops that landed in Gravesend Bay. Earl Cornwallis, to give him his due, was a member of Parliament; a former lord of the bedchamber to George III, vice-treasurer of Ireland, and Constable of the Tower; and a major general by the time he came to America. A Whig like the Howe brothers, he was against the crown policies that had brought on the Revolution; but being a loyal subject of the king and singularly patriotic, he saw his duty and did it. Some historians say that had he done more of the overall running of the war in America, the rebels would have been defeated swiftly; others say that his mistakes, which included allowing himself to get boxed in at Yorktown, cost Great Britain the war. He went on to become one of the greatest of all British generals, though at the moment he is only doing his best to catch the Americans at Fort Lee before they can get away.

As for this building being his headquarters! All the general did was take his ease here and sample the local refreshments while his men sweated and toiled their way to the top of the cliffs. Since he undoubtedly conferred with his officers during that time, however, and may even have issued an order or two, we will stretch a point and allow that this was indeed Cornwallis's headquarters for at least several hours.

In my early teens, I passed this building on many a hike with com-panions following the shore path upstream. We usually began our walk at a point on the Jersey bank opposite Dyckman Street (200th Street) in Manhattan where a ferry connected with the Jersey shore. We would stop here to fill our canteens at the water pipes and adjust our packs in preparation for the rough, rock trails ahead. The same sign was over the door, so we would pause before moving out to peer in through the windows, but the rooms were empty and the door was always locked.

Today the house is filled with period furniture donated by various New Jersey historical organizations, and the building is a museum, open to the public during the summer months only and maintained by the Palisades Interstate Park Commission. Its exhibits describe its long history as a riverside inn, some of it during the Revolution, as well as the history and lore of the surrounding area. A plaque beside the front door says the original building was a one-room, stone structure, now the lower, south end (the downstream end), and was built about 1750, The wooden half was added during the nineteenth century. A lengthier description hung near the plaque gives an interesting account of the era when the inn offered its hospitality to travelers and boatmen passsing up and down the river.

According to this account, the British "attempted" to scale the cliffs up a treacherous trail after assembling on the east shore opposite Closter's Landing on the night of November 19. The force consisted of two battalions of Hessian grenadiers, two companies of jägers (a German word meaning "hunters" which describes German light infantry originally organized by Frederick the Great), eight battalions of British reserves—at least 5,000 men. They came across the river early the next morning on a fleet of flatboats accompanied by "heavy artillery." The account says the story of Cornwallis's visit was handed down from generation to generation among the local people until the inn became known as Cornwallis's Headquarters and that local fishermen, having nothing better to do between shad runs, sometimes took up the floorboards looking for buried treasure. They turned up only the usual uniform buttons and bits of clay pipes.

So much for local folklore. A little north of the house, near a refreshment stand and comfort station, look for a large **boulder** bearing a metal plaque beside a path leading up the cliff face. According to the plaque, this is the beginning of the trail the British forces climbed to the top. From there they marched six miles to Fort Lee.

The scene to some extent is as it was then; the cliffs and the river remain as they were. The eastern bank, then heavily forested with an occasional farm patch showing amid the trees, is now the Yonkers waterfront. The cliffside is probably more heavily wooded now; a contemporary watercolor of the scene shows a sparsely wooded, rocky slope. The artist was a British officer who witnessed the landing; his scene may be found in several pictorial works on the Revolution, but he seems to have left out the inn. Nevertheless, the old house with the river at its front door and the cliffs frowning overhead evokes a feeling of the era. This is another good spot for a picnic and break for recreation and rest. Be forewarned, however, that the facilities may be strained on Sundays and holidays in good weather; the Palisades Shore Trail has always been a favorite with picnickers and hikers from both New York and New Jersey.

Reassembling his men on top of the cliffs, Cornwallis marched south as quickly as he could, trying to cover the six miles to Fort Lee before the two thousand Americans in the fort could escape. Warned by a patrol, however, General Nathanael Greene got his men out in the nick of time and joined Washington, who had prepared a position on the west side of the Hackensack River guarding the only bridge. The situation was precarious, with Greene returning to the fort to round up stragglers and get them to safety. The British stormed into the fort to find the rebels' food still cooking on the fire, several hundred tents standing, and about fifty cannons and most of the baggage left behind. They also captured a number of stragglers who had been indulging themselves on the abandoned rum rations and others in the vicinity, altogether between 100 and 150 men.

You can easily follow Cornwallis by returning to the top of the cliff and 9W and taking it into the town of Fort Lee, a busy spot with much north-south traffic pouring through its business center and getting onto and off the approaches to the George Washington Bridge. Where 9W intersects Main Street, turn left (back towards the river) onto Main, which goes up a rise of ground and down into Edgewater, the southern anchor of the line Cornwallis established while he was foraging in New Jersey at the time of the Baylor Massacre (Volume I). Turn onto Old Palisades Road and look for No. 141, a white frame house standing opposite what may be a new high-rise apartment building when you get there. **Fort Lee** stood behind what is now 141.

When I visited the site the high-rise was about to be built, although efforts were afoot by a few local inhabitants to delay it. The building was going to be erected on the very spot where the soldiers in Fort Lee may have had their bake ovens. Some history-minded Fort Leeites were trying to get the builder to allow state archaeologists to go over the site for artifacts and to determine if the bake ovens actually were located on that spot. The story made the pages of the *New York Times,* but I learned subsequently that though archaeologists did go over the site, they found nothing to indicate that anybody's bread was ever baked there.

Old Palisades Road dribbles away into a dirt road that goes down a slope and eventually comes out at the top of the Palisades immediately south of the George Washington Bridge. That is Palisades Interstate Park land and on it is where the fort's outer *batteries* are believed to have been located. The entire area along the top of the Palisades at that point has been much worked over and disturbed. During the late 1800s a luxury hotel occupied the site, which accounts for some of the stone retaining walls.

The fort itself, a star-shaped affair, stood behind 141 on ground now occupied by one-family homes and their backyards and front lawns. If you want to trace its outlines, turn left off Old Palisades Road onto Federspiel Street. The southeast bastion of the fort was located just at the intersection of Federspiel and English streets. Following Federspiel will take you along the fort's eastern wall (parallel to the river). Turn left on Cedar Street to drive along what was the fort's northern wall. Another bastion, the northeastern, was just west of the intersection of Federspiel and Cedar. Cedar takes you to Parker Avenue; the northwest bastion was situated at that intersection. Turn left onto Parker and you are driving right on top of the fort's western wall. At the intersection of Parker Avenue and English Street is the site of the southwest bastion. Turn left onto English, which goes along the southern wall of the fort. If you drive west from Parker Avenue to Palisades Avenue, which parallels it, and then turn left, you will see a modern school to your right. A road from Palisades Avenue toward the school takes you into the area where the garrison's huts stood.

The Palisades Interstate Park Commission is a bi-state agency that administers extensive park lands in both New Jersey and New York along the Hudson. The park extends to the Bear Mountain and Harriman Park areas, and the Commission also administers a number of Revolutionary War sites including Stony Point, Forts Montgomery and Clinton, Washington's Headquarters at Newburgh (the Hasbrouck House), the Senate House at Kingston, the New Windsor Cantonment, the Knox House at New Windsor, and Fort Lee. The Palisades Commission has drawn up plans for an interpretative development of the Fort Lee site which includes a Visitor's Center with a 200-seat auditorium where a fifteen-minute film will explain the history of the site and the British strategy in which it played a part. Out along the bluff, a simulated gun battery will be constructed according to the best archaeological and historical evidence, to give visitors an idea of what the fort's outer works may have looked like. A small parking area capable of accommodating about 120 cars and a picnic ground will be included, with an access road leading from Hudson Terrace. All of this may be awaiting you by late 1975, in plenty of time for the bicentennial of the Fort Lee action, November, 1976—provided that sufficient state and federal funds can be found to add to the Commission's investment.

Now retrace your route to Main Street via Palisades Avenue. Turn left onto Main and take it east to the entrance onto U.S. routes 1–6–46. Those three roads will take you west to the northern terminus of the New Jersey Turnpike, which you should take south. As you do, you will be roughly following the path of Washington's retreat as he gave up his Hackensack River position in the face of Cornwallis's relentless advance and retreated to Newark. Washington then wrote to Charles Lee at North Castle ordering him to bring his men across the Hudson into New Jersey to rendezvous with the rest of the army. Lee ignored the command, perhaps to make Washington look bad in the eyes of the Congress; for he argued that his 7,000 men were of greater strategic value where they were, east of the Hudson. For almost two weeks he made no attempt to obey his commander in chief's order while Washington's army retreated from Newark to New Brunswick and then to Princeton, putting first the Raritan River between themselves and their pursuers, then the Watchung Mountains. From Princeton they continued south to Trenton where, on December 7, they crossed the Delaware River and went into defensive positions along the west bank of the river in the low hills of Pennsylvania near McKonkey's Ferry.

WASHINGTON'S CROSSING: NEW JERSEY AND PENNSYLVANIA

Take the New Jersey Turnpike to Exit 9; then follow the signs to U.S. 1 south which will take you, after about an hour's drive, to State Route 546. Take 546 west (toward Lawrenceville and Pennington) to the banks of the Delaware River at **Washington Crossing State Park** in New Jersey. A narrow, steel girder bridge goes across the river to Washington Crossing State Park in Pennsylvania; the scene of Washington's historic crossing is now occupied by two parks separated by the river, each maintained by its respective state and each containing quite different historical features. They both offer picnic facilities, rest rooms, recreational facilities, nature trails, and generally pleasant, green park surroundings. It was in Pennsylvania, however, that the ragged, half-starved Continentals camped and later embarked on the crossing, and in New Jersey that they landed and marched on Trenton.

The retreat across New Jersey from Fort Lee had been a nightmare. Buffeted by freezing rain, the men had been forced to keep moving from one defensive position to another, giving up each in turn and destroying bridges and blocking roads with fallen trees as the British came on against them. By December 3 the advance guard was in Trenton and, acting under Washington's orders, were collecting all the boats they could find up and down the river. Lee, who had finally moved 4,000 men across the Hudson, was still several days away, so there was no chance of making a stand; when the British got to Trenton, Washington ordered his men across the Delaware. As the last American troops boarded their boats and pushed off into the icy current for the Pennsylvania shore, the first British troops coming into Trenton just missed giving them a send-off.

All through the rest of December, Washington's men lived from hand to mouth and from day to day, as did the Revolution. Faced with the prospect of the fall of Philadelphia any time the British wished to take it, Washington could do little to stop them. Had Howe ordered Cornwallis to move across the Delaware instead of allowing the army to go into winter quarters, as was the universal practice at the time, he might have ended the entire business right then and there. A convenient excuse for Howe was the lack of boats, thanks to Washington's foresight; but a local Pennsylvania historian, Ann Hawkes Sutton, in her account of the Delaware encampment and the ensuing crossing, quotes contemporary sources as saying there were 48,000 feet of lumber in Trenton that could have been used to construct rafts. Whether it was the charms of Mrs. Loring (Howe's mistress) in New York City, or an attempt by Howe to keep the door open to peaceful negotiations, Howe again did not move ahead when he should have. Food, clothing and morale were at their lowest in the rebel ranks. Many of the men were just sweating out the rest of the month; their enlistments would be up December 3, and several refused to wait, took French leave and headed for home. Several New Jersey militia units had left during the retreat as their enlistments ran out, and though they were replaced by another 5,000 militiamen, Washington was still woefully short of enough men fit for duty to protect Philadelphia and Congress should the British cross the river.

To make matters worse, Lee carelessly allowed himself to be captured in a tavern in Basking Ridge near Morristown. This was a particularly hard blow, for Lee was one of the few officers in the Continental Army who had had professional military experience before the Revolution, and he was considered the army's ablest commander in the field. His command stalled in its tracks, 4,000 men Washington badly needed only a day's march from the Delaware. They stayed there until General Lee's second-in-command, Sullivan, brought two thousand of them to Washington in time for the attack on Trenton.

Desperately, Washington issued appeals to Congress and to the state of New Jersey for more men, but most of the Jersey militia failed to mobilize; Loyalist-minded citizens by the hundreds flocked to Howe to take advantage of his offer of amnesty.

The situation called for a gamble, some bold, audacious move to rally the men who were left and give new heart to the Revolution. Before you follow Washington through the nine or ten most brilliant days of his military career, cross the bridge over the Delaware River into Pennsylvania to inspect the sites on which his starving, ill-clad troops shivered their way through December, 1776.

THE PENNSYLVANIA ENCAMPMENT

Drive slowly across the bridge, for its width allows two cars to pass each other with barely inches to spare. In fact, any vehicle more than six feet six inches wide requires a police escort to get across, so if you are pulling an extra-wide trailer be forewarned. On the Pennsylvania side of the river, the park area extends both south and north of the bridge, but the major sites are concentrated to the north or right. The general appearance of the river on both sides is rural. The hills are still quite heavily wooded, and beyond the park lands the river is lined with private homes on large plots of ground. The character of the countryside has not changed essentially; both Mercer County in New Jersey and Bucks County in Pennsylvania are still very agricultural.

Parking is available adjacent to the **Ferry Inn,** the first building to your right as you come off the bridge. The Ferry Inn is a large, three-story fieldstone building with a dormered attic making the third floor. It is open daily from 9 A.M. to 5 P.M. and on Sundays from 2 to 5 P.M. It was probably always an inn. The present building was built in about 1780 or 1790 on the foundations of a previous inn, which was probably built about 1740; only the foundation walls and a basement kitchen of the first inn remain. It catered to river travelers and to those taking the McKonkey Ferry, which crossed the river at this point. Samuel McKonkey bought the inn and the ferry in 1774, and he was on the scene when Washington and his officers stopped at the inn the night of the crossing.

The inn is furnished with colonial furniture of the period but none of it, as far as I could determine, was in the building in 1776. The bar in the tavern, however, was in use when Washington was here, and the basement kitchen is probably the room in which he had his evening meal on the night of December 25, 1776, before crossing.

After you leave the Ferry Inn, walk north for a short distance to examine a reconstruction of a *Durham boat* surrounded by a white picket fence, the boat the Continentals used when they braved the Delaware ice floes. This is a true replica of a type of boat that was built at the Durham ironworks here in Bucks County in the hills of Riegelsville where an iron ore deposit had been discovered in 1727. First built in 1750, it was designed to carry iron ore and pig iron down through the rapids of the Delaware to Philadelphia. It became so popular as a local means of transportation that at one time more than two thousand men operated more than three hundred Durham boats carrying iron ore, iron, whiskey, and grain in a steady stream downriver from Easton to Philadelphia and manufactured goods back upstream. As long as its popularity continued—until about 1860—the scenes in and around the bars and taverns of the Trenton and Philadelphia waterfronts must have resembled those of the fabled Far West.

The boats varied in length from forty to sixty feet; the one on exhibit is forty feet long with an eight-foot beam and a depth of about three feet six inches. When empty it has a draft of about five inches (it can float in five inches of water); when fully loaded with fifteen tons, it has a draft of about thirty inches. Somewhat like the Ohio and Mississippi river keelboats, the Durham boat depended on the current to take it downstream and a crew of six men and a captain to man poles and oars against the current and through the rapids, using a stern-sweep oar of twenty-five to thirty feet in length to guide it. Naturally, the boat carried a far lighter cargo on its return trip than it did going down to market.

The size and carrying capacity of these boats were what made them so valuable to both the British and American forces. Washington, in his directive to secure all boats along the Delaware, specified that Durham boats in particular were to be denied to the enemy since they were capable of carrying horses and cannon as well as large numbers of men. This reconstructed specimen seems extremely well made and, at least in the eyes of this landlubber, looks river-worthy.

A short distance upstream from the Durham boat is the **Memorial Building**, a keystone-shaped fieldstone building with Georgian pillars on the front, a statue of Washington looking toward the spot on the riverbank where his men embarked, and a long reflecting pool lined with flags. The prospect it overlooks is a lovely one: the gently sloping river-bank leading down to the river, the river itself, and then the low hills of Jersey beyond.

The Memorial Building serves as a reception center for the park. There is a souvenir shop in the lobby, which, among the usual postcards and souvenirs, displays a number of models of interest, including one of the *Philadelphia*, a boat Benedict Arnold used on Lake Champlain. The main room is an **auditorium** where a huge copy of Emanuel Leutze's famous rendition of *Washington Crossing the Delaware* has been placed on a stage. A ten-minute recorded narration may amuse you as you sit and contemplate the picture, but it offers little historical information, being mainly concerned with the painting of the picture and the artist. You might, however, detect several obvious differences in the boats shown in the painting, supposed to be Durham, from the reconstruction you saw just a short while before. You might also reflect on Washington portrayed as standing up in a small craft loaded to the gunwales with men, while miniature icebergs threaten it on all sides. Washington, who had considerable experience on frontier rivers during his youth, would probably be embarrassed by the picture; the ice on the Delaware must surely have been only flat cakes, floe or surface ice, which may be seen on any river in the winter.

Before you leave the Memorial Building grounds, walk down to the river beyond the reflecting pool to visit the site of the embarkation. A plaque marks the spot, which has been made into a wide, fieldstone pavilion with steps leading down to a stone landing flanked by stone pillars, each of which holds a metal lantern. The whole effect is too decorative to evoke the wooded, wintry shores of 1776, but the river current is probably as swift today as it was then, and Malta Island remains, close to the Pennsylvania shore; many of the boats were hidden behind it prior to the embarkation.

The army was camped along the flatlands that lie between the river at this point and a range of hills a short distance inland. Most of the area is taken up today with farmlands, roads, houses, filling stations, and the like. About five miles upstream from the ferry area, however, is another section of the park which gives you a much better idea of what the campsites were like. The same road that skirts the riverbank in this area will take you to the other park zone. If for some reason the road is closed off, as it was when I was there because of a washed-out bridge, go back to the road leading west from the bridge—Route 532—and take it to the first major intersection, which is marked by a traffic light. Turn right onto Route 32, which will take you to the upstream park.

The first site you should visit upstream is **Bowman Tower,** a 100-foot stone tower on top of **Bowman Hill,** which was used by the rebels as an observation post to watch the Jersey shore. The tower is a modern innovation the Continentals would have given their eyeteeth for, since from the top, reached by a circular stone stairway, you get an excellent view of the surrounding countryside. Bucks County is spread out behind you and to either side; the Washington Crossing Bridge may be seen clearly downstream, and so may the rapids beyond. The countryside probably bears a close resemblance, at least in general appearance, to what it was two hundred years ago; though the character of the woodland was probably quite different. In 1776 this was well-settled farming country, just as it is today, unless the homes on both sides of the river increase in number. Time and technology have wrought one great difference in this landscape, however, and that is the almost total absence of river traffic. In colonial times, during those months when the river was free of ice, there must have been a fairly steady stream of Durham boats, flatboats, and rafts carrying produce and ore down to market and manufactured goods back upstream and into the farmlands.

Bowman Tower may be reached by a paved, automobile road which goes to a parking area a few feet from the entrance. The area around the front of the hill was a camp area for units of the Continental Army. Leaving Bowman Hill, proceed along 32 for two miles until you see a sign for Washington Crossing State Park and then a sign for the **Thompson-Neely House.** Turn right into the parking area, which is close to an old stone barn. The house is open every weekday from 10 A.M. to 5 P.M. and on Sundays, 1–5 P.M.

As you walk toward the house, note the red cedar tree on your left with a sign informing you the tree was twenty-seven years old at the time of the encampment; that makes it 227 years old by 1976. The house itself is a long, two-story fieldstone building, quite impressive because of its size, with four brick chimneys. The first room to your left, as you enter, was used as a hospital and is now furnished with straw mats to give some idea of what it may have looked like. The rest of the house is furnished with period antiques; some of the items on display belonged to the families who lived in it. The oldest part of the house was built in 1702 by John Pidcock, the first white settler in the area. A plaque on a boulder near the house marks the spot on which Pidcock built his first home, gristmills, and a trading post in 1684. The present building is a partial restoration of the second house.

At the time of the encampment two families, the Thompsons and the Neelys, occupied the house until it became the headquarters of General William Alexander, Lord Stirling, and several other officers, including Captain William Washington, one of George's relatives, and Lieutenant James Monroe, who would become the fifth President of the United States. Alexander was that same general whose men bore the brunt of the fighting during the Battle of Long Island. A son of the man who defended John Peter Zenger, Alexander had claimed the earldom of Stirling in Scotland. The House of Lords refused his claim, but an Edinburgh jury had recognized and accepted it and he was so proclaimed at the market cross in Stirling, and he was referred to as Lord Stirling throughout his life. He was a noted mathematician and astronomer and once a governor of King's College, now Columbia University. During his military career he served in the Pennsylvania and New Jersey campaigns and also presided over Charles Lee's court-martial and served on André's board of inquiry. It was Lord Stirling who alerted Washington to the Conway Cabal, a notorious attempt to replace Washington with Gates as commander in chief.

Of particular interest in the Thompson-Neely House is the kitchen, known as the Council Room; it was here Washington met with his commanders to plan the Delaware crossing and the attack on Trenton. Because of these consultations, the house is sometimes called the House of Decision.

As you come out of the house to the rear, proceed through the gate in the picket fence just before you; cross the back lawn; go through an opening in a split-rail fence; and you will be just across the road from *Pidcock's gristmill.* The stream that powered the mill wheel is behind the mill; the water must have been carried to the wheel, still in position on the outside of the building, through stone channels you will find nearby.

There are several other small outbuildings on the grounds, one or two of them probably necessaries. Across the road are some of the picnic facilities which may be found throughout the park. They are all pleasant, shady places with open, grassy areas, tables, and fireplaces.

A sign takes you to a *burial spot* that, according to the park literature, contains the first unknown soldier to be buried in the United States. A dirt road leads to a bridge which crosses part of an old canal, then past another picnic area called the General Sullivan Pavilion. The Delaware River to your left may be seen through the trees; on the right you can see the tower on top of Bowman Hill. Also on your right is the Bucks County Canal.

Fieldstone steps lead up between two stone gate pillars to a wide grassy area surrounding a flagpole. Beyond on a raised bank of earth is a colonial tombstone, the sunken remains of other stones, and a row of twenty small American flags of the kind used to mark the graves of veterans. Beyond this first row is a second row of tombstones, most of them with just their tops showing above the ground. A plaque identifies the site as the burial place of a number of unknown Continental soldiers who, having died of exposure and disease while camped along the Delaware, were buried here on Christmas Day, 1776. Just beyond the graves flows the river their comrades crossed without them. Standing with your back to the graves, you face the army's main camping area, extending inland from the river for about a mile and including the line of hills on the near horizon which culminate in Bowman Hill.

The solitary visible tombstone is that of Captain James Moore, son of Benjamin Moore of New York City, who died on December 25, 1776, in the Thompson-Neely House, aged 24 years and 8 months, while his company was on its way to the ferry. Thirteen pie-shaped pieces of stone have been placed around the base of the flagpole, each bearing the name of one of the original thirteen states and the date on which it obtained statehood.

CROSSING THE DELAWARE

Now return to the east side of the river and New Jersey's Washington Crossing State Park, which marks the site where the Continental Army landed. The park covers much more territory than just the landing spot; it contains 714 acres and extends north along the Delaware for almost a mile. Unlike its Pennsylvania sister, this park is a single, self-contained area with four main picnic areas, refreshment stands, playing fields, rest rooms, nature trails, and an open-air theater which presents a summer festival of the performing arts.

The features you are particularly interested in are the spot on the riverbank where the army came ashore, the roads they followed to Trenton, and the museums. Route 546, which you took from U.S. 1 to get here, meets Route 29 at the bridge which skirts the park on its western, or river side. Between 29 and the river is the Delaware and Raritan Canal; a feeder lock is located just upstream of the bridge. Between the canal and the river is a wide, grassy slope known as Washington Grove, with trees, picnic tables, and fireplaces. It was in this area that the army came ashore in the first moments of what was to be a nine-day ordeal of marching, freezing, and fighting.

On Thursday, December 12, the Continental Congress removed to Baltimore lest it fall into the hands of the Hessians. For the rest of that month the American army lived mostly on courage, though many of the men were undoubtedly counting the days until their terms of enlistment would end on December 31st and they could leave, honorably, for the warmth of their own hearths. On December 20 Washington wrote to Congress expressing his opinion that unless some drastic steps were taken, the army would cease to exist within ten days. What he was looking for was some effort by the Congress to get him troops to replace those he knew would leave. Congress did not respond until December 27, when they conferred on Washington, for six months, the power to raise troops on his own, to appoint and promote officers, to go directly to the states for levies of militia, to gather stores of supplies for the army, and to take whatever the army needed from local inhabitants. The last provision was probably the most important as far as the men in the ranks were concerned; the local merchants, tavern keepers, and farmers had refused to honor Continental money and therefore to sell them supplies and food.

On December 19 the first of Thomas Paine's *The Crisis* papers appeared in printed form. "These are the times that try men's souls. The summer soldier and the sunshine patriot will, in this crisis, shrink from the service of his country; but he that stands it *now* deserves the love and thanks of man and woman."

The words were written by the light of a campfire on the head of a drum during the winter of 1776; Paine is supposed to have been inspired by Washington, who, though he freely acknowledged the seeming hopelessness of the army's position, never faltered in his efforts to find a way to keep the cause alive.

Sullivan marched into camp with his two thousand on the twentieth. Then Gates came in with about 500 men followed by 1,000 members of a unit called the Philadelphia Associators and a battalion of German-Americans from Pennsylvania and Maryland. Altogether this gave Washington about 6,000 men fit for duty. By Christmas Washington knew that he had reached the point of no return; after the December 31 exodus he would be left with about 1,400 men. The river was freezing over; once it did, the British would no longer have to rely on boats, but would be able to move men and artillery over the ice and on to Philadelphia. At the moment redcoats and Hessians were in winter quarters in three scattered locations at Trenton, Pennington, and Bordentown, far in advance of the regular British line which stretched between New Brunswick and Newark. Most of the army was snugged down in New York with Howe for the rest of the winter. Cornwallis at this time was so contemptuous of the Americans' ability to take advantage of the situation, particularly of his overextended lines of communications and supply, that he did not take the most ordinary precautions to guard against surprise attacks. On the night of December 25–26, Christmas night, Washington gave the order for the army to march.

The Durham boats hidden behind Malta Island moved out and up to the banks as Glover's Marblehead fishermen, called upon to practice their native vocations, plied oars and poles. They had played the same role when the army was evacuated from Long Island to Manhattan. The men had been paraded during the late afternoon, but instead of being returned to their quarters were marched down to the riverbank. At 6 P.M. they began to board the boats, 2,400 of them with eighteen cannon. A snowstorm was swirling into the area and the temperature was well below freezing. Many of the men left bloody prints of their feet on the snow, for shoes and boots were almost non-existent in the ranks. The snow became mixed with sleet. McKonkey, the innkeeper and ferry master, and Glover tested the river before Washington risked his command to the current. Then he gave the order for the boats to push off.

His strategy, discussed and decided on some weeks before, called for Colonel John Cadwalader to cross the Delaware below Trenton with 2,000 men to attack the British at Bordentown as a diversion to prevent the reinforcement of the Trenton garrison. General James Ewing with 1,000 men was to cross at the Trenton Ferry and hold the banks of Assunpink Creek to prevent the enemy in Trenton from retreating to the south. Washington and the rest of the command would march into Trenton from the north and take the Hessians stationed there by surprise. The whole plan depended on secrecy, darkness, and the enemy's low opinion of the capabilities of the rebel army. From Trenton, Washington planned to go on to Princeton and New Brunswick, striking hard at the British supply bases; he hoped to come away with enough clothing, food, and other supplies to inject new heart into his men and attract recruits. If he succeeded, he would give the Revolution a needed shot of hope; if he failed, the Revolution was over and he faced complete personal disaster.

The embarkation at McKonkey's Ferry went slowly. The men stumbled their way through the storm into the boats; and the guns, their wheels and barrels slippery with ice, were difficult to manhandle in and out over the gunwales. The river was becoming choked with ice. By 11 P.M. the storm was at its height. The entire crossing was supposed to be over by midnight, but the last man was not landed on the Jersey shore until 3 A.M., nine hours after the first man had embarked in Pennsylvania. A few hours of darkness remained, but that advantage would fast disappear during the nine-mile march that still lay ahead.

If you really want to get the flavor and feeling of this moment, perhaps you should visit the crossing site in the winter; the park is open year-round. I have been to Valley Forge in various seasons, but the visit I remember best was a winter visit, an all-day affair spent out in the open. Except for the picnic area, the riverbanks are very much the same as they were in 1776; this river has not changed its course or width over the years. It still flows swiftly; there are still rapids, and in the winter it still freezes over.

Turn north up 29 from the bridge and look for an entrance to the park within a few hundred feet on the right. A parking area lies between the **McKonkey Ferry House** on the right and the **Flag Museum** on the left. The McKonkey House was actually the house to which McKonkey moved after he gave up his occupations as ferry master and inn proprietor. This is a little complicated because, in truth, there were two ferries in operation at this crossing at the time. The one operated by McKonkey was licensed by the state of Pennsylvania and crossed the river eastward; the other, operated by Rut Johnson, was licensed by the state of New Jersey and crossed the river westward. One wonders whether either picked up passengers on the rival shore and took them back on the return trip.

The Ferry House is now a museum open from Tuesdays through Saturdays from 10 A.M. to noon and again from 1 to 5 P.M. It is open 2-5 P.M. on Sundays and closed on Mondays. There is a small admission charge which helps pay for maintenance. A small frame cottage with a peaked roof, it was a tavern in revolutionary times. All it serves its visitors at the present is a collection of period furniture and some colonial household utensils contained within two main rooms and two bedrooms on the upper floor. An interesting feature are the bedroom doors, each of which has a four-pane window inset.

The first room you enter on the first floor is the tap room with its bar, this one featuring a wooden railing from ceiling to bar which closes the publican inside. It can be swung or lifted out of the way. The other room on this floor was the main public room with a cooking fireplace, where Washington and his officers came to get in out of the cold and snow while the crossing continued. Washington is said to have retired to one of the upstairs rooms for an hour or so of sleep, an event that seems likely given the duration of the crossing.

The Flag Museum exhibits a history of the flag and a large diorama, about twelve by fourteen feet, of the Delaware crossing. It was constructed with great care for authenticity of detail and is an excellent graphic representation of the event. Smaller dioramas show the Battle of Princeton and the march on Trenton.

A little way from the Flag Museum, identified by a sign as **Continental Lane,** is a dirt road leading into the park which approximates the road the army used as it marched inland from the river. This is now a very pleasant, shaded ramble, which runs through the entire park to its eastern boundary and at one point also becomes a bridle path. Another sign a short distance from the museum marks what is probably its limits of authenticity, but that short section between the two signs may have actually felt the bare and rag-covered feet of the rebel troop that storm-filled night.

A number of staged events take place in the park commemorating the crossing. One in particular is a yearly enactment of the crossing on Christmas Day as Oliver St. John, regisseur of the now defunct Lambertville Music Circus, costumes himself as Washington and crosses the Delaware in a Durham boat. He is met by a group of people who accompany him back across the bridge to Pennsylvania. On February 22, Washington's Birthday, various local and patriotic organizations gather here to walk the route the army followed to Trenton, a distance of nine miles.

To follow the routes the attacking Americans took to Trenton, return along 546 to the intersection with 579 at the eastern limit of the park. On the northeast side of this intersection stands an empty white building with a long porch and a fieldstone retaining wall in front. This was the **Bear Tavern** where Washington and his officers conferred briefly before the attacking force split up: one group marching under General Greene took Pennington Road, now Pennington Avenue and State Route 31; the other force, under Sullivan, used the river road. At that time the entire area along these roads was rural; today it is semirural with some suburban development in evidence. The present Pennington Road, or 579, is not the road General Greene's column used. If you go farther east along 546 back toward U.S. 1, you will come to Route 31, Pennington Avenue, which will take you into the heart of Trenton right to the battle monument where Greene positioned his artillery during the attack.

To find Sullivan's route, take Pennington Road south toward Trenton, looking for a road marker just outside of Trenton. It will appear on the left side of the road after a railroad underpass in front of the Marie H. Katzenback School for the Deaf: a brick, Dutch colonial building set back on large spacious grounds and so identified by a sign. The blue and white marker which faces south identifies the road as **Sullivan's Way,** the road Sullivan's command used to reach Trenton. There is some controversy among local historians as to the roads the army followed and whether the staff meeting took place at Bear Tavern or at a church.

Before you move on into Trenton for the battle, you might want to spend a little more time exploring the area around the crossing parks. Bucks County is a well-known exurb of New York City, home of colonies of writers and theatrical people, site of a Frank Lloyd Wright house, and replete with a number of historic sites listed in a pamphlet put out by the Bucks County Historical Tourist Commission, Main Street and Locust Avenue, Fallsington, Pennsylvania, 19054. This pamphlet outlines three different historic tours in three sections of the county, which will take you to more than a hundred old homes, inns, roads, canal locks, towns, museums, mines, and covered bridges. The commission also publishes a soft-cover *History of Bucks County,* which is filled with local lore and history.

Just a mile or two upstream of Washington Crossing on the Jersey side, following Route 29, you will come to Lambertville, the site of a ferry called Coryell's Ferry that was frequently used by the Continental Army. A bridge has replaced the ferry and leads directly into New Hope, a charming town with some very good restaurants and the Bucks County Playhouse, which plays an extensive season and frequently features Broadway tryouts.

There are few motels in this area north of Trenton. New Hope has several quaint-looking hotels. Trenton, only nine miles below Washington's Crossing, offers a wider range of accommodations and could serve as a base from which to explore the Delaware River country. Besides, your presence is now required there along the come-back trail Washington and his men are following.

THE BATTLES OF TRENTON: I

Plural is correct—battles—as two engagements were fought in Trenton. Since there was a lapse of only a few days between them, and since they were part of the same campaign, you will not have to make great mental allowances for the passage of time and events. You will, however, be faced with the usual results of urbanization, as you cover events in the midst of a modern city that was once a village of 100-odd houses.

The town was held by a brigade of Hessians that included elements of the Knyphausen and von Lossberg regiments. They were under the command of Colonel Johann Rall, a very competent officer who had led the German units that descended on Fort Washington across the wild northern part of Manhattan. Colonel Rall, however, had two weaknesses: he loved the bottle and he was contemptuous of Americans to such an extent that he refused to order trenches dug or fortifications built around the town.

The Americans still had surprise on their side; but they had lost the cover of darkness, because of the time it took to cross the river, and did not get to the town until after daybreak. Cadwalader got some of his men across, but not his artillery, and so the attack on Bordentown never took place. Ewing could not get across at all which left the Hessians with an open escape route to the south.

These setbacks to the Americans were more than offset by the attitude and actions of the town's defenders. Tory sympathizers in the region had warned Rall an attack was being planned and had even told him the day and time, but American patrol activities on December 25 made the cocksure commander think his informers had their information all wrong—that the patrol was all he had to worry about, not a general attack. Add to that the holiday celebration that had begun on Christmas Eve and gone on all Christmas Day and into the night, during which the Hessian soldiers had debauched themselves on rum and other local hospitality. Rall himself spent Christmas night drinking and playing cards at the home of a Loyalist townsman and did not get to bed until about 6 A.M. What was on guard that morning after Christmas was a collection of hung-over pickets and their officers who were not expecting anything out of the ordinary. During the night's partying, however, a Tory farmer named Wall came into town looking for Rall. He had information concerning the movements of the Americans; but, though he sent a note in to the Hessian commander, that gentleman was too far gone in his cups and too engrossed in his cards to read it. Instead, he stuffed the message into his pocket and forgot all about it.

You have two options as you join the advance on Trenton. You can follow Sullivan's Way, also Pennington Road, keeping in mind that this is the river road Sullivan followed, not Route 29 which actually runs along the riverbank. If you do, be forewarned that in West

Trenton (north of the city proper) Pennington Road runs head on
into an interchange that was not there two hundred years ago. At the
interchange get onto State Street and take it to Calhoun Street, which
you will recognize by the Holiday Inn at the intersection and the exit
from the John Fitch Parkway (Route 29) immediately to your right.
As you drive along State Street, notice the intersection at Hermitage
Avenue where The Hermitage once stood, home of Philemon Dickinson, a general of local militia. A jäger detachment was stationed on the
grounds that Christmas night and was driven off by Sullivan as he advanced on the town. Turn left onto Calhoun and take it to Pennington
Avenue.

Alternate routes you might follow into Trenton are Pennington
Avenue (Route 31), which was Greene's road in part (this will take
you right to the battle monument), or Route 29 into the John Fitch
Parkway, which you should leave at the Calhoun Street exit and take
Calhoun to Pennington Avenue.

At this point, you must decide if you are going to drive from site
to site or walk. You can probably do the walk in two or three hours,
allowing time to stop to read markers and examine sites. If you drive,
you will be faced with the usual problems posed by the downtown
section of a modern city: heavy traffic during rush hours and at lunch-
time, municipal buses, pedestrians, one-way streets, traffic lights, and
restricted parking. Parking lots and garages in Trenton are cheap. At
the time I visited, private parking garages and lots were charging $0.50
for the first half hour and $0.25 for every hour after that; municipal
lots charged $0.10 per half hour or fraction thereof.

Begin at the corner of Calhoun and Pennington Avenue. The action
began a quarter of a mile or so up Pennington Avenue where a Hessian outpost spotted the first Americans coming out of the woods and
fired. As the attackers pressed forward the outpost fell back on its regimental position, where more fire was exchanged. At the same time Sullivan's men on the river road routed the outpost of jägers at The Hermitage and pressed on into the town. The Hessian pickets ran down
Queen Street as the Americans raced forward, bayonets at the ready.

Now turn right onto Pennington Avenue and follow the attack
to the **Battle Monument**, a tall column surmounted by a statue of Washington and an observation platform. An elevator goes to the top when
the monument is open—on weekdays and holidays from 10 to 12 A.M.
and from 1 to 5 P.M.—but since it was closed at the time of my visit
I cannot vouch for the view. From that height, you can probably see

the approach routes of the Americans, the scene of the main action now in the heart of the town, and the surrounding areas to the south and west. The bronze plaques on the monument are by Thomas Eakins and were recently appraised, as they were being cleaned for an exhibit at the Corcoran Gallery, at about $150,000.

The Battle Monument is situated on what is now and was then the highest point in the town, overlooking the downtown area. From this point two streets lead downhill: today they are called Broad and Warren; then they were known as King and Queen streets. Washington ordered the artillery to take up a position where the monument now stands and the guns opened fire on the lower town. Solid shot and grape whistled down King and Queen streets as the Hessians tried to rally against the attack. Rall was roused out of bed and came into the street to find it raked by American fire and his men completely disorganized.

None of the buildings you now see around you were there at the time, but as you go down Warren Street, just past Perry Street, you will find **St. Michael's Church** on the left. Here in the churchyard behind the church Rall attempted to form his troops into an orderly formation. Artillery fire and flanking fire from American units closing in was too much for them, however, and the Germans broke and ran. On King Street the Hessians managed to get a couple of guns into action, but a determined charge led by Lieutenant James Monroe put them out of service. The lieutenant and his commanding officer, Captain William Washington, were both wounded, but their men went on without them into the lower town.

Walk down Warren Street to State Street. The battle raged through and around the houses then lining these streets. In the meantime, Sullivan's men coming into the village from the south met up with the Knyphausen Regiment at the Old Barracks (which you will visit later) and drove them to Assunpink Creek, which today flows through the lower part of the city. A bridge across the creek, about where South Warren crosses the creek near Goldberg's Department Store, allowed the fugitives to escape to the south; for Ewing, as you know, was not there to cut them off. Most of the fighting was close-in bayonet action. The only weapons using gunpowder were cannon; the storm had made it impossible to fire rifles or muskets. In fact, during the march to Trenton Sullivan had sent word to Washington that the snow and sleet would soon make it impossible for his men to use their guns. Back came the word from Washington: "Tell General Sullivan to use the bayonet. I am resolved to take Trenton!"

At that time, the area south of what is now State Street was an open field. Here the Hessians tried to form for a counterattack, but the American artillery stopped them cold. With Sullivan now behind them at the bridge over the creek, Rall tried to get his men into an orchard, but was hit and fell mortally wounded. He died shortly after the battle, the unread note still in his pocket. Turn left off Warren Street onto State Street and walk two or three blocks to the Public Service Building on the left side of the street. A large *plaque* on an iron post near the curb identifies this as the approximate site of the Hessian surrender.

The last shot was fired about 9:30 A.M., after a fight that had lasted either thirty-five minutes or an hour and three quarters, depending on which account of the battle you read. The Hessians lost 106 officers and men killed and wounded; 918 were taken prisoner, including the wounded. About 500 Hessians escaped. The Americans lost four wounded (two privates and Monroe and William Washington), and about four killed, three of whom are said to have frozen to death during the withdrawal. Some historians insist, however, that the Americans suffered no deaths at all in this battle.

The effect of the victory was immediate and dramatic. Congress and the country were instilled with new courage at the news; the army was starving, frozen, and exhausted, but alive with hope. Howe was astounded, and Cornwallis, who was about to return to England for a short leave, was ordered to march to the Delaware to make matters right again.

Since neither Ewing nor Cadwalader had joined him, Washington felt unable to carry out the rest of his plan to attack Princeton and New Brunswick and so withdrew across the river to Pennsylvania with his prisoners. Because of the weather and the exhausted condition of his men—many had not rested for more than two days and had marched more than forty miles—the withdrawal was not completed until late the following day, December 27. That same day Cadwalader finally got his men and guns across the Delaware and occupied the town of Burlington. Washington then considered joining him in an attack on Bordentown, but his men were in no condition to undergo another crossing and march, so the opportunity passed. On December 30, however, having sent their prisoners to Philadelphia, the Continental Army crossed the Delaware again, under worse conditions than previously, and marched back to Trenton; Washington had persuaded the militia to extend their enlistment by six weeks by offering them an unauthorized bounty of $10.

Of the 1,600 troops that reoccupied Trenton, about 1,100 were militiamen serving out those six-week enlistments. Against them, 8,000 British were coming from Princeton. Up to this point the British had thought of the Jersey campaign as a fox hunt, with Cornwallis the hunter and Washington the fox. The fox had turned on the hounds, however, and made some of them run; so he had to be punished. When the hunters began to close in from New Brunswick, Princeton, and Amboy, the fox went to ground. Calling in Ewing and Cadwalader, Washington dug in along Assunpink Creek, while picked detachments did what they could to delay the oncoming British on the road from Princeton.

THE BATTLES OF TRENTON: II—
ASSUNPINK CREEK

To join Washington on Assunpink Creek walk down Broad Street until you come to an open area of boulevards near the river with several state buildings ahead of you. Near the spot where the street crosses the creek, a marker identifies the site of **Washington's stand.** Facing across the creek, Washington's men were dug in on what was then high ground ahead of you. (The Delaware is on your right.) Cornwallis stayed the night of January 1 in Princeton and took the road to Trenton, only twelve miles away, the following morning. Along the way he had to deploy time and again to fight American harassers. By 4 P.M. Tuesday, January 2, he was fighting his way into Trenton from the north against stiff resistance from the American delaying force under the command of Colonel Edward Hand, who fell back slowly and in good order to the creek. It took the British eight hours to cover the last eight miles. At the creek Cornwallis tried three times to get across, but rebel guns placed to cover the bridge and American rifles threw his redcoats and Hessians back each time. A mill stood on the American side of the creek at this point. Several Hessian soldiers managed to get across and take cover in the mill, where they were cooped up until after dark and then captured.

When it became too dark to see, Cornwallis called off his attacks and decided to wait until the next day, when he expected to finally nab his fox; for now he had him cornered with the river behind him. But Washington had yet another trick hidden up his sleeve. Picked men kept the campfires burning and made the night noisy with the sound of pick and shovel; while Washington, with rags wrapped around his gun carriage wheels to muffle the sound and with his men barely breathing, moved out and around the British left and, following deserted and little known back roads, marched on Princeton. When Cornwallis awoke the next day, he found the American positions deserted and heard from the north the distant sound of cannon. The fox had gotten out of one chicken coop and into another.

Before you leave Trenton for Princeton, take half a day or so to visit two colonial landmarks connected with the first battle. The **Old Barracks** is on the grounds of the State House on South Willow Street. You can reach it by following West State Street from Calhoun Street and turning right onto South Willow, the first intersection after the State House. There is parking along the street in front of the barracks and a municipal park and lock garage about two blocks farther down State Street.

The barracks is an E-shaped building fronting on South Willow with a formal lawn and shrub arrangement taking up what used to be the barracks' yard. A Revolutionary War cannon mounted on a fieldstone pedestal in the middle of the lawn points in your direction. The two wings were originally built as officers' quarters; the long main section, with the second-floor balcony running its length, contained the enlisted men's quarters. At one time the wings were moved away to other sites; an extension of Front Street was built right through the main barracks building, and the remainder became a tenement house. The work of restoration was begun in 1902 and completed in 1917.

The first part of the barracks was built in 1758 as one of five barracks erected in five different New Jersey towns, all at the behest of the citizens, who objected to soldiers being quartered in their homes. Trenton barracks is the only one of the five to survive. Today it serves as a *museum* housing a collection of antiques and weapons. One of the rooms in the main building has been restored as enlisted men's quarters, with triple-tiered bunk beds, freestanding fireplaces, and all the accouterments of barracks life during the colonial period. On the upper floor one room exhibits five dioramas, accompanied by an excellent recorded narration that, with the help of lights, tells the story of the ten-day campaign, from the crossing of the Delaware to the Battle of Princeton. In the main entrance room, notice at the head of the double stairway part of the triumphal arch through which Washington walked in Trenton while on his way to his inauguration as President. He walked through such archways in every city and town he passed through on that route.

The entire barracks building was originally surrounded by a picket fence; the formal garden in front was a bare barracks yard where soldiers formed for inspections and drill. Sullivan's men came from behind the barracks and encountered the Knyphausen regiment in front of the building. The Hessians fired one volley, then ran for the creek and safety.

Walk down to the far corner of the barracks to see a granite monument bearing a tablet that gives an account of a most interesting sidelight to the events of the winter of 1776. Despite Howe's guarantee of safety for all inhabitants of New Jersey and Pennsylvania who proclaimed their allegience to the king, the Hessians knew no such distinction and plundered the local inhabitants with such a lack of discrimination that many a Tory became a Whig and not a few became out and out partisans of the revolutionary cause. Much of the plunder was kept in the churches, jail houses, courts, and old barracks in Trenton. After the American occupation of the town, Washington had the loot returned to its rightful owners.

Follow Warren Street down to the complex of official buildings on the river, then follow the signs for the **William Trent House**, where a detachment of Hessians was stationed at the time of the battle. Ewing was supposed to have come across to this point to seize the eastern terminus of the Trenton Ferry. The house, built in 1719 and restored in 1934, was the home of William Trent who owned the land on which the original Trent Town was built. This is one of the most beautiful colonial homes I have seen. Many of the furnishings are of the William and Mary and Queen Anne periods, and you might want to devote an hour or two to their inspection before you follow the Continental Army to Princeton.

THE BATTLE OF PRINCETON

In later years General Arthur St. Clair insisted that the idea of slipping around the British left and marching to Princeton was his idea, that he proposed it on the night of January 2 during a council of war in which Washington asked his officers for advice. Some historians believe that Washington had Princeton in mind when he took up position on the Assunpink, that it was part of the overall strategy that had been discussed and decided on before the army moved across the Delaware into New Jersey. Whatever the planning, the night of January 2–3, Washington marched his army north along backcountry roads of which the British were not aware and that no longer exist. One contemporary description pictures them as little more than dirt tracks not quite cleared of tree trunks. An early January thaw had turned the roads to mud, a factor that had slowed Cornwallis on the way south from Princeton almost as much as the delaying tactics of the Americans. The temperature dropped again, however, that night, and the mud froze solid giving the rebels a good, hard surface to walk on. Nevertheless, it was a nightmarish march, beginning at 1 A.M. with the officers pushing the men as hard as they could all the way. By 3 A.M. they had covered ten miles and were at Stony Brook, just two miles south of Princeton.

You can get to the Stony Brook position by taking Route 583 north from Trenton. Keep an eye open for the **Princeton Battlefield Monument** on your left at about the ten-and-a-quarter-mile count on your odometer; it's a four pillar, Greek colonnade standing by itself on a rise of ground about three or four hundred feet off the road.

If you have not been following the Delaware basin tour but are coming directly from the north, take the New Jersey Turnpike south to Exit 9 and pick up U.S. 1 south to Route 571 west into Princeton, home of Princeton University. You will pass university buildings for several blocks before you come to Nassau Street, where you should turn left and go through the town. Note on your left Nassau Hall, which you will visit during the last stages of the battle. It is the university's first and oldest building and is set back off the street beneath huge shade trees, behind an iron picket fence. Watch for Palmer Square on your right, a quadrangle bordered by one-way streets with a sign directory listing its shops and services. Between the first and second traffic lights after the square (very soon after the first light), you will see Mercer Street going off at a diagonal to your left. Turn left onto Mercer Street (Route 583) and follow it out of town until you see the Greek colonnade battlefield monument on your right.

The only parking facility in this park, which stretches across Mercer Street and takes in all the open ground you see on both sides, is the shoulder of the road. On either side are wide grassy lawns with the ground sloping up from the road in both directions. The monument marks the higher ground known as **Mercer Heights.** A flagpole on the opposite side of the road marks the high ground on that side. The field on the flagpole side is divided by a windbreak, to the right of which, as you face the flagpole, is **Mercer Oak** with its huge trunk and magnificent spread of branches. To the right of the monument, as you face it, and close to Mercer Road, a plaque between two large yews marks the burial place of the British dead. The monument itself bears several commemorative plaques and one that designates the site a national landmark. Behind the monument a gravel path leads to a circular area paved with pieces of slate in the midst of a grove of tall pines. An inscription identifies this site as the burial place of the American dead. Beyond are a number of suburban and country homes.

There are no paths in this park and nothing to stop you from wandering across the lawns from site to site at will. The local residents come here to picnic, fly kites, exercise dogs, and take wedding pictures in front of the colonnade. Near the flagpole is a tile map of the battlefield with a full diagram and blow-by-blow description of the action. Before you consult the map, however, go through the opening phases of the battle.

Keep in mind that Mercer Road did not exist in 1777; that the road along which Washington and his army marched is no longer to be found; that Route 206, which runs along Mercer Heights beyond the monument, was then called King's Highway; and that Princeton was a small village with Nassau Hall the only university building. Now go south along Mercer Road, away from the town, to the first intersection, at Quaker Road. Turn left onto Quaker Road (which also existed then) and proceed until on your left you see the sign for the **Quaker Meetinghouse.** The meetinghouse is at the end of a long driveway which ends in a parking area.

A small, fieldstone building with a Quaker cemetery next to it, this house served as a hospital after the battle. It is still in use as a meeting-house and the cemetery contains tombstones dating from the Revolution to the present. As you enter the cemetery, to the right of the gate is the burial place of Richard Stockton, a signer of the Declaration of Independence. Most of the old colonial stones have sunk into the earth and their inscriptions are illegible. Several are marked by small American flags and one or two mark the resting place of veterans of the Revolution.

Just before dawn, Washington's men stopped to rest on the banks of **Stony Brook,** which parallels Quaker Road a few feet to the south. Princeton was only two miles away, but Washington wanted the army as rested as possible without losing the element of surprise. King's High-way (Route 206), the road Cornwallis had taken to Trenton, was just a half mile to the west. In the town were 1,200 troops under the command of Lieutenant Colonel Charles Mawhood, left there by Cornwallis to guard his supplies. During the night Mawhood had received orders from Corn-wallis to join him in Trenton for the expected assault on the Continental Army which Cornwallis planned as the last engagement of the war; he felt sure of capturing Washington at last. Mawhood started south at dawn leaving one regiment of about 400 men to guard the stores. Both forces were now within a half mile of each other, but not yet aware of each other's presence.

As Washington stood beside **Quaker Road** watching his men march by the meetinghouse, he detached General Hugh Mercer and a brigade to the left to guard his flank and to destroy the bridge which carried

King's Highway across Stony Brook. They were also to act as a delaying force should Cornwallis's men appear from the south. Leave the meeting-house and return along Quaker Road toward Mercer Road, following the Continental line of march. Continue on past Mercer Road, noticing as you go that the brook comes closer to the road, appearing on your left at the foot of a shallow ravine. As Mawhood's men crossed the bridge head-ing south, Mawhood caught a glimpse of Mercer's men approaching the bridge and turned his command to meet the threat. Both forces saw each other at about the same time, deployed immediately, and raced to reach high ground east of the brook, probably Mercer Heights, now marked by the monument.

Before picking up the story from the battlefield map, you should continue along Quaker Road to the intersection with 206 (King's High-way), along which Mawhood marched. Turn left and cross a stone bridge built in 1792 as a replacement for the original bridge. Notice on your right at the south end of the bridge, the tall, fieldstone remains of a grist-mill. Unfortunately, the road is too narrow and curved to permit you to park and examine the site.

Return along Quaker Road to Mercer Road; turn left; park again along the road; and walking to the flagpole, turn to face the map, with the battlefield spread out before you. Orient yourself by the monument, Mercer Oak, Mercer Road, and other landmarks, all of which are clearly shown on the map. The **Thomas Clark House** shown on the map is behind you beyond the trees. The Quaker Meetinghouse is beyond that and to the left. Mercer Heights is about where the monument stands. At the time most of this was cornfield, covered with the stubble of the previous year's crop. Mercer and his men were in an orchard which spread across what is now Mercer Road to the left of Mercer Oak. A belt of trees be-tween the Quaker Meetinghouse and the orchard hid the rest of the rebel forces from Mawhood.

Accounts of what happened differ considerably, according to how familiar the writer has made himself with the terrain. For example, one account I have read describes the orchard on high ground, which is non-sense for the orchard area is in the low ground between two slopes. The most likely account is that Mercer, seeing he could not reach Mercer Heights before the British, turned to join Sullivan's men who were fol-lowing a road (no longer in existence) that cut across the battlefield at a diagonal toward Nassau Hall in Princeton. As Mercer's men reached the orchard, a small detachment of redcoats behind a fence fired at them. Mercer led a charge that drove the British back up the slope. At that point Mawhood, seeing how small in numbers his opponents actually were, turned his line and charged across the field from the other side of present Mercer Road. Armed with slow-loading muskets, the Continentals did not have time to get off another volley before the British were among them with their bayonets. Mercer, cut off from his men near the oak, was stabbed repeatedly and fell mortally wounded. His men panicked and ran toward where you are standing.

Two American guns in another orchard off to your left stopped the British advance and additional American troops coming out of the woods behind you to the left, from the direction of the meetinghouse, caused Mawhood to turn to meet them. The new arrivals, members of Cadwalader's militia thrown in by Washington, received one volley from the British and turned to run. But now units of Washington's rear guard appeared off to the left advancing to the scene. Cadwalader, Greene, and Washington dashed out onto the field to rally the fleeing Continentals in the area immediately in front of you.

Shouting to the men to follow him, Washington got them back into line and led them toward the British. The redcoats fired when he was about thirty yards away. The Americans returned the fire and Washington was lost to sight in a cloud of smoke. When the smoke cleared away, he was still on his horse urging the men on. His aides rushed to him as he shouted for the troops to come on. As the line of Continentals behind him advanced, the rear guard elements moved to outflank the British. Mawhood's men fell back toward Mercer Heights. As the British left the field, American units tried to cut them off from the bridge, but Mawhood rallied them and led a bayonet charge that cleared the way. Washington sent a troop of the Philadelphia light horse in pursuit and shouting "It's a fine fox chase, my boys!" led them himself across the bridge and down the road after the fleeing British.

It was a fox hunt, indeed, but it was the hounds who were the hunted, not the "old fox" as Cornwallis had called Washington on the banks of Assunpink Creek just the day before. The redcoats scattered into the woods, but Washington called off the pursuit. Advance units sent out by Cornwallis, who he knew would have heard the guns and would be on the way back to Princeton, would find the Americans spread out along the road in a highly vulnerable condition. According to one story, as he rode away Washington saw a wounded British soldier being robbed and came to the man's aid. Leaving the field of victory behind him, the commander in chief led his men on to Princeton.

With your back to the map, walk through the trees to the granite memorial to Mercer, which was erected by the Mercer Engine Company

No. 3 of Princeton in 1897. You can also walk along a wide, grassy opening between the trees which will take you to the Clark House, now privately owned. This is the house in which Mercer died, and though you cannot enter to inspect the premises, you can get a good look at this well-preserved reminder of that January day.

Then walk back across the field to the great oak where Mercer was placed before he was carried to the house. Another living witness to history, this magnificent tree, obviously well taken care of by the park attendants, has a full spread of branches, every one in full leaf.

One more action remains to be accounted for before you leave here to cover the action at Nassau Hall. The Fifty-fifth Foot had been drawn up in formation on Mercer Heights, probably to the right of the memorial as you face it. When Mawhood retreated, the Fifty-fifth fell back toward Princeton in a circular path that brought them down into what is called Frog Hollow about where Alexander Road crosses Mercer Road. When Sullivan moved against them, they retreated toward the town without a fight.

The entire action lasted less than half an hour, costing the Americans about forty killed and wounded; but what an expensive half hour it was for the British. They lost much more than the eighty-six killed and wounded and the two hundred or so taken prisoner at Nassau Hall. Though Cornwallis came back in haste from Trenton, entering Princeton from the south as the last Continentals were leaving the town, Howe's campaign aimed at destroying the Continental Army, capturing Washington, and taking Philadelphia was at an end. In just ten days, the ragged, hungry rebel forces, less than 5,000 strong, had crossed the Delaware three times in the dead of winter, taken Trenton after routing crack Hessian regiments, held Cornwallis at bay; then outwitted him and struck again at his rear, proving they were far from beaten. But even more than that, this brilliant, fast-moving campaign had cleared most of New Jersey of the enemy except in New Brunswick and Amboy (now Perth Amboy) where they posed no threat, and it had all been done against an army of professional, trained, and battle-tested officers and men.

Take Mercer Road into town and, turning right at Nassau Street, look for parking at one of the meters near Nassau Hall or in a municipal lot. Situated at the edge of the university grounds and facing onto Nassau Street, **Nassau Hall** was completed in 1756. For fifty years it was the university's sole building, housing classrooms, dormitories, teachers' quarters, dining rooms, and so on. During the Revolution it was alternately occupied by the British and the rebels and was used as a hospital and barracks by both forces. The Fifty-fifth Foot and the regiment Mawhood left in town to guard the supplies retreated into Nassau Hall after the battle and barricaded the building. Sullivan came up with his men and it looked like a long and bloody siege, until Alexander Hamilton rolled up two of his guns and sent a couple of shots against the buildings. The first glanced off, but the second crashed through the main room on the ground floor and the British, about two hundred strong, promptly surrendered.

The university's Orange Key Society conducts tours of the university which begin with a visit to Nassau Hall, meaning that you can go along for Nassau Hall and drop out of the rest of the tour if you wish. These tours, however, are not conducted on a regular basis; you must write to make arrangements beforehand. Inside Nassau Hall, the room in which the British tried to hold out is directly across from the main lobby. Modeled on the House of Commons, the room has a long table down the middle, tiered pews on either side, and a presiding officer's bench on a dais at the front. To the left of the bench is Charles Willson Peale's portrait of Washington, painted in 1783 showing the commander at the Battle of Princeton with Nassau Hall in the background. Originally the frame held a portrait of George II which occupied the wall to the right of the bench. It was through this wall that Hamilton's cannonball entered, decapitating the king's portrait, so the story goes, and bringing about the British surrender in the face of so obvious an omen. The Continental Congress sat in Nassau Hall from June to November, 1783, at a special session during which it gave its personal thanks to Washington for his service during the war, received the news of the signing of the Treaty of Paris, and officially received the first minister accredited to the United States, Peter van Merckel of the Netherlands.

If you've done the battlefield in the morning, as you might after spending the previous day in Trenton, you will find Princeton a good place for lunch before moving north to Morristown.

Washington had planned to go on from Princeton to raid the British stores at New Brunswick, for though his men had captured some supplies, the results were meager at best and many were still without clothing in the middle of winter. But the army had marched too far and too fast and fought too many engagements in too few days; after resting the men for a few hours and allowing them to fill up on captured British rations, Washington decided to take them north into the protection of the hills around Morristown.

ROCKINGHAM: THE HOUSE AT ROCKY HILL

On the way to Morristown, take an hour to find and see Rockingham, the house General and Mrs. Washington occupied while the general was in the Princeton area in 1783. Continue along Nassau Street in the opposite direction from the battlefield as it becomes Route 27 north. A short distance out of Princeton you will see the first sign for "Washington's Headquarters," directing you left onto a country road to Route 518. Turn right on 518 and within a mile, turn left at the sign onto a driveway. The driveway leads to a parking area at the rear of **Rockingham**, a two-story, white frame colonial farmhouse with a kitchen addition.

Originally the house was located almost a mile away on what is now 518 in the direction from which you came, but when a quarry company threatened to destroy it during the late nineteenth century, local residents aware of the house's history raised sufficient money to have it moved to its present site and restored. Admission is $0.25 for adults, but free for children under twelve and senior citizens.

The house originally stood on 360 acres of land along the Millstone River, on what was then the main road between Princeton and Morristown. It was built by John Berrien, who came here in 1735 from Long Island as a surveyor, married, and built himself a home. At first the house had only two rooms, the dining room on the first floor and the room above it known as the Blue Room. By 1772, Berrien and his second wife (his first wife died, childless) had six children and he had extended the house to accommodate them. On April 22, 1772, Berrien, a judge by this time, invited several friends to the house to witness the signing of his will. Among them was Richard Stockton, whose grave you saw in the cemetery at the Quaker Meetinghouse. Having signed the will and seen it witnessed, Berrien then drowned himself in the Millstone River, in the presence of his witnesses.

When Congress came to Princeton in 1783 to hold its sessions free from the threats of mutinous soldiers in Philadelphia who were demanding their pay, they invited Washington to meet with them so they could have the benefit of his counsel. The presence of Congress and its attendants and petitioners, added to the student body at the university in a town of only seventy-five houses, a good number of them taverns, placed accommodations at a premium. The Widow Berrien had placed her home on the market, but buyers in those unsettled times were not crowding to the gate. When she was approached by an army officer who had been delegated by Congress to find a place for Washington, she agreed to let the general and his official family use the house as his home and headquarters during his stay in Princeton.

Actually a rather sticky situation had arisen between Washington and Congress. While still in Philadelphia, Elias Boudinot, the president of the Congress, had written to Washington requesting that he attend the session. Washington, then in Newburgh, New York, sweating out the peace treaty, wrote back to say he would be delighted to attend. He was then kept waiting for weeks for final word on when to come, while his troops were sent home on furlough to await discharge. Tired out from the long years of war, anxious to get back to the peace and tranquility of Mount Vernon, Washington wrote again on July 16: "Finding myself in most disagreeable Circumstances here, and like to be so, so long as Congress are pleased to continue me in this awkward Situation, anxiously expecting the Definitive Treaty, without Command and with little else to do, than to be teazed with troublesome Applications and fruitless Demands, which I have neither the means nor the power of satisfying . . . I have resolved to wear away a little Time in performing a Tour to the Northward, as far as Tyconderoga and Crown point, and perhaps as far up the Mohawk River as fort Schuyler."

This gentle hint brought quick action to relieve the general of his "awkward situation," and when he returned to Newburgh after his two-week tour he found an official invitation from Boudinot waiting.

Washington and his wife, who had had a fever and was still ailing, left Hasbrouck House in Newburgh on August 19, and by August 23 were installed in Rockingham. It was from this house that, on Monday, August 25, 1783, the hero of the Revolution rode into Princeton to receive the tumultuous reception its citizens had prepared and the gratitude and thanks of the Congress. At the admissions counter inside the entrance, which is actually the back door, you can buy a little book called *Rockingham—Washington's Headquarters* by Genevieve C. Cobb, a local historian, which contains an excellent and colorful account of what went on in Princeton during this period between war and peace and something of what occurred at Rockingham during Washington's tenure in the house.

As is the case with many restored colonial homes, none of the furniture now in Rockingham is original to the house, but is a collection of antiques representing the period and the area. On the ground floor, to the right of the entry hall, is a long room now used to marshall visitors for the tour. Beyond that is a small bedroom in which Martha Washington slept. She was probably placed in the ground-floor room because of her illness, which persisted, causing the general to send her on ahead to Mount

Vernon the first week in October before the onset of bad weather and worse roads. Note just outside the door to this room the odd placement of some of the floorboards, indicating that formerly the room had an adjoining dressing room, exactly the size of the general's dressing room on the floor above, heated by a corner fireplace.

The entry hall leads ahead into the main living room in which the family spent most of its time. To the left a door leads to the outside and the cookhouse from which the food was carried to the table. In an adjoining room, the paneling has been cut away to reveal the lathe and plaster construction usual at the time, but what is not shown is the insulating layer of brick between the inner and outer walls.

On the second floor are the room in which Washington slept, his dressing room, and the room he used as a study; here he handled all his correspondence and wrote the farewell address he eventually delivered to his troops. Known as the Blue Room, it is the one room that was not threatened with destruction when the quarry company owned the house. According to local accounts, the company filled the house with Italian immigrant workmen who were endowed with greater sensitivity than their employers. Knowing something of the house's history and the significance of the study, they scrupulously avoided using that room, crowding into the other rooms instead, preserving the study as a shrine to Washington. The study opens out onto a balcony running the length of the front of the house. Though the prospect is a pleasant one of lawn and trees, it cannot compare to the view Washington enjoyed when the house stood on its original site on the Millstone River, with the hills of the river valley disappearing into the distance toward Princeton.

In Washington's drawing room, note what seems to be a large, corner chair with a high back. It is actually a commode with a seat that can be raised to reveal the chamber beneath. Also take a close look at what looks like decoupage on the wall of the main room on the ground floor, just to the right of the door as you enter. Actually that framed series of scenes with its tiny figures, buildings, trees, shrubs, and animals was created with a scissors out of heavy paper and then pasted on to a cloth background. The longer one looks at it, the more amazed one is at the skill and patience that went into its creation.

It is a little difficult for us to realize the extent of the affection and regard with which Washington was held by the general populace after the war. William Dunlap, the artist who at the age of seventeen spent some time at Rockingham and in Princeton during this period, gave this account of the first time he saw Washington:

"As I walked on the road leading from Princeton to Trenton . . .

ascending a hill suddenly appeared a brilliant troop of cavaliers, mounting and gaining the summit in my front. The clear autumnal sky behind them relieved the dark blue uniforms, the buff facings, and glittering military appendages. All were gallantly mounted—all were tall and graceful, but one towered above the rest, and I doubted not an instant that I saw the beloved hero. I lifted my hat as I saw that his eye was turned toward me, and instantly every hat was raised and every eye was fixed upon me. They passed on and I turned and gazed as at a passing vision. I had seen him."

CAMPING OUT AT MORRISTOWN

Before turning to the east to cover Jersey sites to the south and east, take a ride up to Morristown to round out the story of the winter of 1776–77. Coming out of the Rockingham driveway, turn right onto 518 and take it to U.S. 206 north, which will lead you to Interstate 287. Use the interstate north as far as you can. At the time I used it last it did not quite make it to Morristown, only to a point a little north of Basking Ridge. If you want to save time, take the interstate; but if you have the time to drive leisurely through the gently rolling, wooded hills of this part of Jersey, then stay on 206, which is joined by Route 202, which takes you into Morristown.

The present town of Morristown is a bustling, crowded county seat filled with shops, department stores, and traffic. In 1777 fifty or sixty buildings made up the entire town and the total population was 250. Washington brought his army here for several reasons: two or three regiments originally stationed at Ticonderoga were there to provide him with additional strength; with the British still at New Brunswick and Amboy, Morristown was a good strategic position from which he could move east, north, or south to meet whatever move they might make; the inhabitants of the town and the surrounding country were known to be friendly and, since the area was largely agricultural, might keep the men fed; and there were several important iron mines and foundries west and north of the town at Ringwood and Hibernia which he hoped would supply his army with necessary metal equipment. It would also have been a difficult position for the British to attack, since it was protected by great swamps to the east and the Watchung Mountains beyond, two lines of them curving from the west to run along a north-south line for more than thirty miles right up to the New York border where they join the Ramapo Hills. Though the British sent probing forces toward Morristown from time to time—the later Springfield Raid in June, 1780 was such an attempt—their efforts were concentrated mainly on getting their hands on the cattle and farm produce Washington's occupation of these rich farmlands denied them.

On his part, Washington kept up constant and vigorous patrol activities based on Morristown. From here he again sent out urgent appeals for men and supplies and recruiting officers to help raise the eighty-eight battalions Congress had finally authorized. And here in Morristown he met one of the most serious attacks his army had to withstand: smallpox struck the army as it had in 1776 and ran like wildfire through the ranks and the civilian population. Taking what was then a calculated risk, Washington instituted a program of inoculations, at first secretly; then, as the results seemed favorable, openly, even extending it to the civilian population in the Morristown area. Though many civilians failed to take advantage of the inoculation program and became ill, most of the soldiers so treated who contracted the disease came down with mild infections and survived.

There are three sites to visit in the Morristown area, two of them within the town and the third, the scene of the major encampment in 1779–80 and the one best remembered, a short distance south. The Continental Army, or units thereof, spent three winters at the Morristown encampments; yet despite the area's importance, there are at this writing no signs in or around the town to guide you to the sites. The National Park Service has placed markers along the roads—small, white discs about four inches in diameter—but they hardly do the job. Members of the staff have told me new signs are in the making and by the time you visit Morristown, you may not experience the difficulty I encountered.

Begin by going first to park headquarters on Morris Street. Route 202 goes to one corner of Morristown Green in the center of town. Turn right onto Washington Street, then left onto Morris Street. Morris Street will take you past the railroad station, under the tracks, past the George Washington School on your left, around a curve, and past a traffic light, at which point you will spot a sign on your left reading "**Morristown National Historic Park**—Washington Headquarters." On the opposite side of Morris Street, to your right, an equestrian statue of Washington is poised for a canter down Morris Street and back into town. A short distance up Morris Street past the statue is the site where Washington's life guards encamped while their commander was in residence in the Ford Mansion.

Ford Mansion is set off the street in the midst of tree-shaded grounds, with a fence along the street. There is no parking area set aside for visitors, so you will have to find parking on the side streets. A sign on the front lawn puts the building of the house at 1772 by Colonel Jacob Ford, Jr. and cites it as the home of General and Mrs. Washington and the general's headquarters from December, 1779 to June, 1780. The house and the *museum* behind it are open daily from 10 A.M. to 5 P.M. Admission is $0.50 for adults, free for anyone under sixteen.

Once past the admission desk in the entry hall, you begin a self-guided tour with the first room on your left, the dining room where the general and his lady dined and where he conferred with various officers and dignitaries, including, among others, Lafayette; the French ambassador, Chevalier de La Luzerne; and Don Juan de Miralles, who was traveling with him. These foreign gentlemen arrived during the spring of 1780, but during the elaborate celebrations heralding their arrival Don Juan became so ill he could not attend. By the end of April he was dead, and he was buried temporarily in the common burying ground of the Morristown Church. The account of this incident in the National Park Service handbook on Morristown describes Miralles as a "Spanish grandee" and states his presence was unofficial. According to the Chevalier de Chastellux, an officer on the staff of French commander Rochambeau, who traveled extensively in America from May, 1780, to January, 1783, Miralles was the first Spanish minister appointed to the rebellious states, a fact Chastellux learned when he stayed in the unfortunate man's apartments in Philadelphia later that year.

This is one of the largest colonial homes you will visit, aside from Mount Vernon and Monticello: large in the number of rooms it contains and in the size of the individual rooms. There are stairways that connect half-stories, rooms beyond rooms, back hallways, odd little nooks of rooms, and rooms that were obviously servants' quarters. At the time Washington stayed, the widowed Mrs. Ford gave over most of the house to the general and his "family," as he referred to his staff, keeping only two rooms on the ground floor for herself and her four children.

There is a short, printed legend posted at the door of each room describing the uses the room was put to. This is a decided change from the usual rule in landmark houses, where signs describe the furniture, going into detail concerning its design, antiquity, and function. Those of you who are antique buffs may obtain from the park office, upon request, a listing of the mansion's furnishings and further details. The rest of you presumably belong to what the National Park Service considers the majority of tourists and sightseers, those more likely to relate to a house and its contents in terms of the people who lived in it. I think a happy medium should be struck, particularly in a house like the Ford Mansion where 80 percent of the furnishings are original to the house and many of the pieces, like the secretary in the dining room, are known to have been used by George or Martha Washington, their guests, and other historic figures who came here on official business.

One of the most interesting single items in the house is in an upstairs room used by the general's aide de camp: a colonial version of a folding army cot, complete with canopy. A photograph on the wall near the bed shows what it looks like folded up. This oddity was designed to be carried in the field and must be the forerunner of our modern army folding cot. I have seen other beds, usually made of wood which were designed for the same purpose and had to be disassembled to move, but never one that collapsed as this does. Also notable is the large kitchen on the ground floor with its huge, brick, cooking fireplace, Dutch ovens, and cooking utensils. Take an especially good look at this kitchen, for here one night during the terrible winter of 1779–80, the Washingtons and their family and Mrs. Ford and her four children huddled together in front of the fireplace all night trying to keep warm.

Since this tour ends back in the main entry hall, I suggest you stop at the desk and ask the attendant for the small pamphlet that contains maps of the other sites and directions for getting to them. Behind the Ford Mansion, beyond a wide, terraced lawn, a large, stucco building designed in Dutch colonial style houses a museum that exhibits a small but select number of items connected with the Morristown encampments, the Washingtons, and colonial life and warfare in general. I found most interesting a case of relics concerning the Society of the Cincinnati and another case filled with items that had been personal possessions of George and Martha Washington. Also of interest are several paintings of the Morristown area before and during the encampment, showing what the town and countryside looked like and what the army huts were like. An auditorium on the second floor offers, every half hour, a slide film which gives the history of the encampments. In this day of multi-media presentations—especially in comparison to the slide film at Fort Chambly in Canada, a site not half as big or as important—this presentation leaves something to be desired visually, but it can orient you to the sites you are going to visit.

Your next objective is **Fort Nonsense**, which you reach by going back along Morris Street into town. At the Green, turn right and follow the one-way signs. As you come to the main street of the town, with Bamberger's Department Store to your left front, turn left and head toward Route 24 east, according to the signs. At Washington Street, having by now gone around two sides of the Green, make a right and begin looking immediately for the courthouse on your left and the Y.M.C.A. just beyond it. Between the two runs Western Avenue. Turn onto Western Avenue and find a Morristown Historic Park sign a few feet from the intersection indicating Jockey Hollow straight ahead and Fort Nonsense to the left. This sign is somewhat misleading. You do have to turn left onto Ann Street to get to the fort, but then you must turn right almost immediately onto the road that leads to the top of the hill. Be sure to avoid the turnoff for the jury parking field.

The road loops back at the top; pull off to the side onto a widened area that serves for parking. Beyond the parking area, on a grassy knoll, is a map of the area showing the various sites and your present position. Beyond that a large stone bears an inscription identifying the site as that of Fort Nonsense, an earthwork built by the Continental Army during 1777. A popular myth has sprung up about this site, to the effect that Washington put the men to work on this position to keep them occupied, hence its name. Actually, it was built at Washington's direct, practical order by a detachment left behind to guard supplies when the army moved out into the field in the spring of 1777.

Thirty-five years ago a reconstructed earthworks was here, but that has either been done away with or allowed to suffer the fate of the original construction, crumbling away to nothing. Now there is only a round grassy area surrounded by the woods, the granite marker, the road, and little else. A reconstruction is on the drawing boards, and by the time you come you may find a reasonable facsimile of the original. At the time this fortification was built the men stationed here were able to look out over the town and the surrounding countryside. This indicates that the hill, or at least its summit, was bare of trees. Today the woods make it difficult to get anything but glimpses of the view; the town which lies around the foot of the hill is completely obscured from view when the trees are in full leaf.

JOCKEY HOLLOW

Return to the foot of the hill and take Western Avenue to Jockey Hollow, the site of the 1779–80 encampment, as indicated by the park sign. Western Avenue becomes Jockey Hollow Road, which leads through hilly and wooded country with private homes along both sides, many of them hidden from the road. Jockey Hollow, about three miles from town, announces itself by the markers you begin to see along the road marking the sites where units of the army were encamped.

Jockey Hollow Road ends at a stop sign, where you make a right turn onto a road that leads to Route 24, passing the New Jersey brigade campsite marker on the other side of the road. A short distance farther you will see the **Wick House** on your right, a weathered cottage with a peaked roof. This is your first stop on the tour road that winds through the Jockey Hollow site. A parking area behind the house has a gate exit which takes you onto the farm grounds close to the barn. Just beyond the gate is a Jockey Hollow Encampment map and a weatherproof plaque with accompanying explanatory text and pictures. According to this map, much of the encampment occupied the hillsides to your front and right. A facsimile of an old map drawn by Captain Bichet de Roche Fontaine (a French volunteer who also drew up a number of other historically important maps, including several of West Point fortifications) pinpoints the sites where some of the encampments huts stood.

This is a lovely spot, with something of the feel of the frontier about it because of the wooded hills just beyond the fields, the split-rail fences, and the kitchen garden close to the house. You should remember, however, that those wooded hills were probably denuded of trees once the army moved in and built its huts. Close to the back door of the house, another plaque describes it as the home of Henry Wick, who built it about 1750. Major General St. Clair used the house as his quarters in 1779–80. At the time St. Clair was commander of the Pennsylvania Line, Anthony Wayne's old command, which was encamped on a hill about a mile behind you, a site that is blocked from view by trees.

Enter the Wick House by the back door, which leads you into a big, old, colonial farm kitchen. To your left is a pantry and storeroom you can look into through a glass door, then the dining room at the far left with a small bedroom off that. The room to the right off the kitchen is the master bedroom and is identical in shape, size, and detail to the dining room, even down to the small fireplace to the left of the door. Another glass door to your right permits a look into the tiny bedroom of the Wick's daughter, Tempe, who was about twenty-one years old at the time of the encampment. A traditional story says that at the time of the mutiny of the Pennsylvania Line, which was occupying huts in Jockey Hollow in 1781, Tempe hid her horse in the dining room for fear the mutinous soldiers would commandeer it for their march on Philadelphia.

This farmhouse is high on my list of the colonial homes I have visited for authenticity and atmosphere. The house itself, with its dimly lit interior and dark paneling, its weathered shingles, the fields around it, and the hills beyond evoke the colonial farm for me with greater conviction than the larger, more spacious Hasbrouck House, for instance, or Knox's Headquarters at New Windsor. Perhaps the simple, homemade and home-spun furnishings like the patchwork quilt on Tempe Wick's bed have something to do with the feeling that real people lived here. In fact, as you look around, you almost expect someone to walk in and ask you what you are doing there. Interestingly enough, this house was an occupied residence continuously from the time it was built in 1750 until 1935, when the Park Service took it over. As might be expected, it had under-gone some remodeling over the years—for example, a door that no longer exists led directly from the kitchen into the kitchen garden—and it took some reconstructing to get it back to what it was like, particularly the interior.

At the far end of the Wick House parking area, a sign directs you onto the one-way tour road, similar in intent to the tour road on the Saratoga battlefield. A twenty-mile-an-hour speed limit keeps you down to a safe speed as you drive through what is now a lovely, semi-rural park area that during the winter of 1779–80 was hell on earth for ten thousand Continental soldiers.

Your next stop is a restoration site in an open, grassy area, with a reconstructed army hospital just off the parking area and up on a hillside, overlooking the hospital, a row of reconstructed log huts. This is the site of the Pennsylvania Line encampment and the hill is **Sugarloaf Hill**. A plaque gives you some idea of what the site looked like and the condi-tions the men had to face during that terrible winter, when the snow lay on the ground four feet deep and higher and boiled shoe was part of their diet, according to Joseph Plumb Martin, a soldier who lived to write about the experience fifty years later. The descriptive matter also includes facsimile, enlarged copies of pages from journals kept by some of the people who lived through the winter. The plaque at the Pennsyl-vania brigade site, for example, describes life in the encampment as experienced by Doctor James Thatcher, a Massachusetts doctor who served in the army from 1775 to 1783.

The day I was there, a park attendant in colonial costume was demonstrating the making of paper cartridges as part of a new program at the Morristown restoration. During the summer months, similarly uniformed attendants will be on hand to answer questions and give talks and demonstrations concerning the kind of life the soldiers of the

Revolution led there. A Brigade of the American Revolution unit, Morgan's Rifles, which comes from this neighborhood, has in the past lent its colorful services to this project.

The *hospital* is made of huge, peeled logs notched at the ends and chinked between the cracks with clay and mud. There is a large, central section and projecting wings at either end. On the plaque in front is a reproduced page from a journal kept by Dr. James Tilton, who designed the structure, explaining why he designed it in this fashion. According to the doctor, it was built in the style of an Indian hut with a central fire but no chimney. The smoke was carried off through an opening between the roof and the sidewalls that ran all around the building. Patients lay with their heads to the walls and their feet turned to the fire. According to the good doctor, the smoke, which hung above the patients' heads under the roof before it left the building, helped to fight infection without affecting the patients. He was "well satisfied with the experiment."

You can enter all three sections of this army hospital, though they are almost identical in detail, with open fireplaces, windows cut into the walls with shutters hanging over them, and bare, dirt floors. The big difference is in the fireplaces; those in the wings have high, fieldstone back walls; the one in the central section is just a low, stone arrangement very like a campfire.

Behind the hospital is a large circular enclosure set off by a continuous chain hung from low, cement posts. In the enclosure is a plaque on a large boulder which marks the site of the **Jockey Hollow Cemetery** where more than one hundred men who did not survive the winter are buried. The hospital is a good exhibit, but is not historically accurate. According to the park's historian, it was actually located at Basking Ridge. If it's not there when you visit, historical accuracy has triumphed.

A dirt path leads up Sugarloaf to five reconstructed *log huts.* Four represent a line of enlisted men's huts; an officer's hut is placed above them. Each has a stone fireplace with a stone chimney on the outside, topped above the roof line by a narrow chimney pot made of logs with clay chinking. They are all equipped with triple-tiered bunks and all but one can hold twelve men. The officer's hut is divided into two quarters with a party wall in between. These Jockey Hollow huts are similar to those at Valley Forge and must have been a standard form of army architecture. The roofs are shingled with cedar shakes with half a log nailed down along each line to hold them in place. A peculiar feature is the highest row of shakes on the front slope of each roof which has been allowed to project over the roof line by a good six inches.

Continuing along the tour road you will find on the other side of Sugarloaf a large open area now known as the **Grand Parade,** where guard details reported for instructions before moving out to their posts and the army occasionally paraded for inspections or to witness punishments or executions. Throughout the area are markers denoting the campsites of the units stationed here, though usually there is nothing to see but the area itself, long since overgrown with trees and grass. As you walk about exploring the Jockey Hollow site, you should keep in mind the paintings at the museum and in the slide film showing the area during the encampment: how bare of trees it was; how the snow was piled high in an even, white blanket; how the huts looked in their even lines with the officers' huts out in front, as though the buildings were on parade; and how the smoke from the inadequate fires hung over the scene like a dirty pall.

There are picnic facilities throughout the area as well as rest rooms; the woodlands and meadows are crisscrossed by hiking and nature trails and bridle paths that are a delight to follow. An additional site to visit is on Route 24 west which you can pick up in that tangle of streets around the Morristown Green. It is that of **Knox's artillery camp** and is marked by a plaque on a large boulder on the right side of the road about a mile out of town.

One thing you should remember about the Jockey Hollow site is that it was the scene of the mutiny of the Pennsylvania Line in 1781, the most serious of the many mutinies that plagued the Continental Army from its inception until after the final battles. These mutinies were usually caused by the same things: bad winter quarters, the inadequacy of food and clothing, no pay, and long enlistments. The Pennsylvania troops marched on Philadelphia, where they meant to confront the Congress. Wayne tried unsuccessfully to stop them and the men marched into Princeton, which they took over. Negotiations with representatives of Congress and Pennsylvania went on for days. The British sent two agents into Princeton to try to persuade the mutineers to come over to the crown, but the two were eventually handed over to the army and executed.

The mutiny was finally quelled by allowing soldiers who had been in service most of the war to leave if they so wished; the other grievances were met as far as possible. This mutiny was followed by a mutiny of the Jersey Line at Pompton Lakes which was squelched by a stronger force of men and guns. Three of the ringleaders were condemned to death and executed. Several Connecticut militia units also mutinied during the 1779–80 encampment, but it was also suppressed.

The souvenir shop in the museum behind the Ford Mansion sells a small $0.25 volume entitled *A Soldier at Morristown,* an excerpt from Joseph Martin's original journal, covering his experience during the 1779–80 encampment. It is a great value for the price and a highly enlightening and entertaining account of the life of a Continental Army soldier.

A word of caution. If you want to do the Morristown sites right, allow yourself at least one full day. The distances in between are not great, but unless there are new signs directing you through the town, you must maneuver back and forth through a very busy shopping area, with its traffic, one-way streets, and numerous signs for the state highways that feed in and out again. You can expect to spend more than an hour at the Ford Mansion and museum; less than a half hour at Fort Nonsense, unless the expected reconstruction is completed in time for your visit; and several hours in Jockey Hollow, especially if you plan a picnic. The nearest motels are in Morris Plains a few miles to the north and Dover to the northwest, or an hour's drive to Elizabeth and New Brunswick and less than two hours to Trenton. There are comparatively few motels and motor inns in the hinterlands of New Jersey. Most of them seem to have congregated along the Jersey Turnpike and the Garden State Parkway.

THE SPRINGFIELD RAID

In June, 1780, Baron von Knyphausen led a force of 5,000 men, including British, Hessian, and New Jersey Loyalist units, across the Arthur Kill from Staten Island and began an operation intended to reestablish the British in New Jersey. He had been led to believe that sympathy for the crown was on the upswing in New Jersey and that his men would be greeted with open arms by the local populace. He was quickly disabused of the notion as soon as he got to Elizabethtown where local militia and farmers by the dozens rushed to block his advance. He was repulsed at Connecticut Farms, now Union, where he expressed his disappointment by burning down most of the town. He then lay on his arms waiting for his boss, Sir Henry Clinton, to return to New York from Charleston, where he had beaten the Continentals under General Benjamin Lincoln.

Clinton was planning to invade New England again and to make another attempt at the Hudson Valley. When he feinted in that direction, by sending ships up the Hudson, Washington moved his army from Short Hills to Pompton, where he was in position to move either toward West Point or into central and southern New Jersey. In response, Clinton had Knyphausen advance west again in the direction of Morristown to keep Washington off-balance. The feint almost worked. Washington started to move his men to support General Greene, who met Knyphausen at Springfield, but Greene's men did so well, Knyphausen was forced to break off the action and return to Staten Island.

Some histories of the Revolution either completely ignore or merely mention this raid, but since it occurred over a period of seventeen days —from June 7 to June 23—a fairly long period for a single military operation, it has an important place in the annals of the Revolutionary War in New Jersey. You can acknowledge its importance by spending a half day covering the few remaining sites connected with it.

Begin in Elizabeth, whose exits from the north or south via the New Jersey Turnpike are clearly marked. If you are coming from the west, or from Morristown, take Route 24 east to Route 82. Follow Route 82 east into Elizabeth. The town was originally built on the shores of the Arthur Kill and was known as **Elizabethtown.** Since then it has grown far beyond its original limits and become a very modern city with its downtown area and traffic problems. The two sites you should look for are downtown in the official buildings area on Broad Street near the intersection of Rahway Avenue. As you come down Broad Street from 82, there is a tall, imposing building on your right, the courthouse, and next to it a church and cemetery. Parking is available in a lot on Broad Street two blocks before Rahway Avenue; otherwise look for metered parking on the side streets off Broad.

Before you look at the church on Broad Street check out the gun on the courthouse lawn. It's a small *cannon* mounted on concrete. According to the plaque, this is the gun that killed General Richard Montgomery at Quebec. The gun was made in Strasbourg in 1758 for Louis XV of France and sent to Canada for the defense of Quebec. It remained in Quebec after the French surrendered the city to the British and eventually, if the plaque is correct, was placed in the blockhouse on the lower road below the cliffs on the St. Lawrence. It fell into American hands at the capture of Stony Point and was given to the reserve force of Elizabethtown militiamen who brought it home with them.

Though I have gone through the Elizabeth library looking for corroborative evidence or at least some clue as to how the gun got from Quebec to Stony Point, I have come up with nothing. For the time being at least, take the plaque at its word, but with reservations.

Leaving this unexpected relic, turn to the **First Presbyterian Church** next door to the courthouse. A marker on the front lawn identifies this as the site of an earlier church, built in 1724, which was burned by the British. A plaque to the right of the front entrance gives January 25, 1780, as the date the church was destroyed, but does not explain the act as one of retaliation for pillaging and looting carried out on Staten Island by Jersey civilians during an abortive raid commanded by General Alexander, Lord Stirling. The Reverend James Caldwell, who was known as the Fighting Parson, officiated in the old church from 1761 to 1776. The present structure was erected in 1786. Caldwell was the chaplain of a New Jersey brigade of the American army, and thirty-six members of his congregation fought in the Revolution. Take a minute to wander through the shady churchyard, a delightful oasis of peace on busy Broad Street. Many of the tombstones are colonial, and not a few have inscriptions that are still legible.

On the corner opposite the courthouse, just across Rahway Avenue in front of the public library, a plaque identifies the site as that of a popular tavern in which Washington stopped on his way to New York City in 1789 on the occasion of his inauguration. A second plaque mentions the fact that the old York Road, then the main road between New York and Philadelphia, passed along this way.

Knyphausen's men were looking for friendly supporters as they passed through Elizabethtown, and so had no use for the torch. To follow their progress, take Route 82 west out of Elizabeth and about a mile and a half from the center of town, look for the grounds and buildings of Newark State College. On the right side of 82, just at the curb in front of a high wall surrounding some of the college grounds, a *marker* identifies this as the site on which Liberty Hall stood, a residence built by William Livingston, a leading New Jersey Patriot and close friend of Washington. Knyphausen paused here long enough to burn Liberty Hall to the ground before proceeding to Connecticut Farms. He probably had less to worry about getting there than you do however, as far as the road was concerned. Look for the turnoff onto Route 22 west, which comes up just after a Two Guys shopping center on your right. Bear right coming off 82, or you may find yourself on the ramp leading onto the Garden State Parkway.

After a quarter of a mile on 22, you will see a sign for the Union exit. Once off the exit, turn right onto West Chestnut Street at the foot of the ramp and continue down an incline with high ground to your left until you reach an overpass. Make a left onto Stuyvesant Avenue just before the overpass and immediately look for a church on your left. Parking here is on the street, and it is possible to make a U-turn and park directly in front of the church.

The marker at curbside reads "**Connecticut Farms**—Settled by Yankees 1667—Scene of Hardest Fighting Against Invading British and Hessians June 6, 1780. Became Union in 1880." The present Connecticut Farms Presbyterian Church sits on high ground and is reached by a flight of cement steps. Another plaque on the front of the church identifies it as standing on the site of a former church "where was fought a battle on June 7, 1780, between American forces under General Maxwell and Colonel Dayton and the British army in its advance to Springfield. The church and the village were burned by the British during their retreat on June 23, 1780. The British second advance here formed into two columns and advanced to Springfield where they were repulsed." The date of the battle was probably June 8 or 9 instead of June 6 or 7, according to most accounts, and Connecticut Farms seems to have been burned at the time of the battle, rather than later.

The church sits on a bluff overlooking the streets below and the Connecticut Farms School across the way. The village once spread out around it is now a contemporary suburban area filled with comfortable homes and shaded lawns and gardens. Not far away up Stuyvesant Avenue is a neighborhood shopping and business area.

Maxwell, who was known as "Scotch Willie" because of his Scottish burr and his love of whiskey, had taken part in the Canadian invasion at the head of five companies of New Jersey troops and had fought at Trois Rivières. He took part in the battles of Brandywine and Germantown and was eventually court-martialed for misconduct and drinking; however, since the charges were not proved, he was let off. He was at Valley Forge and then at Monmouth and in 1778 was with Sullivan on his march into Iroquois country. He submitted his resignation in a pique in 1780 but before he could withdraw it, Congress accepted it. Elias Dayton, on the other hand, had an absolutely clean record and went on to become a major general. He, too, had served at Brandywine and at Monmouth and with Sullivan. A close friend of Washington, whom he is said to have resembled, he later served in the state assembly and in Congress.

During the hard fighting here, Knyphausen was entrenched on the high ground while the Patriots successfully opposed his attempt to move on against Springfield. Finally discouraged by the resistance, he withdrew to the banks of the Arthur Kill. When he moved west again, he paused here to divide his men into two columns: with one he tried to envelop the American left while the other frontally assaulted the American position at Springfield.

Pay a visit to this churchyard as well, noting the plaque on the side wall of the church facing the graves; it lists the names of seventy-two men who served in the militia and army during the Revolution and are buried here at Connecticut Farms. They may not all be buried in this cemetery, but a number of colonial tombstones are marked by small American flags. The names on these stones may be found on the plaque.

Return along West Chestnut Street, following it well past the exit-entrance to Route 22, until you come to Caldwell Avenue. A sign at the corner indicates a right turn to the **Caldwell Parsonage Museum.** You will know the parsonage, a white clapboard building which was rebuilt in 1780, by a historical marker in front and a sign on the building. A bronze plaque attached to a stone marks the nearby site of the original parsonage in which Hannah Ogden Caldwell, wife of the Reverend Caldwell, died.

Caldwell had been preaching independence in Elizabethtown as well as religion since he began his ministry in 1761. In 1776 he marched off with the Elizabethtown militia as its chaplain. Known to the British and local Tories, his family suffered threats and intimidation during his absence; by the time Caldwell returned his parsonage had been burned. His Sunday services were marked by armed sentries at the church door and two loaded pistols on the lectern. When the British retreated after their first thrust toward Springfield, they came back through Connecticut Farms. Mrs. Caldwell was sitting in her kitchen with her children around her when a British soldier fired his gun through the window and killed her.

Return to West Chestnut, turn right, and go back and onto 22 west. At the first sign for a U-turn, return east and leave 22 for 82 west, once more being careful not to go off onto the Garden State Parkway. Continue along 82 until you see the turnoff for Route 24. Shortly after, you will see an old, frame farmhouse on your right, set well off the highway. This is the locally famous **Cannonball House.** The marker in front informs you that on and near this spot 1,500 Americans under Greene and Dayton were attacked by 5,000 British and Hessians under Knyphausen and Clinton. (Clinton planned the raid from New York, but was not actually at the battle.)

This is an interesting old house, a very typical colonial farmhouse, built about 1740. Around the left side, notice hanging from a bracket high up on the wall a cannonball. This relic, which gives the house its name, was found after the battle embedded in one of the walls. The old house is the headquarters of the local historical society and is open to visitors on Sundays, 2–4 P.M. Directly in front of it, to the right as you face it, is an old drinking trough; to the left of the front gate just off the sidewalk is an old milestone, now completely illegible. The area is hardly rural any more with traffic pouring east and west along 82, a lumberyard next to the house and commercial properties all about. Behind the house, however, looming on the horizon are the still-wooded slopes of the Watchung Hills, those natural embankments behind which Washington retreated during his long trek across Jersey to Trenton and after his victory at Princeton.

A short distance farther west on 82, look for a church with a *marker* in front, the site of a church destroyed by the British during the Battle of Springfield which may be Knyphausen's high-water mark. Here in Springfield, Clinton's attempt to lure Washington out of position at Pompton and Knyphausen's try for Morristown came a cropper. The cost to the British of the battles of June 8 and 23 is not accurately known. Local people saw a number of wagons filled with dead and wounded being taken away with the withdrawing columns. About twenty redcoats and Hessians fell into rebel hands. The defenders' losses may have been as high as 110 killed and wounded, although some sources say they were considerably less. Since neither side kept an accurate count of their losses, it is difficult to determine the truth two hundred years after the fact. We do know, however, that there was considerable property damage in the area; the Hessians burned most of Springfield as well as all of Connecticut Farms.

It was during the engagement of Springfield that Fighting Parson Caldwell lived his finest hour. While he was with the militia, Caldwell had served seven days a week: on Sundays with the Bible and from Monday through Saturdays with his rifle. Unable as usual to stay out of the action, he was present at the fighting. When a Rhode Island unit ran out of wadding for their cannon, Caldwell rushed into the Springfield Church and came out with his arms filled with hymnals by Watts.

"Here, boys, give 'em Watts!" he is said to have yelled. "Put Watts into 'em, boys." The hymnals were stuffed into the cannon, which continued to fire, bombarding the enemy with iron balls and bits of hymn books.

Caldwell's death in November, 1781, was an ironic end to a colorful career. He was shot by an American sentry at Elizabethtown Point. The sentry was court-martialed and hung, but witnesses told such conflicting stories that the issue of an accidental or deliberate shooting remains clouded to this day.

Now that you have done the Springfield Raid and Washington's campaign of lightning strokes in December–January, 1776–77, it's time to turn your face toward the ocean counties for a swing through eastern Jersey, beginning with the biggest battle ever fought on New Jersey soil.

II.

BATTLE
OF MONMOUTH

You can get to Monmouth battlefield by several routes, depending on where you are coming from. If you go there directly from Morristown, return south on Route 202 and take Interstate 287 south to the Garden State Parkway. If 287 is not yet completed east of the Jersey Turnpike Interchange, Route 440 will take you the rest of the way to the parkway. Take Garden State south to Exit 100, where you pick up Route 33 west into Freehold.

If you come from either the north or south, Garden State Parkway is your best bet; but if you come from the west—say from Trenton—then Route 33 east is the most direct. Coming from Philadelphia, take the Jersey Turnpike north to Exit 8, where you will pick up Route 33 east.

If you come from the east, take 522 out of Freehold on the way to Englishtown, which will take you right through the battlefield proper. You will see markers on both sides of the road, including one on the left for "Molly Pitcher's Spring," but pass them all by for the time being, until you come to an intersection with a white-spired church clearly visible just to your right. That is **Tennent Church** where you should go for a battlefield overlook.

Coming from the west, go off Route 33, at the sign for Tennent, onto Route 527 and take it to an intersection with Main Street. Turn right onto Monmouth County Highway 3, which will take you directly to the church.

The Continental Army reached this area while trailing the British army after it evacuated Philadelphia in June, 1778. The British were on their way back to New York; the Continentals had just come through a rough winter in Valley Forge. They met and clashed in battle around the town of Monmouth Courthouse, now Freehold, more by accident than by design: what was intended to be an attack on the British rear guard turned into a major engagement, the last major battle fought in the North and the longest battle of the entire war.

The main action took place in an area west of Freehold. The opening phase occurred in what is now part of the town, near the present courthouse and around Briar Hill to the east along the road to Middletown. However, I was unable to discover so much as a marker in the Briar Hill area, let alone a site, though I have sinced learned that the first engagement was near the present Monmouth County Welfare Home.

Tennent Church and its graveyard crown a windy hill overlooking the main battlefield, which stretches off to the south and east: that is, with your back to the rear of the building, along your front from left to right and in the middle and far distance. The view is panoramic but, in terms of the battle, indistinct. There are trees, what are evidently watercourses, low hills, buildings, roads seen through the trees, green farmland, and orchards. Comb's Hill, where Greene placed his artillery, is to your right front; the parsonage, where the bloodiest fighting of the day occurred, is to the left of that in the midst of an orchard; the bridge over the marsh is to the left of that; and the town of Freehold is somewhere off in the distance directly in front of you.

Some of the dead who fell on that field are buried in this churchyard. As you face the entrance to the church along the first row of stones to the left, closest to the building, you will find recent headstones, which have replaced the old ones. One is for Lieutenant Colonel Henry Monckton, a British officer who fell at the parsonage. Next to him lie some of his opponents: Captain Henry Fauntleroy of a Virginia regiment in the Continental Line, who was killed by a cannonball at Monmouth on his birthday, June 28, aged twenty-two; next to him is Joseph Huddy, captain of a company of New Jersey troops, who died four years after the battle. Close to Monckton lies Captain William Wilson, the man who took Monckton's sword and captured his regimental colors. Local tradition says that an American soldier sitting on a grave site during the battle was killed by a cannonball that struck a tombstone and knocked off a piece, wounding him mortally. He is said to have been carried into the church and laid in the second pew to the right from the rear, off the left aisle, where he died leaving a stain that is visible to this day.

Before you move off the hill and down into the battlefield, review for a moment the circumstances that brought the two armies to this spot. The British had been in Philadelphia since September, 1777. A month later Burgoyne surrendered at Saratoga. Congress had moved to Baltimore, where it continued the business of government and running the war, proving that the loss of the capital had not meant that much to the cause after all. The Continental Army went into winter quarters in Valley Forge, enduring despite the bitter cold and learning how to drill under the tutelage of Baron von Steuben. In April, 1778, General Henry Clinton succeeded Howe as commander of British forces in America. Shortly after, Charles Lee, captured by the British at Basking Ridge, was exchanged for British General Richard Prescott who was the laughing stock of the American army because he had been captured in bed with his mistress.

Washington had been expecting the British to move out of Philadelphia for some time, but which way they would move remained a mystery. Late in April came news of the French alliance with the United States. By this time the Continental Army had been issued new uniforms and equipment, thanks to the efforts of General Nathanael Greene, and, having finally been brought to a state of military competence under the direction of von Steuben, was prepared when the news came in June that Clinton was getting ready to leave the City of Brotherly Love. Later that month the Carlisle Commission, a group of peace commissioners under the Earl of Carlisle, came to Philadelphia in an effort to get the rebellious colonies to accept something very close to dominion status, but was turned down. On Thursday, June 18, the British began to move across the Delaware into New Jersey. The Continental Army moved after it via Coryell's Ferry (Lambertville, New Jersey), leaving a small force behind to occupy Philadelphia under the command of General Benedict Arnold, who had not yet recovered from the wound he received at Saratoga.

Accounts differ as to the number of men in the opposing armies. The British had from 10,000 to 17,000. In addition, Clinton had assembled 5,000 horses and 1,500 wagons to carry his army's supplies and personal belongings. The wagon train stretched twelve miles along the road, requiring almost half the army to guard it under the command of Knyphausen who, for once, was bringing up the rear.

Washington had about 13,000 officers and men available, including

2,000 Jersey militia who were out in the field as the British began their move. During a council of war held on June 24 there was a sharp difference of opinion among Washington's officers concerning strategy. Lee, who is said to have dominated the meeting, urged restraint. He had dim hopes for the outcome of any confrontation between the trained veterans of the British Line and the Continental Army, despite von Steuben's efforts. He felt that the British should be allowed to go their way if they were going to New York, and, in fact, should be helped to leave Jersey if possible. France was now in the war on the rebel side, he argued, and eventual victory was therefore certain.

Lee was much respected among his colleagues, for he had a long record of military achievement behind him. He had served during the French and Indian War with Braddock, with Burgoyne in Portugal, and then, as a soldier of fortune, with great distinction in the Polish army against the Turks. Retired from the British army on half-pay he had resettled in America, where he joined the Patriot cause, perhaps more out of a desire to capitalize on a situation where someone with his background could rise to the top quickly, rather than from political conviction. He considered himself a better strategist and commander than Washington and he may have been, especially during the early years of the war. He was famous for his sarcastic wit and was almost universally admired for his ability and self-assurance as a military commander. Washington held him in deep regard, but had no way of knowing that during his captivity he had voluntarily discussed with Howe a plan he claimed would easily win the war for the crown. Though treason was never proved against him and not suspected at the time, his behavior at North Castle, when he deliberately ignored Washington's order to move his troops to New Jersey, and his subsequent actions at Monmouth have caused some historians to suspect the worst. Though he did not believe in the agreed upon strategy at Monmouth and acted in a desultory fashion when ordered to move against the enemy, his redeployment in the face of a superior force did save the army from disaster during the opening phases of the battle.

A decision was finally reached to harass the enemy as much as possible and not to attempt battle unless a favorable opportunity to punish him severely arose. The young Lafayette, not yet twenty-one, was to be in command of the advance force, which was to hang on the British flanks and cause as much trouble as possible while the militia burned bridges, blocked roads and made matters as sticky as possible in front of the retreating columns. As yet Washington did not know what Clinton had in mind; it might be New York, but it could be the Hudson Highlands or southern Jersey. Washington's problem was to keep his army in position to move in any direction the situation required.

The weather was hot and sticky. For most of June the temperature never dropped below ninety, and much of the time it hovered around one hundred. It rained almost every day; the humidity remained high; and the British soldiers suffered cruelly, marching under their eighty-pound packs in stiff, heavy uniforms. Local people said the British line of march was marked by exhausted men lying along the road. The Americans, who carried much lighter packs, were able to travel faster and did not have to stop to repair bridges at every stream or guard a twelve-mile-long column of wagons. They followed a route to the north of the British that gradually converged with the British route, until they reached the area around Englishtown at about the time the British reached what is now Freehold. By the time Clinton reached Monmouth Courthouse, he had to stop for a day to give his men a chance to rest. In the meantime, Washington had been increasing the size of the advance force until it numbered more than 5,000. Deciding that it was better to have a more experienced commander on the spot than Lafayette, Washington offered the command to Lee, who at first turned it down but then changed his mind when he learned the number of troops he would command.

Clinton reached Monmouth Courthouse on Friday, June 26. Washington and his main force went into bivouac at Cranbury, twenty miles away, with the advance command in between the two armies. By this time, Washington had made up his mind to strike as hard a blow as he could at the enemy. It was felt by most of his generals that the army had to do something, anything rather than allow the British to retreat at will. Before he got to Monmouth, Clinton had two choices if he was going to New York City: he could go north through Princeton and New Brunswick and so to Staten Island, or he could go east to Sandy Hook and sail his men north. When he reached Monmouth he had only one choice: a single road to Sandy Hook, undoubtedly for embarkation. His two columns and supply train would now be confined to a narrow route, allowing the rebels to strike at almost any point along a highly vulnerable line. If Washington could hand the British a resounding defeat so soon after Saratoga and hard on the heels of the news of the French alliance, the war might end amid the farms of Jersey.

Before you attempt to follow the battle, take another look at your New Jersey road map. Notice that Monmouth Battlefield State Park is marked "undeveloped." In most respects, it is exactly as it was on that fearfully hot day in June, 1778, when British and American soldiers locked in combat succumbed to heat exhaustion and sunstroke as well as to bullets and bayonets. It is still open farmland, most of which has been acquired by the New Jersey State Department of Conservation and Economic Development which intends to develop it as Monmouth Battlefield State Historic Park. Most of its topographical features are intact, despite the intrusion of a road and a railroad embankment.

Though this may stir the hidden archaeologist and explorer in you, let me point out that since this land is about to be developed New Jersey does not want unauthorized persons wandering about the premises, conducting their own digs on likely sites, and walking away with relics for private collections. Unless you are extremely well versed in the history of this battle, are thoroughly familiar with the terrain, and are able to put together the conflicting versions and accounts of what took place and come up with a substantiated story, you will probably never be able to make heads or tails of what took place here, anyhow. About 25,000 men marched and retreated and charged and retreated and charged again for an entire day over more than 1,450 acres of rolling farmland, marshes, orchards, and wooded hills, the longest sustained period of combat of any Revolutionary War engagement. And when it was over, handing the victor his laurels was a matter of interpretation.

At the time of this writing, there are only a few markers along the road between Englishtown and Freehold, a monument in Freehold, this church and graveyard, and some rather general ideas of what took place where. There is as yet no tour road, no overlooks, no weatherproof maps, no museum with its relics and imaginative illustrations, no auditorium, orientation film, or multi-media presentation. All these are yet to come and may happily be awaiting you by the bicentennial of the battle. For the present there are the raw sites with limited access, those few markers, and your imagination. So, like the prologue to Shakespeare's *Henry V*, let me, cipher to this great account, on your imaginary forces work.

On Saturday afternoon, June 27, Washington met with Lee, Lafayette, Wayne, and others and decided to move against the enemy as soon as he marched out of Monmouth Courthouse. Lee was ordered to attack east of the town while Washington moved the main body of the army up to support him. All that was intended was to strike a telling blow at the rear guard. Lee relayed this order to his brigade commanders, but rather than make exact plans decided to play the scene by ear. At 4 A.M. the following morning, Clinton started Knyphausen off on the road to

Middletown with the baggage, while he stayed behind with Cornwallis, who was in charge of the rest of the army. Washington heard of the move by 5 A.M. Lee was up, but he had not ordered any reconnaissance during the night and did not move his command forward until 7 A.M. By the time he got to a point about halfway between Tennent and Monmouth Courthouse, no one knew exactly whether the British had left Monmouth Courthouse. At this point, Lee had to get his men across a marshy area over a single bridge. While he was trying to make up his mind what to do, there was a good deal of delay and milling about, and some units were marched back and forth over the bridge several times. In the meantime, Clinton had Cornwallis move the rest of the army out, except for a rear guard. Lee finally advanced, intending to cut this detachment off. He marched into and through the town and out toward Briar Hill.

Return to Freehold along 522. Shortly after you pass the turnoff for U.S. 9 and a row of houses on the left, look for a sign on the right indicating a left-hand turn for Monmouth County Courthouse. Take that left, and go one block to the next intersection. The courthouse is now directly in front of you. Make a right at this corner onto Court Street and proceed to the Monmouth County Historical Society headquarters and museum, a converted private home on the right side. Directly opposite, in the midst of a small park, is a tall, stone pillar, the **Monmouth Battle Monument.** Parking is available along the street on the museum side. The monument has several bronze plaques around its base depicting the highlights of the battle. It marks the site where the first shots were fired. Here a Pennsylvania brigade in advance of Lee's main force halted to take a break at 7 A.M. that morning. By then the temperature was already in the eighties and climbing steadily. As they rested, a company of Simcoe's Rangers suddenly appeared out of the early morning fog, obviously preparing to charge them. The Pennsylvanians had just enough time to form and present before the dragoons were on them. They got off a volley and the rangers turned and galloped away, with Simcoe and several others reeling in the saddle from their wounds.

By now Lee was deployed at Briar Hill preparing an outflanking movement around Clinton's rear guard. This alerted Clinton to the fact that a sizeable force in his rear was preparing to make trouble for him. He sent to Knyphausen for reinforcements and turned to meet Lee, who ordered a redeployment, realizing he was now faced by superior forces. Clinton came to the same realization at about the same time and decided to teach the American a lesson. He ordered Cornwallis to march back to town.

At this time there was much confusion among Lee's commanders and aides. Lafayette was ordered to withdraw from one position and move to another. Other commanders were not informed of what was happening and upon seeing Lafayette move back, ordered their units back as well. The result was a general withdrawal which Lee was unable to stop. He therefore decided to form a new line on the town, but since the entire community consisted of only twenty or thirty homes (they were all located farther east of where you are now), he decided to fall back to a line along the road that now borders the Catholic cemetery, just past the intersection of 522 and U.S. 9.

The Monmouth Historical Society has several interesting relics connected with the battle in its *museum*, so you might pay it a visit before leaving this site. It is open 11 A.M.–5 P.M., from Tuesday through Saturday, 10–5 on Sunday, but is closed the last half of July and the last half of December. In the entrance hall to the left hang three maps of the battle, two made by British geographers and one that was made for Lafayette. They were drawn soon after the battle and show the disposition of the troops and the roads they used. Immediately to the right as you enter hangs the banner that was captured from the grenadier battalion commanded by Monckton at the hedgerow. In an upstairs room is the sword Monckton waved so bravely before he fell victim to the American guns. When Captain William Wilson captured the sword and flag, he presented the sword to Lafayette, who carried it for the rest of the war and returned it to the Wilson family during his visit to the United States in 1824. The museum hands out a facsimile map of the battlefield showing the roads, troop movements, and positions. It was originally drawn for schoolchildren visiting the site, and you may find it useful should no other map be available.

Go back out along 522 just past U.S. 9 where you may make a right turn onto a road that runs along the Catholic cemetery. This is the site of **Lee's line**, marking his first withdrawal. As Cornwallis's men advanced steadily and in strength, however, Lee ordered his men back again. Before they retired, they repulsed a cavalry charge with a well-directed volley. Lee now decided to get back across the marsh to a new line on high ground where he could hold while waiting for Washington to bring up the rest of the army. It was during this withdrawal that Lee seems to have lost control of his command. He complained about a lack of aides to carry orders and generally bad communications between himself and his unit commanders, a perfectly legitimate complaint at the time.

Meanwhile, Washington, who had been listening for the sound of a heavy engagement, had heard only a few scattered volleys of rifle fire. As he and the army came into the Tennent area, he came upon a frightened young soldier who told him Lee was in full retreat. The boy was followed by a number of other soldiers obviously exhausted and in no mood to stop. Fearing the worst, Washington rode down to the marsh bridge, crossed it, and came upon Lee and his aides.

You can attend this historic meeting, imaginatively that is, by driving out along 522 toward Englishtown to the *marker* on the right side of the road that is supposed to mark the spot. It may not be the exact site, but the encounter certainly did take place in this vicinity; for on the other side of the road, between the road and the railroad embankment, is the suspected site of the bridge. There are several different accounts of what happened. Whether Washington lost his temper and swore a blue streak at Lee may be apocryphal. There definitely was an exchange of some sort between the two during which Washington expressed his disappointment and displeasure over the turn events had taken. Lee, confused and embarrassed, tried to explain that the British were stronger than had been expected and that he felt he had had to withdraw to save his command. Washington remarked that Lee should not have taken the command if he did not intend to carry out orders, an obvious reference to Lee's arguments against the engagement in the first place and a possible dig at his deliberate refusal to carry out orders at North Castle. Nevertheless, Lee was not relieved of his command and Washington left him to ride to the top of a nearby hill to see what was going on.

You can follow Washington to that spot, but you would be intruding on parkland without permission. I crossed the road and almost directly opposite the Washington-Lee marker found a tunnel under the tracks. At that time the tunnel was blocked, probably deliberately, by fallen trees. I climbed the embankment and found a path on the other side leading through an orchard with tall trees on the right and the sloping ground leading up and off to both left and right. The trees probably mark the site of the *hedgerow* around which so much of the fighting occurred. The *slope* is crowned by an old, farm shed and a sunken depression choked with young trees and weeds. This is thought to be the fallen-in *basement* of the old Tennent parsonage that stood here at the time of the battle. It is now in the heart of a commercial orchard, which is maintained and harvested by a local farmer who calls it

Battle Orchard and sells its products at a roadside stand along Wemrock Road, some distance beyond the parsonage site.

This ground is the raw stuff of history. There was an orchard here at the time of the battle and a hedgerow where those trees are in a line along the path. I visited the parsonage site with the acting park superintendent and poked around the depression and the hill. Standing here between the slope and the hedgerow, with the site of the marsh bridge behind you and to your left, you can almost hear in the wind "the very casques that did afright the ear . . ."

From the parsonage hill, Washington saw the rest of Lee's command streaming back across the field and through the orchard heading for the bridge, with the British not far behind and coming up fast. Realizing a disaster was in the making, Washington rallied the men and had them form a line in front of the parsonage under Wayne's command. He placed other units behind the hedgerow and in position to command the road. Then he rode back across the bridge to look for high ground he had been informed of; seeing Alexander and Greene coming up with the main body of the army, he had them form a line along the high ground beyond the marsh, extending far behind the present Route 522 with Alexander on the left and Greene on the right.

The British appeared and charged Lee's line. The Americans fought furiously but were forced to give way and fell back on the bridge. The scene was one of hand-to-hand combat while the American guns fired from the tops of little knolls, then moved back to new positions to fire again as the line fell back. Overhead the sun beat down remorselessly. After an hour of fierce fighting the Continentals were finally driven over the bridge and behind Alexander; Washington sent Lee and his men into reserve at Englishtown while the rest of the army continued to fall into position along the main line.

In the meantime, Greene, who had been sent off to the right with a column of guns and men to guard against a flank movement, discovered Comb's Hill, which is to the right as you stand with your back to the hedgerow facing the parsonage hill. Comb's Hill overlooked the entire battlefield and on it Greene set his artillery with a strong force of infantry to guard them.

Clinton now sent strong forces to attack both of Washington's flanks. The column sent against Greene marched up Wemrock Road, then struck out across country only to be hit by Greene's artillery. The other flanking party, moving against the left, was beaten back by a wild bayonet charge that some historians believe was the turning point of the battle.

At the same time, the units in the center on the high ground behind the hedgerow withstood attack after attack as the British grenadiers tried to crack the line. The heat was so intense that eyewitnesses swore an entire line of grenadiers collapsed from exhaustion as they charged up the slope. In the British ranks that day were the Coldstream Guards, the Hessian Jägers, and the Forty-second Highlanders, The Black Watch, who had been chased on Harlem Heights by some of these same rebels now standing so firm against them, giving them volley for volley, bayonet for bayonet, no longer the untrained, frightened "summer soldiers" who had run at Kips Bay and Long Island. Von Steuben's training paid off at Monmouth, and Clinton, to his surprise, realized he was now facing crack troops every bit as good as his grenadiers and highlanders, the best troops Europe could put into the field.

As the British recoiled from the American line, the Continentals pursued them, urged on by Washington who rode up and down encouraging his men, exposing himself recklessly at times only thirty or forty feet from the enemy. It was probably his finest hour in battle and those who lived and saw old age never forgot the big man who faced everything the British were throwing at his men, riding his white horse to death from heat and exhaustion.

A number of historically notable names were involved in this battle and several almost had their careers cut short. Alexander Hamilton went down with his horse and escaped death by chance. Lieutenant Colonel Aaron Burr pursued the enemy back across the bridge so impetuously that he refused to fall back until the enemy guns got the range and began dropping men around him.

Wayne and his Pennsylvanians got over the bridge and manned the hedgerow again just in time to meet a charge of grenadiers led by Lieutenant Colonel Henry Monckton, whose grave you visited at Tennent Church.

"Forward, charge my brave grenadiers!" shouted Monckton as he led his men forward.

"Steady!" Wayne told his men. "Wait for the word and pick out the king birds!"

They listened to him and waited, and when the grenadiers were about forty paces away, they got the word. Monckton went down and so did a good part of his command; yet on they came, swinging their rifles and pressing bayonets forward into the hedgerow. Now hand-to-hand, the fight raged up and down the hedgerow with Monckton's body the prize, as British and Americans pulled it back and forth in a ghastly tug-of-war. It was here that Captain Wilson captured the banner you saw in the museum in Freehold, wresting it out of the hands of the grenadier color guard; and it was here, after the grenadiers fell back, that Monckton's body, carried behind the hedgerow, gave up its sword to that souvenir-hungry captain.

The grenadiers turned and ran for their lives. Clinton made one more attempt to turn the American left, but thought better of it and called the men back. The artillery dueled for the next two hours, while the exhausted, heat-prostrated men on both sides watched. It was during this grand display of gunpowder and sound that a cannonball supposedly carried up to Tennent Church and indirectly hit the soldier sitting on the grave. Clinton pulled back and rested his men. Washington, still looking for a clean-cut victory, moved to attack again, but darkness fell, making contact with the enemy impossible and so the battle ended. At midnight Clinton quietly moved his men out of Monmouth Courthouse and resumed his march toward Middletown and Sandy Hook.

Before you count up the results, drive back toward Freehold along 522, ignoring again a spring and marker claiming it to be Molly Pitcher's. At Wemrock Road, marked by a large sign reading Battle Orchard, turn right; go under the railroad embankment; and park just beyond. On the left side of the road is a marker for **Molly Pitcher's Well**, and down the grassy slope is the stream and the place where Molly reportedly drew water for the men in her husband's battery. Just where that battery was located and during what phase of the battle, is not yet known. Perhaps it occurred while Lee was defending the parsonage line before he fell back over the bridge. If so, the site along 522 is the more likely, for it would put the line closer to the parsonage. Though that well was dug in 1860, there may have been a spring or a former well on the same site that was used by the parsonage.

At any rate, the story is that Molly, née Ludwig, was married to a gunner named John Hays, who was wounded during the battle. Molly had been drawing water and carrying it to him and his comrades when she saw him fall. An order was given to remove the guns, but was never carried out. Molly, taking her husband's place, loaded and fired at the approaching British. The story is identical to that of Margaret Corbin, "Captain Molly," whose husband John was serving a gun in the redoubt north of Fort Washington when he was hit. Margaret, who was fetching water for him, took over the gun and fired the last shot at the British as they came over the parapet. In another version she was wounded, almost losing a shoulder and breast, was taken prisoner, and then sent with other wounded rebels across the Hudson to Fort Lee.

The historical society museum has a pamphlet on the two Mollys, written by a local historian who seems to have researched both women quite thoroughly. The similarities between the two are remarkable. The name Molly Pitcher might have referred in general to camp followers who often fetched water for the men during combat. There is a Margaret Corbin buried at West Point, who was pensioned by Congress for her services during the Revolution. Molly Ludwig was also a real person who was with the army at Monmouth: Greene presented her to Washington after the battle, and he had her pensioned, so there you are. Legends, which are usually based on some truth, are hard to kill.

Continue along Wemrock Road away from 522, passing the Battle Orchard on your right and parsonage hill behind it hidden among the trees, following the route of Clinton's men as they moved to attack Greene on Comb's Hill. Wemrock Road ends at Route 33. A short distance to the right off 33 is a dirt road, blocked by a fence or steel cable, that leads to the top of **Comb's Hill.** From there one can indeed get a panoramic view of the battlefield. Directly ahead across a ravine and wooded marsh is the parsonage site, easily recognized by the old shed, and behind it the hedgerow and the high ground on which the main line formed. Off on the horizon to the left, Tennent Church pierces the sky with its spire. Here Greene placed his guns and traded shot for shot with the British guns. Below the top of the hill to the left in the undergrowth is a long trench-like depression which may be the remains of entrenchments dug by Greene's men.

As you passed back and forth along 522, you probably noticed a side road leading to the park headquarters and maintenance shops. There is a large, frame house at the end of that road clearly visible from 522. To its right, a dirt road leads to **Craig House,** one of the few buildings on the battlefield that has survived the years. It is hidden from sight by trees and not open to the public, but by the time the park development is finished, it will have been restored. A two-story, frame building, shingled with the elongated Dutch shingles common to this area, it is now a sad ramshackle with a sagging roof. The house Clinton used for his headquarters is still standing in modern Freehold and is being restored by the historical society.

A short drive along 522 away from Freehold will take you to Englishtown. Turn right on Main Street and go to the intersection of Main and Water streets, the town's principal intersection. Turn left onto Water Street and at the next traffic light look for the **Village Inn** on the left, where Washington stayed after the battle. While he was at the inn

Lee wrote to him demanding an apology for Washington's behavior toward him. Washington replied that he was not conscious of having done anything to warrant an apology and insisted that Lee had disobeyed orders. Lee answered by demanding a court-martial, and Washington complied by promptly having him put under arrest. He was charged with misbehaving in the face of the enemy by ordering an unnecessary retreat, disrespect for his commanding officer, and disobeying orders by not attacking when he was so ordered. The court found him guilty on all three counts, and he was suspended from command for a year. The verdict was sent to Congress for review and approved. Lee then wrote an insulting letter to Congress and was permanently relieved of his rank.

The inn is a two-story building with an overhang running the length of its front. At one time fairly recently it was probably a restaurant, but it has now been divided into private apartments and is not open to the public. A marker at the curb draws attention to the site.

Though both sides put out conflicting claims about their own and their opponent's casualties the score seems to have been Americans, 356 killed and wounded; British, 358 killed and wounded. Thirty-seven Americans died of sunstroke (or heat exhaustion) and so did sixty British. According to all sources there were no German casualties, a highly suspicious statement since at least one company of Jägers was in the line attacking the American center. The American army, according to Washington, buried more than 249 enemy dead, which makes the official British figure suspect. Some historians believe the British lost more than 1,200 men in this one battle. Since about one-half of Clinton's ten thousand were occupied with the protection of the wagon train, British losses were about one quarter of the troops involved in the battle, if that figure is accurate.

Who actually won? The British left the field to the Americans, but since Clinton's objective was to get his men to New York, not to occupy Jersey territory, that is a moot point. As far as Clinton was concerned the victory was his, for he had saved his baggage, which was what he thought the Americans were after. Washington did not get the undisputed victory he so badly wanted. There are students of this battle who believe that Lee's intention at the parsonage was to let the British cross that one and only bridge into a position in which they could have been wiped out. That is a matter of conjecture and a debatable point. What is important, however, is that on this occasion the American army met the British in what was then traditional combat and beat them at their own game, standing firm against them, stopping them repeatedly with well-disciplined formations, and driving them back time and again. Militarily speaking, the Patriot cause had come a long way.

Leaving Englishtown and Freehold, turn south for a circular tour of New Jersey's ocean counties that will eventually take you on a small excursion into Delaware and then back into Pennsylvania.

III.

WAR
IN THE OCEAN
COUNTIES

When the British marched into New Jersey in October, 1776, in pursuit of the fleeing rebels, they were received warmly by much of the population, especially in the western part of the state where Tory sympathies ran high among the prosperous farmers of the Delaware Valley. The eastern counties, particularly to the south, however, had been settled by Scottish and Irish immigrants who remembered defeats by the British at Culloden Moor and the Battle of the Boyne.

After Trenton and Princeton, Washington moved most of his men into the camps at Morristown. Sizeable detachments took Garrison, Hackensack and Elizabethtown, while the British maneuvered through central Jersey and Pennsylvania trying to draw him out and then in the fall and winter of 1777–78 sat tight in Philadelphia and Staten Island. It was during this period that the people of the ocean counties found themselves living in a no-man's-land, a rich agricultural region in which rival foraging parties competed for cattle and pigs needed to feed the hungry fighting men of both armies. The Americans were harder pressed for food than the British as the attitude of many farmers in the neighborhoods of their encampments was strictly cash and carry. In Pennsylvania, for instance, the Dutch landowners around Valley Forge saw no profit in selling their produce for Continentals when the British in Philadelphia were willing and able to pay in good, sound guineas. The result was increasing pressure on the farmers of New Jersey. Many gave willingly to either the British or the Patriots, depending on where their sympathies lay. Not a few paid a high price for their allegiance.

Most of the rebel settlements and towns in the ocean counties were particularly vulnerable to attack. British ships could land troops virtually unopposed in any of the numerous inlets and coves that wrinkle the Jersey Atlantic coast, and rivers such as the Mullica and Cohansey offered the invaders easy water routes to inland communities. For the most part, defense of the area was left to the local militia. It was impossible for Washington to spread his army thinly enough to cover the entire state, nor could he afford to send detachments in pursuit of every British raiding party. During most of 1777 his main concern was the defense of Philadelphia, the new nation's seat of government; and when that fell into British hands, he was forced to hold his tiny army in readiness to block whatever move Howe and then his successor, Clinton, might attempt. Rarely did he send detachments of any size beyond the safety of his encampment grounds unless it seemed as though a major attempt was being made against his positions, as in the Springfield Raid. He did manage to keep patrols active in most sensitive areas along the coast.

In his account of life in the Continental Army, Private Joseph Martin tells of being on patrol duty in the Elizabethtown area and mentions that his brigade was stationed at the towns of Springfield, Westfield, and Woodbridge. He and his comrades were kept constantly on their toes even in the dead of the winter by British patrols that came over the Arthur Kill at night from Staten Island to raid stores, kill sentries, and take prisoners.

Most of the sites of these isolated incidents were never marked and are long since lost. Place names have been changed over the years and the original names forgotten, even among the local populace which has itself changed under the relentless pressure of urbanization. Today New Jersey is the most densely populated state in the union, having taken that honor away from Rhode Island after the last census. This will become evident as you travel through the state; real estate developments and industrialization lap at the edges of every Jersey field, wood, and lake, or so it seems, and superhighways and express bus service have made most of the state easily accessible to New York City commuters. In Monmouth County, fast bus service to the big city is bringing an increasing number of commuter families right up to Monmouth battlefield looking for homes they can afford. Local real estate people, builders, and farmers who are tired of being horny-handed sons of toil are responding accordingly.

Nevertheless, a swing through the ocean counties to visit a selective list of sites is highly rewarding. The countryside is green, even if flat;

commercialization has concentrated along the beaches, and some of the sites offer rare touring experiences.

Take the Garden State Parkway to Exit 58 for Route 539 to **Tuckerton,** known in colonial times as Little Egg Harbor because of the small gull eggs found in the area. Little Egg Harbor was also known for its privateers, who preyed on British shipping up and down the Atlantic coast to such an extent that in October, 1778, two regiments of redcoats, including a New Jersey Loyalist outfit, were sent to clean it out. Word of the impending attack got to the Patriots and Pulaski's Legion was sent to protect the town.

A Polish volunteer, Casimir Pulaski had served as an aide de camp to Washington at Brandywine. When Congress authorized the raising of several regiments of dragoons, he was placed in command on Washington's recommendation. Like so many of the foreign volunteers who came to America seeking glory, fame, self-advancement, or whatever else they expected to gain, Pulaski was an aristocrat by upbringing and habit and expected to be given a rank commensurate with his social position. Based on his cavalry training in Poland, which does not seem to have included much combat experience, the young man of thirty was given the rank of brigadier general. Unfortunately, his aristocratic upbringing made it difficult for him to take orders from anyone, including Washington. At first he was given only minor field assignments, one of which was to guard the settlers in the Delaware Valley from Indian attack. He complained about this constantly to Congress and finally resigned his post. He was subsequently allowed to recruit his own mixed infantry-cavalry unit, known as the Pulaski Legion, though he insisted on signing up deserters and prisoners of war without waiting for the commander in chief's consent.

Pulaski's Legion got to Little Egg Harbor too late. The British had already been and gone after destroying a number of vessels in the harbor. They had then sailed up the Mullica River burning everything in sight, from warehouses to the homes of local Patriots. Pulaski stationed his infantry on Mincock Island near the town, perhaps planning to waylay the raiders as they returned to their ships. The British, however, discovered that Pulaski was careless about posting sentries, sneaked up on the Legion infantry during the early morning hours of October 5, and attacked. Fifty officers and men were bayoneted to death before Pulaski could get there with the cavalry and drive the attackers off. Always at odds with Congress, forever complaining about his fate,

Pulaski was finally sent with his legion to the South, where we shall meet up with him again at Savannah.

Route 539 will take you into Tuckerton to a traffic light at an intersection with Main Street, which is also U.S. 9. Turn right onto 9 and follow it out of town past a lake on your right until you get to Center Street. Turn left onto Center Street and follow it to its end at a T-intersection with a nameless road bordered by woody tracts and small homes. Turn left and head for a tall, yellow watertower or chimney which has the words "Mystic Island" printed on it in huge, black letters. Mystic Island is a private development of small homes bordering the old harbor. When the road curves to the right, watch for a triangular piece of ground on the left bordered on three sides by road. Beyond it, on a rise of ground close to a one-family house, is a *tablet* which commemorates the massacre of the Pulaski Legion.

The action, however, took place farther down toward the harbor. In fact, it seems as though the Mystic Island development has completed the massacre by wiping out the site. Mincock Island does not appear any longer on local maps, but you can explore about a bit through the development streets and down to the water here and there on the shores of Little Egg Harbor where privateers once anchored their ships. Incidentally, the leader of the British force was Captain Patrick Ferguson. You will meet him again at Brandywine and later at King's Mountain. Serving under him at Little Egg Harbor were Simcoe's Rangers, a unit you encountered recently at Monmouth and will encounter again at other Jersey sites and later in Virginia.

Retrace your route to Garden State Parkway and take it south to Exit 36 to U.S. 40/Route 322 west to McKee City. At this point, you are a few miles west of Atlantic City and just north of the delightful Cape May area with its excellent beaches, swimming, and fishing.

At McKee City, U.S. 40 splits. Part of it continues northwest along with 322; the other part swings west by itself. Take it west to State Route 552 and then 552 to Millville. Take Route 49 out of Millville into Bridgeton and onto Broad Street where, in the heart of town on the right side of Broad Street, opposite the courthouse, you will find **Potter's Tavern,** a white, frame building with a flag flying in front. According to the marker, it was in the tavern that local Patriots published the *Plain Dealer* during the 1770s, which advocated independence for the colonies. The old inn is in fine condition and is obviously well taken care of, judging by the fresh coat of paint on its exterior. Since it was not open to the public when I was there, it is impossible to say what the interior is like. In the lobby of the courthouse on the opposite side of Broad Street is the local liberty bell, which was rung when the news of the Declaration of Independence arrived in Bridgeton.

Bridgeton is a brief stopover on the way to one of the most interesting and best preserved sites in Jersey. Continue along Broad Street (you are traveling west) to the next traffic light where a sign for **Greenwich** indicates a left turn. Two blocks after the turn, a similar sign will take you to the right. Follow the signs for Greenwich through the charming countryside until you reach the town.

The road you are traveling goes into Greenwich, eventually arriving at a T-intersection with a tree-shaded street along which, in both directions, are a number of quite obviously colonial houses. To your left is a general store, which is also the town's post office. Parking is along the street just about anywhere; so leave your car in the most convenient spot and explore.

In one sense, Greenwich might be compared with colonial Williamsburg. It is authentic, but where Williamsburg is, by and large, a reconstruction, Greenwich is a preserved site. It is also quieter and less crowded—I doubt if more than a comparative handful of people have known about it up to now—and for that reason a walk along its one, main street, with a few side streets branching off, is really a step back in time. What a street this main street is! It is lined on both sides with colonial homes all in excellent repair and most of them occupied. Each house exhibits a plaque or sign giving the date of its construction, the name of the original owner, and sometimes his occupation. I heartily recommend that you spend at least an hour in Greenwich just strolling. Despite the occasional car driving through, you will feel you have made the transition back two hundred years to a cleaner, sweeter air free of industrial noises and pollution to a more relaxed pace of living.

As for the homes themselves, some were also shops for the candlemaker, the shoemaker, the rush weaver, and so on. One building is a *museum* run by the Greenwich Historical Society; another is the headquarters for the Cumberland County Historical Society. Many of the buildings are open to the public on special days when tours take visitors through the town. For further information, write to the Greenwich Historical Society, West Avenue, Bridgeton, New Jersey. In particular ask for information about the yearly colonial crafts festival during which you may see leatherworking, rush weaving, wool carding, spinning, and cane weaving as they were practiced in colonial times.

Using as a point of reference the intersection of Greenwich's main street with the road that brought you here, turn to your left and walk along the street, looking on the right side for a *monument* to local Patriots who, disguised as Indians, on the night of December 27, 1774, burned a cargo of tea that had been brought to the town on a British ship. As you continue along the street, notice on your left the all-brick Quaker meetinghouse built in 1771. The oldest house in town, built in 1636, is at the foot of the street on the left, a brick structure with prominent chimneys and a frame addition in the rear. The street ends on **Cohansey Wharf** where a historical marker informs you that here at Shepherd's Ferry on December 12, 1774, the British brig *Greyhound* unloaded a cargo of tea, the tea that was burned by the rebellious inhabitants of the county. Another marker identifies Cohansey Wharf as the landing place of Watson's Ferry in 1733, indicating a change in the ownership of the ferry. The wharf is a pleasant, tree-shaded area with a turnaround for cars and private land bordering it on two sides. Beyond the end of the wharf is the estuary of the Cohansey River, along which ships moved under half-reefed sails as they made their way to their moorings.

After you have treated yourself to a reviving dose of Greenwich, drive down the main street away from the wharf, and after passing the Morris Goodwin School on your left, take the first right onto the road to Roadstown. At a fork in the road, go to the right. Less than a quarter of a mile farther, you will come upon a marker at the foot of a lane leading to a large colonial farmhouse. This is the **Fithian House** in which the tea burners donned their Indian disguises. In their honor, the farm is now called Tea Burners Farm, according to the sign the present owners have erected.

Retrace your route to the fork in the Roadstown road; turn right, and follow the signs for Roadstown. At the crossroads in Roadstown, turn left and follow the signs for Quintan. To your left beyond the low hills and fields is the Delaware River widening as it flows into Delaware Bay, which is behind you to your left. You are now traveling through the Jersey backcountry along county roads which are for the most part unmarked. I have recorded carefully all the turns we took and the roads we followed, but don't be surprised if you find yourself taking a wrong turn or two, just as we did. Stop and ask directions if you are at all doubtful (there are plenty of homes along the way); otherwise you may drive for hours through these Jersey fens.

The road to Quintan eventually meets up with Route 49. A left turn takes you into the town. Continue through Quintan until you come to the bridge over Alloway Creek. Just before the bridge is a memorial tablet on the right side of the road. The present bridge is of iron girders, but in 1778 it was made of roughhewn planks. Here on Wednesday, March 18, came Colonel Charles Mawhood, promoted to full colonel since the affair at Princeton fourteen months before, with a command of regulars and Simcoe's Rangers. Mawhood's mission was to forage and do what he could to stop rebel foragers. Anthony Wayne had been foraging through this part of Jersey gathering 300 head of cattle for empty rebel stomachs. Mawhood did not yet know that Wayne and the beef were well on their way back to Valley Forge and beyond his reach, but some local Tories had tipped him off to a force of 300 militia under the command of Colonel Asher Holmes stationed near the **Quintan Bridge.**

The road you are on, which leads over the bridge, is a busy thoroughfare, but you can probably pull off onto the shoulder on the far side of the creek. Mawhood concealed most of his men farther down the road away from the bridge. A smaller detachment hid in the rear of a nearby tavern close to the bridge. The rebel militia, who had taken up the bridge planks, were on the side of the creek you first approached.

A militia officer named Smith saw movement around the tavern and decided to investigate. He had his men replace the bridge planks and without reconnoitering led them over the creek. Leaving 100 men behind, Smith led the rest along the road, past where you are now standing, until they suddenly made contact with Mawhood's concealed force and realized they were in a trap. Turning back to the bridge, Smith and his men found themselves cut off by the British in the tavern who had emerged from concealment behind him. Smith ordered his men to ford the creek below the bridge, but the water was so high thirty or forty of them drowned. Luckily another company of militia armed with two cannon arrived in time to keep Mawhood from crossing the bridge, thus saving the remainder of the Quintan militia from destruction.

The tablet was erected in memory of Holmes, Smith, and the militiamen who defended the bridge on the site of the Smith homestead. The area on both sides of the road is all open fields and woods now, indicating that it resembles at least in part the terrain as it was two hundred years ago.

Now continue in the direction you have been following across the bridge until you come to a road going off to the left marked by a sign, indicating it will take you to the town of **Hancock's Bridge.**

Angry because his scheme had not worked, Mawhood decided to hit Hancock's Bridge, where he had been informed another company of militia was stationed. First, however, he went to Salem, a town about six miles from Hancock's Bridge that he had been using as his base of operations. There he laid his plans for the Hancock's Bridge attack.

When you come into Hancock's Bridge, drive down the town's main street for four or five blocks until you come to the bridge over the creek for which the village is named. The entire village consists of that one main street and a few side streets and roads. It is surrounded by estuary marsh on three sides with Alloway Creek cutting it off from the mainland on the fourth side.

At the bridge, you will see **Hancock House** to your right set back from the road amid trees and lawn. A small parking area just off the road is provided for visitors.

Hancock House was built in 1734 by Judge William Hancock. Originally a thousand acres were attached to the house, which took in most of the land in the immediate vicinity, including the land on which the village stands. It had all been part of a royal land patent given to a man named Fenwick, who sold it to the Hancock family.

In 1778 the house was being used as a barracks for the militiamen stationed at the bridge. Notice the huge sycamore tree on the front lawn which was there when the house was built. The house is a two-story colonial brick structure with a one-story frame L-shaped part to one side. At present it is maintained by the state. Visiting hours are 10–12 A.M. and 1–5 P.M., Tuesdays through Saturdays, and 1–5 P.M. on Sundays. It is closed on Mondays, Thanksgiving, Christmas, and New Year's Day. Adult admission is $0.25; children under twelve are admitted free.

Inside Mrs. Mary T. Hewitt, who is in charge of the site for the New Jersey State Department of Environmental Protection, has the history of the house and everything in it right at her fingertips. Small wonder, for she lived in Hancock House as a little girl. Her parents were its original custodians for the Salem Historical Association and made the conservation of the house their lives' work. They searched out and collected all the antiques and relics now in the house, and Mrs. Hewitt knows the history of each.

On the day of the attack, Mawhood sent Simcoe and his Rangers, plus a number of local Loyalist volunteers, down the Delaware River on barges with orders to come up Alloway Creek from the west while the rest of the command marched overland from Salem. Simcoe's detachment landed on the bank of the creek about two miles from the present bridge on the night of March 20. Both forces approached Hancock House under cover of darkness. Early Saturday morning, March 21, they were in position for the attack. Sleeping in Hancock House at the time were thirty men, all Quakers according to Mrs. Hewitt and therefore unarmed. (Other sources say there had been as many as 200 to 400 militiamen at Hancock's Bridge, but that they had withdrawn earlier that night.) The Quakers were local people as were many of the attackers. In fact, several of the people on both sides knew each other as neighbors, a fact that makes only more horrible what happened.

As Mrs. Hewitt tells the story, the only reason the men were stationed there was to attend to the bridge. It was a drawbridge and required fifteen men on each side of the ropes to raise and lower it. As Quakers they could not bear arms or fight except in defense of their lives and property. However, they had probably helped Wayne collect some of the cattle he was taking back to Valley Forge and every night they raised the drawbridge to safegard the food stored in the village from the British.

When the attackers reached the house, 300 strong, they were divided into two bodies, one going to the front door, the other to the back. In his *Encyclopedia of the American Revolution,* Mark Boatner says a seven-man militia patrol along the creek was ambushed by the British and six were killed. The two sentries posted outside the house were bayoneted and the attackers burst into the house and savagely attacked the sleeping men. Most of them were herded upstairs into the attic or fled there of their own accord, only to be mercilessly bayoneted to death against the sloping eaves. Judge Hancock, who was in the house at the time and was known to be a Loyalist, was stabbed along with the rest and died a fortnight later in a nearby house to which he had been carried.

When the attack was reported outside the village, it was immediately labeled a massacre by the Patriots. The victims were asleep at the time of the attack and no quarter was given. One of the unwritten laws of civilized warfare during that period, however, made it perfectly all right to give no quarter during a night attack if the only weapon used was the bayonet.

The house is a museum now, filled with a collection of antiques, relics, and memorabilia of the period and locality. Upstairs in the attic is a collection of colonial weapons and farm tools. Bloodstains are still supposed to be seen on the old floorboards and on the lower portions of the roof where it meets the walls. There is a darkening of the wood where the bloodstains are supposed to be, but whether it is due to weathering or to unnatural causes, I leave to your judgment.

After listening to Mrs. Hewitt tell the story of the massacre, however, you may very well come away a believer; out of her mouth, the story comes as fresh as though it had happened only yesterday. She is especially good with an audience of schoolchildren. I guarantee she will raise the hairs on the back of the neck of the most hardened young television fan as she describes the dreadful work that was done in that house.

Another story connected with the place is that of Denis Daily, the hero of a popular legend. Denis and his brother Darius were twins, natives of Scotland. Darius was stationed at the bridge that night. Denis, who lived in North Jersey, had a sudden urge to see him and came to Hancock's Bridge for a visit. Both were sleeping in the house at the time of the attack. Darius suffered his fellow militiamen's fate, but Denis followed one of the men into the downstairs fireplace, the very one you can see to the left when you enter the house, and climbed up the chimney. Another man attempted to follow him but was pulled down and bayoneted to death amid the ashes. The man ahead of Denis was shot by a Scottish officer on the ground as soon as he climbed out of the chimney.

Hearing the Scotsman speak, Denis called out in his best burr, "Dinna shoot! Dinna shoot! I'm a countryman of yours!"

The officer heard him and held his fire. Denis was taken prisoner and marched away to Salem and was never heard of again, or so the legend goes. To prove there was a Denis Daily, however, there on the wall just to the right of the souvenir counter is a framed document, the minutes of a Friends' Meeting at which Denis Daily, who was a member, was given a letter of recommendation to the meeting on Cork Island where he was going to visit his parents.

Before you leave Hancock's Bridge, follow the signs for the local marina. The road will take you out into the open fields and marshes around the town and down Poplar Lane. Along the lane are a number of very substantial homes of the revolutionary period, all privately owned and lived in at present. The second of these houses belonged to Judge Hancock's brother-in-law and it was there he was taken after the attack and died. Known today as the **Thomas Shourd House,** you will recognize it by its red and blue brick. It was built in 1758 by Joseph Ware, but it is associated with Shourd because in it he wrote a history and genealogy of Hancock's Bridge.

Now head northwest from this bridge with its bloody history to a small bridge in the state of Delaware. From Hancock's Bridge, take the road across the bridge and on to Moore's Corner where you should follow signs to either Route 49 or the town of Salem. Route 49 will take you through **Salem,** another center of colonial activity in south Jersey where the Salem County Historical Society conducts tours of the old homes in the town and vicinity. Many are of the colonial period, though none figured prominently in the Revolution. There is also a five-hundred-year-old oak in the Friends Burying Ground at West Broadway and Oak Street. You might write to the historical society, whose headquarters are in town, for more information.

IV.

HOWE'S PHILADELPHIA CAMPAIGN— 1777–78

Having covered the New Jersey sites, it is time to flash back in time to spring, 1777, when Howe moved again to capture Philadelphia after his unsuccessful 1776–77 New Jersey campaign. Finding it too difficult to confront Washington in his strong central Jersey positions, Howe embarked his army on transports in New York Harbor, sailed out of sight of land, and for almost a month, kept Washington wondering when he would reappear.

Continue on Route 49 to Interstate 295. Take 295 across the Delaware Memorial Bridge to Interstate 95. Take 95 south four exits to the interchange with State Route 896 and go off onto 896 south. About a half mile down the road you will come to a traffic light. Make a left turn at the light and in less than a mile, look for a small, concrete bridge crossing a creek. Just before it is a historical marker flanked by four cannon on the left side of the road. This is Cooch's Bridge, site of the only Revolutionary War engagement fought in the state of Delaware and a milestone along the British line of march toward the Brandywine and Philadelphia.

COOCH'S BRIDGE

This may not be the best place in the world to catch up on Howe's progress because of the lack of parking facilities. That is to say draw off the road as best you can, and since it is a quiet, country road, it is a safe bet you can stop here for a while undisturbed.

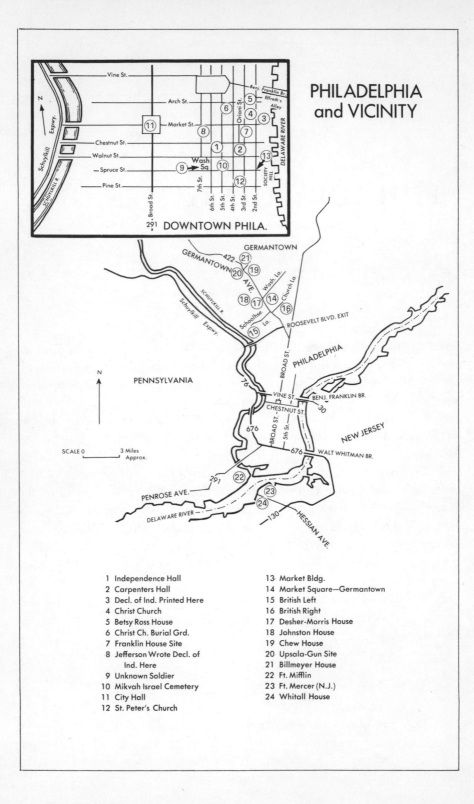

PHILADELPHIA and VICINITY

DOWNTOWN PHILA.

1 Independence Hall
2 Carpenters Hall
3 Decl. of Ind. Printed Here
4 Christ Church
5 Betsy Ross House
6 Christ Ch. Burial Grd.
7 Franklin House Site
8 Jefferson Wrote Decl. of Ind. Here
9 Unknown Soldier
10 Mikvah Israel Cemetery
11 City Hall
12 St. Peter's Church

13 Market Bldg.
14 Market Square—Germantown
15 British Left
16 British Right
17 Desher-Morris House
18 Johnston House
19 Chew House
20 Upsala-Gun Site
21 Billmeyer House
22 Ft. Mifflin
23 Ft. Mercer (N.J.)
24 Whitall House

It was September, 1777. After sailing from Staten Island on July 23, General William Howe finally put in to land August 25 at what was then called Head of Elk, near the present town of Elkton in Maryland at the head of the Elk River. Washington's dilemma when Howe first sailed consisted of not knowing whether he was going to march on Philadelphia, move on Charleston, or head up the Hudson River toward Burgoyne, who had already captured Fort Ticonderoga and was heading down the Hudson Valley toward Albany. On August 24 Washington marched his army through Philadelphia and took up positions around the city of Wilmington, but as the British began to move north, scattering local militia units as they went, he too moved to the north to take up a position at Chadd's Ford in Pennsylvania.

Five miles northeast of Head of Elk, British advance units met up with Maxwell's Light Infantry, a special detachment of men under the command of General William Maxwell of the New Jersey militia, otherwise known as "Scotch Willie." This is the same Maxwell who later opposed Knyphausen during the Springfield Raid, tended his resignation to Congress, and then tried, too late, to withdraw it. The creek you are now on is Christiana Creek, which flows into the Christiana River a few miles to the south. Maxwell tried to stop the British advance, under the immediate command of Cornwallis, along the creek, but the Hessians sent against him in the advance units had the advantage of several light cannon and turned his right flank with a bayonet charge. To his credit, Maxwell tried to retire in good order, pausing at several positions to turn and fight; but though he did some damage to the enemy, his men were eventually forced into a rout and did not stop running until they reached the main body of Washington's army on White Clay Creek, four miles north of Cooch's Bridge.

The road you are now on was part of the old Baltimore Pike, a major north-south artery which connected Philadelphia and Baltimore. The plaque is guarded by four small cannon and a flag is flown over the spot. It stands at the foot of a private driveway leading to a handsome old house on the top of a rise. According to the plaque the American forces included some cavalry. The American units were probably spread out along the creek, 654 men commanded by about 54 officers, all expert marksmen drawn from six of Washington's brigades. This was one of the first combat actions in which the Stars and Stripes were flown, hence the flag that is flown here. The advance British units moved along the road you used toward the bridge, which at that time was made of wood. The banks of the creek are now covered with young trees and bushy undergrowth.

BATTLE OF THE BRANDYWINE

From Cooch's Bridge, you can follow the route of the British army toward the scene of its violent confrontation with Washington's men at Chadd's Ford on the Brandywine by getting to U.S. 1, which is still marked on county maps in Pennsylvania as the Baltimore Pike. The most complicated but possibly the historically most accurate way of doing that is to return to Route 896 and follow it north to State Route 72. Take 72 north to State Route 7. Turn left on 7 and take it to Valley Road; follow Valley Road to Route 41. Make a right turn onto 41; go for a short distance to Yorklyn Road. Turn left onto Yorklyn Road which will take you to Route 82. Make a left onto 82 and follow it across the state line into Pennsylvania and into **Kennett Square** where Howe encamped September 10.

This was a wise move on Howe's part, for his men were not yet over their thirty-odd days of confinement on board ship, nor were his horses. In Kennett Square, just five miles west of Chadd's Ford where he knew the Continental Army awaited him, he paused to allow his men to rest before the day of battle.

Take 82 into town, but look for a point well before the center of town where 82 becomes Union Street. Off to your right on a hill there, you will see a large, brick school building with a porticoed entrance. It is known as the Union Consolidated School and it was here the British camped, on the very hill now occupied by this school and the elementary school behind it.

The Hessian campsite is at the other end of town on top of another hill, which you can see off in the distance in the direction in which you have been going. You can reach it by continuing along 82 into the center of town. At the second traffic light, you will be at East State Street, the town's main thoroughfare. To your left, diagonally across East State Street is Connor's Pharmacy in a contemporary brick building that stands on the site of the Unicorn Tavern, where Knyphausen made his headquarters.

Continue across east State Street until, a short distance farther on your left, you will notice the Kennett Meetinghouse off the road. This is not to be confused with the old Kennett Meetinghouse in which General Maxwell ensconced himself while his men probed General Howe's intentions. Just before the meetinghouse, turn left until you see a large, old house with a sign in front identifying it as the Presbyterian Home. This area, and this hilltop, is known today as **Hessian Hill**; it was here Knyphausen's compatriots camped while their commander made himself comfortable in the inn at the foot of the hill. Hessian Hill is now covered with one-family homes, lovely tree-shaded lawns, and well landscaped grounds.

Returning to East State Street, look off to your left and notice a glass-fronted department store called Newberry's, which stands on the site of the old Shippen Mansion where Cornwallis, field commander for General Howe, made his headquarters.

THE APPROACHES

To follow the British army, you will have to take into account one-way streets, something that never bothered them. Continue a block or so beyond East State Street to Cypress Street, which will take you out of town to the point where it meets U.S. 1. Just before you reach that point, you will see two historical markers at the side of the road on your right. One marker merely cites the Battle of the Brandywine in a general way, though it is several miles from the actual scene. The second marker explains Howe's strategy, which was to reenact the Battle of Long Island. At this point the British army divided. One unit under Knyphausen, 5,000 strong, marched east to Chadd's Ford, the center of the American line; the second, 7,500 men under Cornwallis with Howe overseeing, marched about six miles north and then three miles east to circle around the American right flank. The encircling force followed Great Valley Road, no longer in existence, before turning east. It is impossible to determine which, if any, of the contemporary roads winding their way through Pennsylvania's Chester County duplicate that route, though I took a stab at it. You will be able, however, to find the fords, with a fair degree of accuracy, where the wily British crossed the two branches of the Brandywine, and you will be able to follow their route from the second ford on as they came up behind the main American line.

For the present, follow the doughty Hessian as he leads his men down the old Baltimore Pike into the valley of the Brandywine. Turn east onto U.S. 1 and go to the intersection with Route 52, about two and a half miles farther. U.S. 1 is a four-lane highway, and since it is still a principal north-south route along the eastern seaboard, it requires caution for what you are about to do. At the intersection with 52, turn left onto 52 and look for a little blue sign at the intersection on the southbound lane of U.S. 1. The sign informs you that this is the site of the Anvil Tavern, where the first skirmish of the Brandywine took place.

Thursday morning, September 11, 1777, began in a fog which lasted from dawn until the sun burned it off. During that time, the movements and positions of both armies were partially concealed from each other, though thanks to superior intelligence, Howe was far better informed concerning his opponent's position than was Washington. Nevertheless, soon after the British left Kennett Square, at about 5 A.M., Washington was alerted. Washington's overall problem was to keep the British from invading the rich farmlands and iron mines of interior Pennsylvania and to prevent, if possible, the capture of Philadelphia. His immediate problem was to prevent Howe from crossing the Brandywine, or at least to make the crossing a costly affair.

Unfortunately, though the Brandywine was wide and deep enough to present a serious obstacle to armies, it was amply blessed with fords. Chadd's Ford was where the Baltimore-Philadelphia Pike crossed the Brandywine; so Washington established his headquarters and the center of his line there and spread the rest of his forces up and down the stream for some distance, with the heaviest disposition on his right or north flank along the eastern bank of the stream. Maxwell's Light Infantry, reinforced to 800 since the affair at Cooch's Bridge, had been stationed on the west bank, the enemy side, to cover the ford. When word reached Chadd's Ford of the British advance, Washington ordered Maxwell to make contact and fight a delaying action. Maxwell went as far as the old Kennett Meetinghouse, our next stop, then paused with most of his men and sent a patrol ahead to Welch's Tavern, later known as the Anvil Tavern. The patrol deployed along the bar and were enjoying a quiet beer when someone glanced out the door and noticed the British advance guard quickstepping it along the pike. Snapping off a token shot or two in the direction of the enemy, the patrol skedaddled out the back door, leaving their horses behind them, and hightailed it back to the meetinghouse.

At present, the general tavern site is occupied by a number of contemporary, one-family homes. On the opposite side of Route 52, however (opposite to the first sign you found), is a marker for the Liberty Trail which tours this part of Pennsylvania. Just beyond it you will see an old blacksmith's *anvil* sitting atop a granite block, marking the exact site where the tavern stood. Most of the site is now occupied by a house, probably dating to the early nineteenth century, which was built after the Anvil Tavern was torn down. A lawn and garden surrounds the house enclosed by a low, whitewashed, ivy-covered wall. Beyond the wall another whitewashed wall may be seen beneath a group of shade trees. It is part of the original foundation of the tavern.

Continue now along U.S. 1 toward Chadd's Ford to cover another event in the career of Scotch Willie and the next action preliminary to the battle proper. A short distance from the Anvil Tavern site you will pass through a small hamlet with single rows of frame, one-family houses lining the sides of the road. Immediately after, be on the lookout for a two-story, white stucco building with a sloping roof on the left side of the road. A driveway leads off U.S. 1 onto the grounds around it and to the small Quaker cemetery behind it. To the right of the building as you face it, close to the road and hidden by the high grass, is one of the old Pennsylvania state historical markers, a keystone-shaped piece of bronze. This one informs you that here at the **Kennett Meetinghouse**, Maxwell's men opened fire on the advancing Hessians, opening the Battle of the Brandywine. Although there were Hessians in the column, Ferguson's Rifles and the Queen's Rangers were out in front of Knyphausen's main advance. The marker is an old one and probably needs to be replaced by something more accurate.

Maxwell learned of the enemy's approach from his frightened patrol, placed his men in ambush behind the cemetery wall, waited until the enemy came up to the wall, and then opened fire. Keep in mind, however, that although U.S. 1 is known as the Baltimore Pike, it only approximates the old pike in places. In fact, in this neighbor hood small bits of road are still known as the old Baltimore Pike, very much like pieces of the old, battle road between Concord and Lexington which still exist. The point is that the old road may not have paralleled the cemetery wall, but might have approached it at an angle so that Maxwell's position might have been across Knyphausen's line of march.

While this was going on outside the meetinghouse, the Kennett Monthly Meeting was in session inside. One of those who attended, Jacob Pierce, noted that there was an engagement of some sort between the forces of General Knyphausen and General Maxwell outside on the lawn of the meetinghouse, but "while there was much noise and confusion without, all was quiet and peaceful within."

Shaded by hickory trees, the old meetinghouse and its cemetery form a small oasis of green and quiet alongside busy U.S. 1. Though you might like to tarry a bit to read the names on the old stones, remember that Knyphausen's advance is driving Maxwell's men back toward Chadd's Ford and you must move on with them. Follow the

British advance along U.S. 1 toward Chadd's Ford, now just a mile or two east, remembering that the British advance units moved through the woods and ravines that lay along both sides of the road. Notice a local pub on the right side of the road called Dario's bar. There is an old, stone house set off the road just east of it. As Maxwell's Light Infantry fell back on the ford, reinforcements came to their aid; and the combined American forces succeeded in driving the British back as far as this stone house, before the pressure increased and they all had to retreat across the Brandywine.

Just before the highway bridge that carries U.S. 1 over the stream, at the western end of Chadd's Ford, you will see a traffic light suspended over the middle of the highway. It operates only when school buses come down off the driveway immediately to the left leading up to the Unionville-Chadd's Ford School. When Knyphausen reached the Brandywine at Chadd's Ford, he did not attempt to cross, but, according to the plan, deployed his men to north and south along the stream and placed his artillery on the *hill* directly behind the school.

We drove up to the school, parked in the parking lot (on a Sunday) and I climbed to the top of the hill with my son, Richard. It is now covered by a pasture. Cowpaths led us through the tall, wild grasses, bushes, and hickory trees until finally we got to the top, where in an open area we were able to look across the Brandywine just as the Hessian artillerists did that September day. Below the river can be seen through the trees as it winds through the rich Chester County bottomlands. Beyond the ground rises to a long, wooded ridgeline with open fields and an occasional old, stone house showing between the trees. One of those houses is the John Chadd House, which you will visit shortly, marking the position of the American guns.

Chester County must be one of the prettiest in the country. Its rolling hills, winding creeks, wide, green pastures, woodlands, and old stone houses and barns, many of them authentic colonial and a good many pre-Revolution, not to mention its Penn Oaks—huge, old trees so called because they were here when William Penn drew up his treaties with the local Indian tribes—bear a close resemblance to what it must have been like in revolutionary times. To some extent where there were farmlands then, there are farmlands now; where corn grew then, it grows now; and where the British and Americans marched past or fought around old, stone buildings, many still stand today where they did then. Standing on this hill and looking across the river, listen for the sound of the guns echoing across the years; mark with your eyes the puffs of smoke issuing from the distant trees and fields as the American guns answer; feel in your bones that down there along the riverbank men in homespun, buckskin, and white cloth wait silently, clutching their heavy rifles and muskets, their eyes fixed anxiously on this very hill; while somewhere to your left rear, a column of men, horses, guns, wagons, and camp followers sweating under the late summer sun perspires its way toward Birmingham Meetinghouse.

Now cross the Brandywine on U.S. 1 and enter the American center position, **Chadd's Ford.** From here the American line extended south for a short distance only as far as Pyle's Ford about a mile downstream, where the Pennsylvania militia were holding terrain considered too rough for Howe to attempt a crossing. The Brandywine is fed by twin creeks, east and west branches, which join above Chadd's Ford. Most of the American forces guarded Chadd's Ford and extended north to cover the fords known to them. Unfortunately, there were a number they knew nothing of and left unguarded.

Chadd's Ford Village is where **Brandywine Battlefield Park** is located. Though the park is fifty acres in extent and contains the reconstructed building in which Washington made his headquarters and the restored building in which Lafayette resided, the battlefield proper is outside the park limits. However, it is a good place from which to begin your tour of the battle area.

Chadd's Ford village has a great deal within its limited boundaries to attract the outside world. As you enter, going east on U.S. 1, one of the first buildings you will see is the Brandywine River Museum, a tall, brick building on your right overlooking the Brandywine. Originally a turner's mill, it was used by Howard Pyle, the illustrator, to house his studio and school. In it N. C. Wyeth, whose pictures along with Pyle's served so well to illustrate the books of R. L. Stevenson and James Fenimore Cooper and other romantic classics, attended classes. Today the old mill is a very successful art and regional museum. Though opened as recently as June, 1971, it has already attracted national attention, as its attendance records prove. On exhibit when we were there were paintings by Howard Pyle, N. C. Wyeth, Andrew Wyeth (mostly his Pennsylvania canvasses), and Andrew's son, James. The museum itself is worth seeing for its architectural features, which include promenades with floor-to-ceiling windows at the rear connecting the galleries on each floor. These promenades overlook the Brandywine which bathes the foot of the building as it flows past; the effect when the trees along the stream are in full leaf is entrancing.

Almost directly opposite, on the other side of U.S. 1 where Route 100 meets the pike, is the Chadd's Ford Inn established in 1736. It was always closed when we were there, so I cannot vouch for the food. Behind the old inn is a courtyard lined with shops and artisans' workshops which deal in antiques and regional handicrafts.

The entrance to the park is about a mile east of the inn, on the southbound lane of the pike. There are two entrances, one at the west end to Washington's Headquarters, and one at the east to Lafayette's. The park provides ample parking space, picnic facilities including barbecue pits, rest rooms, and recreation areas, all connected by one paved road. There are no food concessions except for automatic soft drink machines. The park provides an excellent place for your midday meal and a good place to relax, weather permitting, after you have fought the battle to its conclusion.

There is a large weatherproof map posted on the side of the rest rooms near the Lafayette House which shows the park and the battle area in detail, including the battle lines and the route followed by Howe's outflanking force. Near the Lafayette House stands a huge sycamore tree under which, according to local legend, Lafayette's wound was dressed after the battle. The tree is probably as old as 1650 and was certainly here when the house was built. The spread of the branches at the widest point is just a little less than a hundred feet.

The **Lafayette House** was originally the property of the Gilpin family. Three successive houses have stood on this site; the present one, which was recently restored, is the one Lafayette occupied at the time of the battle. It was the home of Gideon and Sarah Gilpin, Quakers who did not openly support the war, but did not object when the young Frenchman asked for the use of their home. When Lafayette and his son, George Washington Lafayette, visited Chadd's Ford in July, 1825, they stopped at the house and the elderly marquis paid his respects to his former host, who was then on his deathbed.

This is a handsome, two-story stone house, typical of the area. None of the present furnishings are original to the house or connected with Lafayette, though they are all antiques of the period. Two life-size figures in tableau portray the young Lafayette and a servant attending to his needs at table. The ovens are beehive ovens, and you can see how they got their name when you walk around the outside of the house to the outer wall of the kitchen. In the coachhouse, behind glass, is the coach Lafayette rode in during his tour of the United States in 1825.

Washington's Headquarters is a restoration of the original house which was, at the time of the battle, the home of another Quaker, Benjamin Ring. Inside another tableau of life-sized figures represents Generals Washington and Sullivan listening to farmer Thomas Cheyney as he brings them the news that alerts them to Howe's right flank end run. It would be nice to say that the tableau is displayed in the very room in which it happened, but the original house was destroyed by fire some years ago. A photograph of it is on exhibit in the restoration. Christian Sanderson, a local teacher who associated himself with the battle to such an extent that he became a local tradition in his own right, moved into the earlier house with his mother and lived in the eastern wing. For the next sixteen years, Sanderson showed visitors around the place, conducted tours over the battlefield, and lectured extensively on the events that took place in the neighborhood. When Sanderson moved out of the headquarters house, he moved into a house which you can visit near the John Chadd House; it is packed full of all kinds of historic memorabilia, not all of which is connected with the Revolution.

The site had been nothing but a pile of rubble for almost twenty years before the Brandywine Battlefield Park Commission put its architect to work digging out the old foundations. The present restoration was built according to the data deduced from the old foundation stones and it is believed to be an accurate restoration. The original house, a one-room, frame house was built early in the eighteenth century and was added onto over the years and enhanced with stone walls; by the time Washington used it, it was probably one of the biggest and finest homes in the area.

Having visited the center and headquarters of the rebel army, drive back into Chadd's Ford proper and look for State Route 100 which follows the Brandywine north and south of the village. The site of Pyle's Ford, the southernmost ford guarded by Washington's men, is not marked at this time. You can drive south along 100 through a lovely, mixed rural-exurban area with the Brandywine winding along on your right, but though in a mile or less you will come to where Brookfield-Cossart Road crosses the creek, there is no evidence available to show that this particular spot was Pyle's Ford. It must have been difficult country for an eighteenth-century army to make its way through. For that matter, it would present difficulties to a modern army were there no roads, for it is even today an area of ravines and creek beds.

Traveling north from Chadd's Ford on Route 100 takes you along the line where the major part of Washington's army was stationed. A short distance north of U.S. 1 you will see on your right a two-story fieldstone house off the road with a wooden porch in front and an American flag flying over it. A small parking area on the opposite side of the road allows a few cars to pull off. This is the **Sanderson House** which you might want to visit to view the numerous artifacts Sanderson and others picked up on the battlefield: cannonballs, swords, pieces of bayonets, spent bullets, and so on.

A short distance farther is the **Chadd House.** John Chadd operated a ferry over the ford as early as 1738 and for sometime also operated a tavern in his home until his death in 1760. A number of people seem to have followed this practice, probably as a means of earning additional income. Both Gideon Gilpin and Benjamin Ring did so in the homes you just visited; in fact at one time Gideon was read out of his meeting because of it. The ferry Chadd operated was typical of the period and area. It consisted of a flatboat secured to a line strung between the two banks by a wooden block and tackle. The ferryman poled as hard as he could forward and the boat, held against the current by the block and tackle, inched its way across the stream. Flatboats were big enough to carry horses and wagons. A replica is being constructed by local people in Chadd's Ford who hope to have it in operation by the bicentennial of the battle.

The Chadd House is a two-story, fieldstone building with a wooden porch in front covered by an overhang which was being restored when I visited. A flight of stone steps leads up to the porch on one side; the house is built into the side of the hill and the foundation wall is exposed to the front. You must keep your eyes open to spot it high above the road, partially hidden by trees and shrubs. A steep, dirt driveway leads up to it and one of the old keystone-shaped markers near the house identifies it as the site of the American artillery position under Proctor. The restoration of the interior may be completed by the time you get to Chadd's Ford. The artillery was placed on the ridgeline behind the house and one particular battery of guns was placed on the hill directly behind the house. I tried to walk up to the spot, but was blocked by a chicken-wire fence, which marks the limits of an adjacent house and property.

THE BATTLE

At this point you have a choice. You can take the long tour by returning to the point on U.S. 1 where Howe divided his forces, then following an approximation of the flanking forces' route to the Brandywine fords they used and their route to the main engagements at Birmingham Meetinghouse and Sandy Hollow.

The alternative is to continue along Route 100 as it parallels the Brandywine to Meetinghouse Road, which comes in from the right. Meetinghouse Road will take you to the Birmingham Meetinghouse, a midway point on the battlefield opposite the plowed hill. From there you can go first to the left to find the place where the British attack began, Osborne's Hill; where Cornwallis and Howe paused to plan the next move; Sconneltown, which they passed on their way to Osborne's Hill; and so on back to the fords. Turning left from the meetinghouse will also get you to the sites where the Americans formed their second and third lines of resistance; the spot where Lafayette was wounded; Sandy Hollow, the site of the last, furious encounter; Dilworthtown, the scene of the final phase of the battle (then called Dilworth) and the point from which the Americans retreated to Chester.

By going the long way around, you will do the battle in sequence, the other way in a somewhat piecemeal fashion, but saving yourself almost an hour.

Whatever you do, don't pass up the opportunity to drive along Route 100 north of Chadd's Ford, particularly between Meetinghouse Road and the village. It is a lovely drive along the creek through beautiful vistas of fields, woods, and water. Keep in mind that on one side —to your right as you drive toward Chadd's Ford—on the high ground is where Knyphausen stationed his guns while his men were deployed out of sight under the trees at the foot of the ridge; on the other side the American guns were stationed on the high ground and American troops all along your side of the creek. During the early part of the battle, shells and balls flew overhead in a continuous stream back and forth as the two forces dueled at long range for hours.

Also keep in mind that according to eighteenth-century accounts, the Brandywine wound through a dense forest and its banks were overgrown with trees and bushes. Many of the open fields you now see along the stream were not cleared two hundred years ago.

No matter which route you follow, this is the battle story you should keep in mind. Washington had posted his forces on high ground commanding the fords over the Brandywine, or so he thought. Unfortunately, there were a few more places the British could get across the stream than he was aware of and so he had posted far too few pickets.

He also had a somewhat imprecise idea of just where the fords he knew of were located.

Sometime after Knyphausen drove Maxwell back across the stream and deployed along the Brandywine, he opened an artillery duel which did very little damage on either side. Washington knew that Howe had to cross the Brandywine and expected him to try a ford north of Chadd's Ford where Sullivan's command formed the right flank. When he received word that scouts had seen Howe's division with Cornwallis in command marching north along the Great Valley Road toward the forks of the Brandywine, Washington decided on a bold strategy. He would send Greene across the Brandywine just south of Chadd's Ford to turn Knyphausen's flank, send Sullivan with the right division across to attack the British while they were strung out along the Great Valley Road, and reposition the reserves under Generals Alexander and Stephen near Birmingham Meetinghouse three miles west of Chadd's Ford along the road the British had to use to turn his flank.

It was a good idea and might have resulted in a smashing American victory, but it had a flaw—faulty intelligence. After receiving word that cavalry patrols had spotted the British on Great Valley Road, Washington sent word to Greene to begin his attack, got Sullivan started across the stream, and ordered Alexander and Stephen to march to Birmingham Meetinghouse. Then came word from Sullivan that it was all a mistake; the British were nowhere near the forks. Washington hesitated, undecided. Had the British split their forces and left themselves open to piecemeal decimation or hadn't they? He could not take the chance of exposing his own men to a trap until he knew definitely.

In an agony of uncertainty, Washington called off the river crossing and halted the movement of the reserves toward the meetinghouse. All this happened between eleven in the morning and two in the afternoon. Suddenly Squire Thomas Cheyney, a local Whig who was known to the British for his unfriendly activities, came pounding into camp on his horse. He had been out riding with a friend on their way to Chadd's Ford to see if they could do anything to help the Americans when they had come upon the British north of Chadd's Ford and east of the Brandywine. Realizing what they were up to, Cheyney first tried to warn General Sullivan, who refused to see him, then rode to Chadd's Ford, argued his way past the guards and told Washington his news. Washington was not inclined to believe him, but when he began to receive messages reporting the British at Osborne's Hill just a few miles north of Birmingham Meetinghouse he realized he was in danger of being taken from the rear. He immediately ordered Greene to call off the river crossing and march toward the developing attack and ordered Alexander and Stephen to get to Birmingham Meetinghouse as quickly as possible.

With that in mind, either follow me or proceed to the meetinghouse for the next part of the story. If you're with me, come along back west and south on U.S. 1 to Longwood Gardens. The entrance to these nationally famous gardens (which are free and feature conservatories, plantings, and fountains built on an ancient colonial property) shows up on your right before you get to the turnoff for Kennett Square. Continue south beyond the main entrance until you come to Schoolhouse Road, which intersects from the right. Schoolhouse Road is almost directly opposite the marker identifying Howe's division of his forces. Turn right onto Schoolhouse Road and proceed north in the direction Howe went. Schoolhouse Road ends at an intersection with State Route 926. Turn right onto 926 for a short distance, then left onto Northbrook Road. You are driving through a mixed area abounding in farms and one-family home developments, but at the time of the battle, it was heavily forested with occasional farms, then called plantations, breaking the expanse of green with open field and homestead sites. Bear right along Northbrook Road when it meets Spring Road and take it to Red Lion Road. Bear left on Red Lion Road to an intersection with Route 842. Turn left onto 842 for a short distance; then take the first right which, according to the county map, is Northbrook Road putting in another appearance. The Brandywine wanders quite a bit in this area and at one point makes almost right-angle turns to form the three sides of an angular figure. We know the British had to ford both branches. According to available maps, they crossed the west branch in this vicinity at a place called **Trimble's Ford,** which does not appear on contemporary maps.

Back on Northbrook Road, you will come to a railroad crossing and then the road curves right before ending at a T-intersection. Turn left and you will be paralleling the west branch of the Brandywine. Then comes a bridge over a brook and then a bridge that goes up and down steeply over the west branch. The bridge is not named on contemporary county maps, but as you proceed along Northbrook Road, lo and behold just past this bridge is a wooden sign reading Trimbleville! Though it is not so marked, it is possible you have crossed the west branch of the Brandywine where Howe and Cornwallis led their men across.

At this point, you are only a mile or two north and west of the forks of the Brandywine. When you come to an intersection with Camp Linden Road, take it to the right. Now you are about a mile above the point where the west branch makes one of those right-angle turns. A quarter of a mile along Camp Linden Road you have reached the northernmost point of its convolution. The stream is just to your right and in a short distance, as the road veers away from it, will turn south, straighten out, then turn south again for a two-mile stretch to its meeting with the east branch at the forks.

Camp Linden Road ends in a T-intersection with North Wawaset Road. If you could continue straight ahead, bearing just a little to the north or left, you would come to the second ford the British outflankers crossed that day, Jeffries Ford. As it is, you have to turn right onto Wawaset Road back to 842. Turn left onto 842 and cross the east branch of the Brandywine less than a quarter of a mile above the forks. This was one of two crossings I had pre-selected on the county map as candidates for Jeffries Ford. The bridge here, however, is called Shaw's Bridge. Continue along 842 until you meet Minor Road coming in from the left. Turn onto Minor Road and there before you is a steel girder bridge clearly marked on the maps as Jeffries Bridge.

If you were to walk due west from here you would come back to the intersection of Camp Linden Road and North Wawaset. The next ford north of here is Copes Ford, so marked on eighteenth-century maps, marked Copes Bridge on modern maps. The relationship between Copes Bridge and Jeffries Bridge coincides exactly with that of Copes Ford and Jeffries Ford. This is **Jeffries Ford** then, and here the British crossed the Brandywine for the second time before swinging east to place themselves behind the Americans at Chadd's Ford. However, bear in mind that the route you followed from Longwood Gardens to this point is an arbitrary one. There are other roads through the area which would have led you to the fords. What you have done is to approximate Great Valley Road, possibly found Trimble's Ford, and definitely found Jeffries Ford.

After recrossing the bridge, Minor Road will take you back to the intersection with 842. Go left or east on 842, noticing on your left below the level of the road a local hunting club with a swimming pool clearly visible, until you see a historical marker at an intersection with a road going right. The road is Birmingham Meeting Road and the marker informs you that here Howe's forces turned southeast to take the American army by surprise from the rear.

From this point on the plot thickens in a very satisfactory fashion for the history buff. Turn right into Birmingham Meeting Road and follow it up onto the high ground east of Chadd's Ford. Close to the top of the rise, on the right side of the road, look for one of the keystone-shaped markers. It sits in front of a small, stucco house and marks the site of **Sconneltown,** where Howe's men paused, probably to refresh themselves after the long hike across country and the climb up the hill.

It was here in a wheelwright's shop that the members of the Birmingham Meeting had come together for their regular weekday meeting that September morning. Their meetinghouse farther south had been taken over by the Patriots as a hospital for some of Washington's men. According to a member of the meeting, Joseph Townsend who published a memoir on the battle in 1846, so many of the Americans had become ill after their long march through the summer heat from Wilmington to Chadd's Ford, that the meetinghouse had been commandeered and was being made ready to receive them on the morning of the battle.

In this account, Townsend tells how he and his brother, William, along with a number of other local inhabitants—Squire Cheyney probably among them—took a ride along the Brandywine to see if they could spot the British army fording the river. Having seen nothing, the Townsends reported to the wheelwright shop in Sconneltown at the hour set for the meeting. The meeting began, but such a disturbance arose outside that it had to be adjourned. The women of the neighborhood were afraid the British soldiers would murder them all. As the men sought to calm them, Townsend says: "Our eyes were caught on a sudden by the appearance of the army coming out of the woods into the fields belonging to Emmet Jeffers on the west side of the creek above the fording place. In a few minutes the fields were literally covered over with them, and they were hastening toward us. Their arms and bayonets being raised shone as bright as silver there being a clear sky on a day exceedingly warm."

At that point, the young Townsends decided to hurry home to see to their own womenfolk. However, if you stay for a moment in Sconneltown at the top of the hill, you might get a clear view of the ford and the fields below the hill which were then so open to the view of the Quakers gathered outside the wheelwright's shop. It is open farmland, as it was then, though there is no orchard now. It was up these slopes that the British army advanced after crossing the creek, hurrying to gain the high ground upon which you now stand.

Continue along Birmingham Meeting Road to Lenape Road, which at this point is Route 52 and Route 100 combined. At the intersection on the far side of Lenape Road is an old stone building, **Strode's Mill.** The great mill wheel is no longer, but a stream flowed across the road and a milldam caught and held it; the water turned the wheel to grind the flour the Continental Army needed so badly, which the British advance sought to deny them. The stream is still there with some free-standing masonry close to the house, probably all that is left of either the milldam or the walls that supported the wheel and the mill machinery.

A short distance farther, you will come to the Mews of Radley Run, a road that comes in from the right and leads to the local country club. Directly opposite is a private driveway going up the rise of ground to the left. Beside it on the bank above the road is another old historical marker. It is too far above the road to read comfortably but don't bother struggling up to get the message. It marks **Osborne's Hill,** the position from which Howe directed the fighting that took place a little farther south. This was also the site of a skirmish between an American scouting party and the British advance troops. It was from here the first message was sent to Washington confirming the presence of the British in his rear and it was here Howe held up his advance to give his rear guard a chance to catch up with the main body. The very top of Osborne's Hill, on which Howe set up his command post, is private property and the driveway is so marked. I walked up for a short distance to see if I could spot the plowed hill opposite Birmingham Meetinghouse, where the Americans dug in to resist the British, but the view is now obscured by trees.

Continue to follow the British advance to an intersection with Route 926, which is known now, as it was then, as Street Road. If you were to turn left here, you would immediately find a new historical marker on the left side of 926 for the spot where the British opened their attack on the plowed hill.

It was here the British deployed and advanced to attack the positions the Americans under Alexander and Stephen had taken on high ground south and west of the meetinghouse, about a quarter of a mile away. It was a good position, but when Sullivan arrived with his division and took command, he found his men considerably in advance of the main American position and had the other commanders shift their men to the right, your left, to make room for the combined American forces to present a solid front.

There is a cornfield to the right on the other side of 926 and open fields on the left, probably as there were in 1777. Joseph Townsend, who seems to have acted as a war correspondent, stuck his nose into all kinds of places in a way that would be denied most correspondents today on any field of battle. As a result, he has passed down some excellent glimpses of an eighteenth-century army in action and in particular a number of details that should add a sense of immediacy to your visit to the battlefield.

Having determined that their women were not in any danger, the Townsends returned and discovered that the British were turning toward Birmingham Meetinghouse. Townsend describes the British front and flanking party as a half mile in extent. Eventually the Townsends were allowed into the British headquarters in "one of the most elegant houses in the town," which is supposedly still standing about three-quarters of a mile southwest of West Chester and about three miles from the meetinghouse. This would place it almost due south of Jeffries Ford.

William Townsend informed the British that "they would soon meet General Washington and his army. They enquired what sort of a man Mr. Washington was. My brother having knowledge of him having been with him at his quarters at Chadd's Ford replied that he was a stately, well-proportioned, fine looking man of great ability, active, firm and of a social disposition, was considered to be a good man. The British officer said that he might be a good man but that he was most damnably misled to take up arms against his sovereign."

Another officer told Joseph Townsend, "You have got a hell of a fine country here which we have found to be the case ever since we have landed at the Head of Elk."

At one point, William called Joseph to the door of the house to see Lord Cornwallis as he passed by.

"He was on horseback, appeared tall and sat very erect. His rich scarlet clothing loaded with gold lace, epaulets, etc. occasioned him to make a brilliant and martial appearance."

The inquisitive Townsends continued to move forward with the troops and eventually found themselves with the advance guard just before the fight at Birmingham Meetinghouse began. Joseph describes the Hessians as "wearing their beards on their upper lips which was a novelty in that part of the country."

They were now between the dwelling of Richard Stroud and Osborne's Hill.

"Being now in the front we walked on considerably until we arrived at a pair of bars opposite the ancient dwelling of Amos Davis to which we went into the fields southwest of the road and walked up to the upper fence being the division line between the two tracts of land of Amos Davis and the heirs of his uncle, Daniel Davis. On turning our backs we had a grand view of the army as they advanced over and down the south side of Osborne's Hill [now directly behind you] and the lands of James Carter scarce a vacant place left. . . . While we were amusing ourself with the wonderful curiosity before us, to our great astonishment and surprise the firing of the musketry took place; the advance guard aforementioned having arrived at the Street Road and were fired upon by a company of the Americans who were stationed in the orchard north of Samuel Jones' brick dwelling house. The attack was immediately returned by the Hessians by their stepping up the bank of the road alongside the orchard making the fence as a breastwork through which they fired upon the company who made the attack. From the distance we were from them though in full view until the smoke of the firing covered them from our sight, I was under no apprehension of danger."

At this point Joseph decided to go back and, leaving his brother, made his way through the crowd (which consisted of a number of curious spectators as well as soldiers) until he came to the bars opening into Amos Davis's field. Here he was met by several companies of soldiers who had been ordered to enter the field and form in preparation for the approaching engagement.

"The opening of the bars was not of sufficient width to permit them to pass with that expedition the emergency of the case required. A German officer on horseback ordered the fence to be taken down and as I was near to the spot I happened to be subject to his requirings as he flourished a drawn sword over my head with others who stood by. On removal of the second rail I was forcibly struck with the impropriety of being acting in assisting to take the lives of my fellow beings and therefore desisted proceeding any further in obedience to his command."

He then went up to the top of Osborne's Hill "as great firing of musketry and roaring of the cannon" took place and saw General Howe "mounted on a large English horse much reduced in flesh. . . . [Obviously the horses were not yet over their ocean ordeal.] The general was a large, portly man of coarse features. He appeared to have lost his teeth, as his mouth had fallen in."

While on Osborne's Hill, Townsend used his powers of observation well and observed "the fields in front of us containing great heaps of blankets and baggage thrown together to relieve the men for action, the regular march of the British army consisting of horse and foot, artillery baggage and provision wagons, arms and ammunition together with a host of plunderers and rabble that accompanied the army. Almost the whole face of the country around appeared to be covered and alive with these objects. The march continued about four hours."

While he was on Osborne's Hill, Townsend heard the roar of artillery signaling Knyphausen's attack across the Brandywine; the Hessians had attacked, according to plan, as soon as Knyphausen knew Howe's division had engaged the Americans at Birmingham Meetinghouse.

As you continue along Birmingham Meeting Road you are paralleling the British attack which surged forward across the cornfield to your right. A cemetery will appear on your left behind a stone wall and immediately after you will see the **Birmingham Friends Meetinghouse** set back off the road in a grove of trees, a one-story, fieldstone structure with a more recent addition, a Sunday School added on at the rear, and a small playground beyond that. This meeting was established in 1690 and the present meetinghouse was built in 1763. According to the plaque next to the front door, it was used as a hospital by both sides both before and after the battle as the ground changed hands. A plaque set into the stone wall along the road in front of the building cites this area as the spot on which the Americans erected their first line of defense. Much of the fighting during the early phase of the battle took place around the meetinghouse, but though the door is supposed to show scars of the fighting, I examined all the doors closely and could see none.

Before you leave the meetinghouse, read Townsend's description of the scenes that were enacted around and in it following the battle:

". . . awful was the scene to behold. Such a number of fellow beings lying together severely wounded and some mortally, a few dead, but a small proportion of them considering the immense quantity of powder and ball that had been discharged. It was now time for the surgeons to exert themselves and divers of them were busily employed. Some of the doors of the meetinghouse were torn off and the wounded carried thereon into the house to be occupied for a hospital instead of the American sick for which it had been preparing some days previous. The wounded officers were first attended to. Several of distinction had fallen and as everything appeared to be in a state of confusion and we being spectators and assistance required some of our number at the request of the surgeons became active in removing them there and of whom I was one. . . . After assisting and carrying two of them into the house was disposed to see an operation performed by one of the surgeons who was preparing to amputate a limb. Having a brass clamp or screw fitted thereon a little above the knee joint, he had his knife in his hand, the blade of which was of a circular form and was about to make the incision when he recollected that it might be necessary for the wounded man to take something to support him during the operation. He mentioned to some of his attendants to give him a little wine or brandy to keep up his spirits to which he replied 'No, doctor, it is not necessary. My spirits are up enough without it.' He then observed that he heard some of them say that there was some water in the house and if there was some he would like a little to wet his mouth. As I was listening to the conversation and waiting for the water to arrive, one of my companions caught me by the arm and mentioned that it was necessary to go out immediately as they were fixing the picket guards and if we did not get away in a few minutes we should have to remain within the lines of the encampment during the night."

Can't you just hear Joseph Townsend answering, "Aw, shucks! Just when he's going to take off the man's leg!"

At least from this we get some idea of battlefield surgery of the period, and we also learn that following the battle, the British army camped on the field.

The *cemetery* next to the meetinghouse can be reached through an opening in the stone wall just to the north. It leads into an outer enclosure which contains a number of imposing monuments. One granite block marked by flags and plaques is in memory of those who fell in the Battle of the Brandywine. A common grave behind the memorial contains the bodies of those who fell in this vicinity and, undoubtedly, some of those who underwent the surgery Joseph Townsend had to miss.

With your back to this memorial, walk away from it to where a stone wall jogs slightly. Just to the left of that are a line of low, flat stones which mark the resting places of members of the Birmingham Meeting. Directly in front of that line is a low, white marker with black letters telling us that on a stone in front rested one corner of the first Birmingham meetinghouse made of cedar logs and flintstones, erected in 1721. You can still see the rim of the stone protruding above ground level by two or three inches. If you return to Birmingham Meeting Road and walk a few feet farther north, you will come to yet another entrance to this odd cemetery between two stone pillars. In this section are a number of huge monuments to several of the participants in the battle, including Lafayette, Pulaski, and Colonel Taylor who served in Wayne's brigade, all of them erected in the early 1900s by John G. Taylor, a descendant of the colonel's.

Directly across the road is a farm called Battlefield Farm and beyond it a broad expanse of open field which falls off to the north, back in the direction you came from and to the west toward Chadd's Ford and the Brandywine about a mile and half away. This open area extends south for some distance and is bisected by Meetinghouse Road a little south of the meetinghouse; the road runs down to the Brandywine immediately north of Chadd's Ford. Meetinghouse Road does not appear on the old maps and was not, I am sure, laid out at the time of the battle. It now cuts through what must have been the *plowed hill* where Alexander and Stephen threw up some hasty redoubts and prepared to meet the British. At present the northern half, on the north side of Meetinghouse Road, is Battlefield Farm; the southern part, on the other side of the road, is part of Skirmish Farm. I drove out along Meetinghouse Road to a point just before it dips down toward the creek and then walked north across the field to where the land falls away into a wooden ravine. Ahead of me to the right front I could plainly see Osborne's Hill; to my direct right was the meetinghouse; and this, the entire hilltop area, was where the Americans met the first British attack.

If you park along Meetinghouse Road as I did and face north in the direction from which you came along Birmingham Meeting Road, you should be standing in the approximate center of the American line. Sullivan, who swung his division from its original position facing west along the creek, came up to join the line from somewhere to your left. As he tried to get into position, the British advancing from the direction of Osborne's Hill, now off to your right front, came over the ground in front of you and attacked his right flank, trying to throw it back and pin him against the creek. It was a difficult position to be caught in, but Sullivan managed to get his men in line with Alexander's and Stephen's. The Americans were then forced to fall back, but in good order and giving a good account of themselves as they did so. The story of the battle as presently printed by the Chester County Promotion Bureau contains two excellent maps of the action, but says that Lafayette was wounded here, which is an obvious error as we shall see.

By this time (about 5:30 in the afternoon) Washington had arrived with Lafayette. Once he grasped what was happening, he started to organize a defense line on the available high ground. The main part of Greene's command was still on the way. When Weedon's brigade arrived about six o'clock, having covered four miles on foot across country in forty-five minutes, Washington threw them into the line and formed second and third lines farther east.

Drive south from the meetinghouse along Birmingham Meeting Road for a short distance until you see the juncture with Wylie Road, which intersects from the right. (To the left it becomes Thornsbury Road.) The mouth of a cannon is sticking out at you from under a planting of trees and shrubs on your right where the roads meet. There is some dispute among local historians as to whether this cannon is of Revolutionary War vintage. It does mark the site of the line along which the Americans tried to rally after their right flank had been driven in and they were forced to retire from the plowed hill.

Proceeding farther south, you will see a tall, granite pillar off the left side of the road, standing by itself about fifty feet from a contemporary, white frame farmhouse. The driveway leading to the house winds around the monument, providing a parking place. The monument was erected by the schoolchildren of Chester County in 1895. It states that on the rising ground a short distance south of the spot was where Lafayette was wounded during the Battle of the Brandywine. The site itself lies beyond the farmhouse in an open field. Walk along the road now for a distance of about two city blocks. Keep to the top of the high bank that borders the road. The people living in the house are used to visitors. In fact when I stopped to make inquiries, they knew just what I was looking for and guided me accurately. My object was a cannon which points to the site of the American third line. The last time I was there, it was an unintentional secret, for it is impossible to see from the road. By walking south, however, along the top of the bank from **Lafayette's Monument,** on the edge of a cornfield you will see it ahead of you—a large, seemingly Revolutionary War vintage cannon or a reasonable facsimile thereof, protruding from the trees and shrubs.

When you reach it, sight along the barrel. It points to a vague depression in the middle of the field with rising ground all around it. This is **Sandy Hollow.** Here the Americans formed yet again as they attempted to halt the British advance, and there, across that field, Washington and Lafayette rode back and forth, exposed to enemy fire, as they attempted to get the men to hold fast in the face of the advancing enemy. Lafayette received a ball in the left thigh and rode up to Washington with his leg bleeding badly. Washington called for surgeons and Lafayette was led away to be treated under the big sycamore you saw in Brandywine Battle-field Park. It was the young Frenchman's baptism of fire.

Taking his cue from the sound of the engagement farther north, Knyphausen launched an attack across the Brandywine at Chadd's Ford. Despite heavy punishment from Colonel Thomas Proctor's guns, the Hessians and British crossed the stream and drove Wayne's brigade from its position along the east bank, the very ground you drove by along Route 100 immediately south and north of Chadd's Ford. Wayne attempted to form another line, but darkness fell; contact with Knyphausen being lost, Wayne pulled his men back to join the rest of the army as the tired, defeated rebels moved on to Chester, leaving the British in possession of the field.

Farther along Birmingham Meeting Road, you will come to an intersection with two other roads, old Wilmington Pike and Brinton's Bridge Road. The few homes and stores collected around this three-way intersection constitute **Dilworthtown** and the two-story, brick building with a shingled overhang is the old Dilworth Inn, built in 1758. It is in the process of being restored and will eventually be opened to the public as a restaurant. Some of the original fieldstone wall shows around to the back as does the old beehive oven. An old state marker in front of the inn informs us that the final actions of the Battle of the Brandywine took place just southeast of this spot before the Americans fell back to Chester. Follow old Wilmington Pike through Dilworthtown to a juncture with U.S. 202, a four-lane highway. Turn right onto 202 and in a short distance (just beyond an Arco service station when I was there last) a new state historical marker informs you that the final action took place a little southwest of this spot. In other words, the final scenes were played out in near darkness somewhere on what is now farmland between here and Dilworthtown almost directly east. Several county roads go off from 202 into the area, but it is all pastureland and cornfields now with nothing to mark the exact location where the final shots of September 11, 1777, were fired.

The best estimates available put British losses at 577 killed and wounded and six missing. The Hessians seem to have accounted for only forty of the total. The Americans lost between 1,200 and 1,300 men, four hundred as prisoners, as well as eleven guns. It might have been worse. The casualties could have included Washington. During the preliminaries before Maxwell was pushed back across the creek, Washington, probably accompanied by Lafayette, crossed to the west bank of the creek for a firsthand look at the situation. As he rode close to concealed British positions, Captain Patrick Ferguson, who had developed the first breech-loading rifle (his men were armed with them) had Washington in his sights at almost point-blank range but did not fire because he did not consider it "pleasant" to kill a fellow officer, even though he was an enemy who had his back turned and who was doing his duty.

In retrospect, Brandywine battlefield resembles Monmouth. It is undeveloped in the sense that there are no tour roads or interpretative displays, no visitor's center, no overlooks, and except for the Lafayette column and the grave near the meetinghouse, no monuments indicating where the various units were positioned. Yet one gets a feeling of immediacy and a sense almost of physical presence that I find lacking at sites like Saratoga and Yorktown. Perhaps it is because there is less intrusion of interpretative elements, helpful as they might be. The area is still the scene of normal, everyday activities as it was when these armies maneuvered and fought across the fields. Unless you were made aware of what happened here, you might just drive by, never suspecting.

There are not an overwhelming number of motels and hotels from which to choose if you wish to stay in the Brandywine area. If you want to do the Brandywine–Paoli–Anthony Wayne House–Valley Forge sites as a group, you can find good accommodations in the Valley Forge–King of Prussia area. Whether you stay at Lionville or use Valley Forge as a base of operations, you will be able to get to any one of these sites from your motel within an hour or less.

After Brandywine, the British occupied Wilmington while Washington moved to Germantown to keep between them and Philadelphia. A possible major battle at Warren Tavern, near the present town of White Horse, was prevented by a heavy downpour of rain. Howe then outgeneraled Washington in a brilliant display of tactics, forcing him to retreat behind the Schuylkill River. Feinting toward the American supply base at Reading, Howe tricked Washington into marching along one bank of the stream to head him off. Then the British turned and under cover of darkness marched down the opposite bank and crossed the river to take Germantown and Philadelphia. The next noteworthy action took place September 21 at Paoli.

PAOLI

You were last at the marker on U.S. Route 202 on the fringe of the Brandywine battle area. If you wish to proceed to Paoli, turn around and take 202 north to 926. Turn right or east onto 926 until you reach 352. A left turn on 352 will take you north to U.S. 202 again in the vicinity of Goshenville. Don't think I'm leading you on a wild goose chase when I now direct you to make a right turn back onto 202. Had you tried to follow 202 to this point, you might have been caught in a maze of small development streets in the village of Chatwood in West Goshen township. The route I am laying out now is much more direct.

Take U.S. 202, called Paoli Pike here, northeast, passing Rush Hospital on your right, Sugartown Road, and the grounds surrounding the Phelps School on the left. Shortly after, you will reach the intersection of Warren Avenue, marked by a traffic light, various signs, and a marker on the left indicating a turn to the site of the Paoli massacre one mile away.

Warren Avenue is bordered by rolling, open fields on the left with split-rail fences here and there and one or two private homes. Soon after crossing First Avenue you will see a church and a graveyard on the right in a completely built-up area. At that point Monument Avenue comes in from the left. Turn left onto Monument Avenue. Shortly after, you will see on the left what appears to be wide fairgrounds or a park with a road, Wayne Avenue, bordering it. A sign identifies it as the **Paoli Memorial Grounds.** Turn left onto Wayne Avenue and look for the park drive to your right. Take the park drive and follow it toward a group of monuments with a large depression falling away to your right. This is the site of the Paoli Massacre, an experience which had a lasting effect on Anthony Wayne and is viewed by some historians as the low point of his military career.

Should you come from Philadelphia or the western part of the state, take U.S. 30 into Paoli and turn onto U.S. 202/Paoli Pike. Should you come from the west, the turn will be an acute right turn; but if you come from Philadelphia, 202 will come as a left turn going off 30 at a wide angle.

Take 202/Paoli Pike to Warren Avenue at the third traffic light after you leave Route 30. From that direction the Paoli Massacre marker will have its back to you at the intersection with Warren Avenue. Turn right onto Warren Avenue and proceed as described above.

It was on this spot, in that hollow ground and along the slopes bordering it, that Wayne's brigade was encamped the night of September 21, 1777, about 1,500 strong. Wayne had grown up in this neighborhood; in fact his home, as we shall see, was only a few miles away and he knew the area well. His mission was to hit Howe's flank or baggage wagon as the British followed Washington north from the Brandywine. The British learned of the encampment and a night attack was planned under Major

General Charles Grey. Grey began the march to Paoli the night of September 20 and did not arrive until after midnight. He led a force of a light infantry battalion and two highland regiments, including the Forty-second, the Black Watch. The men were ordered to either unload their muskets or take the flints out, which gave Grey the nickname by which he was known ever after, "No-flint" Grey. The idea was to let the Americans do all the firing, thus revealing their positions. The attack was to be carried out with the bayonet. Major John André, who took part in the operation, described it in detail in his diary.

The attack was very successful. Wayne lost about 150 killed, wounded, and captured. Many of the Americans were killed as they ran in front of their campfires, while those who tried to hide in the darkness were remorselessly hunted down and bayoneted. Once again, the rule of night attack held in this action. The mangled condition of the bodies after the battle caused the Patriots to refer to this action as a massacre, and so it has been called to this day, but that term fails to take into account the seventy-one prisoners Grey took back with him. The British said they lost six killed and twenty-two wounded.

Wayne is supposed to have been warned of the attack, but a court-martial acquitted him of any negligence or wrongdoing. Nonetheless, he never forgot Paoli as we have cause to know; the very same idea formed the basis of his strategy at Stony Point. Grey used much the same technique again at Old Tappan (Baylor's Massacre), with much the same results, and a bitter feud developed between Wayne's Pennsylvanians and the British Light Infantry. At the Battle of Germantown, just after Paoli, Wayne's men had to be restrained from killing captured light infantrymen. The British light infantry also rioted in Philadelphia against the peacemaking Carlisle Commission, and at the Battle of Monmouth they were so anxious to get at the Pennsylvanians that they overshot their support and had to be rescued.

You can drive up to the monuments and flags and park your car along the park road. To your left, marked by two cannon, is a low, stone wall enclosing a long mound. The mound is a common grave containing the American dead, who were gathered up the next day by local farmers and buried here. The granite memorial was put up in the early years of the nineteenth century. The day we were there, fresh flowers were on the grave site as well as small flags and veterans' grave markers. The wall was reconstructed in 1964 and contains some stones taken from the foundation of the Ezekiel Bowen log cabin, which stood in the area and was occupied by American officers on the night of the attack. There is a cornfield directly behind the grave site suggesting what the surrounding area might have resembled; for if local farmers found the bodies, they probably lived nearby. For the most part, however, the little park, called Malvern Memorial Park, is surrounded by streets of one- and two-family homes, standing where woodlands must have concealed the British as they approached Wayne's encampment. There are also monuments to the dead of more recent wars and a playground and bandstand suggesting the park is a center for community activities.

Wayne got away during the attack, managing to save his cannon as well. The British took off after him, which gives you a good excuse to follow them for a visit to the Wayne homestead, where they went looking for him. Retrace your route along Warren Avenue to U.S. 202/Paoli Pike. Turn left onto the Pike and count three traffic lights. At the third turn right onto U.S. 30 and take it into the town of Paoli. A short distance past the railroad station on your left, look for a shopping center on the right and a large historical marker announcing the Wayne House is within a mile or two of that spot. Turn right at that intersection onto Leopard Road and follow it through a suburban area until a golf club, the Waynes-borough Country Club, shows up on the right. Watch for the intersection with Waynesborough Avenue. Turn right onto Waynesborough Avenue and, with the golf course on your left, watch for the **Wayne House,** a large, imposing fieldstone mansion standing in the midst of tree-shaded lawns with a long, white, rail fence setting it off from the road. A large sign at the side of the road, erected by the present owners, alerts passersby to the building's historical significance.

The house was owned and lived in by members of the Wayne family from the time the original section was built in 1724 until 1965 when it was sold by a direct descendant of the general to an architectural historian, who was married to another direct descendant. It consists of a two-story central structure with a dormered attic floor above that and three wings, one on either side and the third extending from the back. The left wing as you face the house was the original house, built and finished in 1724 by General Anthony Wayne's grandfather, Anthony, who came to this country in 1722 with his ten married children. The main section was built in 1740; the right wing was added in 1792 and called the "new kitchen"; and the rear wing sometime later. The upper part of the right wing was added in 1860.

The entire house was restored to its original condition by the present owners. There are terraces in the back which were built in 1930. The dormers in the back of the house were added at some recent date and were left because of the light they afford inside the house. The dormers

in the front were restored. At some time during the first half of the nineteenth century, a number of European trees and other plantings were
added to the landscaping, including house vines grown from slips taken
in 1840 from Kenilworth Castle in England. The linden trees on the front
lawn came from Germany; the black walnuts are of an American species
that died out in 1880, leaving three survivors here; the pines are Nor-
wegian, Swedish, and Danish and all came from Norway. Together they
comprise the largest stand of trees in Chester County that are not indige-
nous to the United States. There are also Kentucky coffee trees, Ohio
catawbas, and a mountain laurel tree, species that once grew in great pro-
fusion in American forests, but are no longer common. Behind the house
to the left rear is a huge boxwood, which figures prominently in the
history of the house.

This was Wayne's home from the time he was born until he died.
During the Revolution his wife Polly and his children lived here. The
British came looking for him across the fields that are now part of the
golf course, entered the house, tore up and burned the feather beds, and
caused some other damage until Polly Wayne drove them out. Then they
went around to the back and poked their bayonets into the boxwoods,
thinking the General might have hidden himself inside. (He had withdrawn with the survivors of his command from the area.) If these boxwoods were big enough to hide a man then they must be at least three
hundred years old today at a guess. They are held together by guy wires
because of damage done to them by a falling tree in recent years. You can
see them when you walk or drive by the house, behind the left wing.

The original property included 1,600 acres where four of the first
Anthony Wayne's sons settled and built adjoining homes. Mad Anthony's
ancestry is easy to trace; the male members of the family from his grandfather on down shared only two given names, Anthony and Isaac. For
128 years, fathers Anthony named their firstborn sons Isaac, who named
their firstborn sons Anthony, and so on from 1724 until 1852. So Anthony I was the first settler; his son, Isaac I, was the general's father; the
general was Anthony II; and his son was Isaac II. Unfortunately, Isaac II's
four sons died in infancy and so the property was left to his great nephew,
his sister's grandson, William Wayne Evans, on condition that he change
his name to Wayne. He complied and from then on the property passed
from William Wayne to William Wayne II and so on.

Since the house is now in private hands, the interior is not on view
to the public but it is worth a trip just to view it from the outside. The
only items in the house directly connected with the general are a cloak

which he wore at the Battle of Fallen Timbers in 1794 and a set of his drinking glasses. In addition the present owners have amassed a collection of manuscripts, documents, and letters connected in one way or the other with this most colorful of all the Revolutionary War figures.

At one time or another the old house sheltered a host of the leading figures of the times. Franklin visited here in 1764. Young Anthony was nineteen at the time, and the then postmaster of the colonies and agent for Pennsylvania came to enlist the young man's services as surveyor and agent for a land company that had some newly-acquired land in Nova Scotia, an assignment Wayne accepted and carried out. During the Valley Forge encampment Lafayette lived here for about three weeks. In that same period the house was also visited by Jefferson, Hamilton, and Madison, who was all of nineteen and came at the invitation of the general, as did many of the young officers, for a weekend's respite from the rigors of that winter encampment.

The Wayne House is probably one of the finest examples of a home of the Revolutionary War period anywhere in the country and is undoubtedly the best preserved and restored of any in this part of Pennsylvania. It reflects the warmth and solidity, yes, even something of the dash, that must have emanated from its former owner as well as all the charm and beauty attached to only a few of the homes extant from the colonial period.

VALLEY FORGE

It is now most convenient to pay a visit to what is probably the most hallowed site connected with the American Revolution, Valley Forge. After Brandywine, General Howe maneuvered into Philadelphia in September, 1777, while Washington thought he was heading for Reading. Not a shot was fired in the city's defense. What followed next was Washington's almost successful attack on Germantown and the British reduction of the Delaware River forts guarding the water approaches to Philadelphia, which you can cover more conveniently when you get to Philadelphia.

For the present, skip over the fall months of 1777. The British are safe and snug in the City of Brotherly Love. Congress is safe in York, Pennsylvania, and with his army in no condition to attack Howe, Washington must find shelter for his men. At the same time he must protect Congress, do what he can to keep the enemy from getting supplies from the surrounding countryside (Knyphausen has already destroyed a supply depot and iron forge at a place called Valley Forge), and keep his army poised to counter the British when campaigning resumes in the spring.

Twenty miles from Philadelphia is a hilly, wooded area with good water and high ground for defense. It is near a small town with an inn, both called King of Prussia, a most unlikely name for the neighborhood of a Continental Army encampment. Washington orders his army to march to Valley Forge; winter comes down on them with a vengeance. Howe prevents them from getting across the Schuylkill River at Matson's Ford, which adds a week to their precamp ordeal. Finally on December 19, after taking eight days to cover fifteen miles from Whitemarsh, the Continental Army staggers into the area about 10,000 strong and seeks shelter in makeshift huts. Along the way they have left a trail of dead and dying men and the blood of their feet, literally; many had no shoes and none were dressed to resist the snow, wind, and ice that were their daily lot.

You can get to Valley Forge from Paoli with no trouble at all by following U.S. 30 east to State Route 252. Turn left onto 252 and drive until you cross the Pennsylvania Turnpike via an overpass. Just beyond, if you haven't noticed them yet, you will see the signs for **Valley Forge State Park.** You can get there from other points on the compass by taking the Pennsylvania Turnpike to the Valley Forge exit, Exit 24, and then following the signs.

The first time I visited Valley Forge, nine years ago, it was to film a television program. I spent two days in the park, mostly in the area of the reconstructed huts near Fort Muhlenberg, one day surveying and one day filming. It was February. There was snow on the ground. It wasn't a particularly cold winter, just an average one, but there was no place to get in from the wind that blew almost constantly over that open hill. There were no nearby comfort stations; the new Visitor's Center had not yet been built. We were all dressed warmly, but by working inside the huts and standing for hours on snow and ice, all of us who were there experienced in some small measure what the soldiers of the Continental Army experienced during the winter of 1777–78. Continually uncomfortable and cold, despite warm clothes and full stomachs, we didn't find it hard to imagine how they must have felt without adequate clothing and proper shelter, living mostly on gruel; standing guard duty and drilling on the parade ground in mid-winter; sleeping on straw in smoky huts impossible to heat; and subject to typhus, frostbite, smallpox, dysentery, and all the other ills that beset men who are undernourished and constantly exposed to wintry elements.

The park is open year-round, but perhaps the best time to visit it to appreciate the atmosphere and flavor of two hundred years ago is during the winter. Keep in mind that the conditions at Valley Forge that winter were not to be compared with those faced by the army at Morristown in 1778–79. In fact, the winter of 1777–78 was comparatively mild. Even so, about 2,500 of Washington's 10,000 stayed behind when the army moved out in June, 1778, dead from exposure, typhus, and just plain undernourishment. Blame their suffering on the inefficiency and blundering of the people in charge from Congress on down to General Thomas Mifflin, who was quartermaster general until Washington replaced him with Nathanael Greene. Blame it on many of the local farmers who were either just plain hostile to the Patriots' cause or lined their pockets with more silver by selling their produce and livestock to the British.

With Greene in charge of supplies, things began to look up. Greene was an efficient quartermaster who sent out foraging parties not only into the surrounding area but also into Jersey and Delaware. He also knew how to get Congress to come across with some of the things it had promised.

It was here in the Valley Forge encampment that Baron von Steuben offered his services to Washington, who put him in charge of training. Beginning with a model company of 100 men and training them to instruct the others, von Steuben made an army out of Washington's ragtag outfit, teaching them the rudiments and finer points of military drill, instilling in them a sense of discipline and esprit de corps, until by the time they took the field the following summer, they were able to pursue the British across Jersey and meet them on terms of near equality at Monmouth.

When you arrive in Valley Forge State Park at the Visitor's Center, you will find all the conveniences you have come to expect at historic parks: rest rooms, a souvenir counter, an interpretative museum, and an orientation slide film which explains the site and its history.

Present Valley Forge covers a wide area of parklands, which include rolling fields and hills, wooded areas, picnic grounds, and even some recreation areas. Throughout are scattered plaques, statues and memorials marking the sites on which particular army units camped, reconstructed redoubts and redans, the remains of original breastwork defenses, reconstructed huts and hospitals, the house in which Washington lived during the encampment, part of the time with Martha, and several other buildings which were used as residences by other officers. A tour road takes you from site to site. At the Visitor's Center you can buy a tour map that will guide you along the road; you can also rent portable tape recorders complete with cassette on which a guided tour is recorded. The charge for two hours with the recorder and tape was $4.50 plus $0.27 state tax when we were there in August, 1971. The recording is done in a "You Are There" fashion with personal narratives of the encampment performed in character, background sound effects (including a number of bloodcurdling screams and groans to go with the reconstructed hospital), and music. Recorded beeps cue you as you follow, and detailed instructions tell you where to turn and where to park. On the whole, it is well worth the money, though there are one or two somewhat confusing directions. However, you must stick exactly to the speed limits posted along the road; the tape is timed to match them.

It would be futile for me to attempt to duplicate on paper what is spread out so well and explained in such detail on the site itself. You will see the reconstructed company street lined with authentic hutments; Forts Greene and Muhlenberg; Knox's artillery park; the blacksmith shop; the schoolhouse, which is the oldest building in the park; the watchtower on Mount Joy, which you should climb for a wonderful view of the park and the surrounding country; Washington's Headquarters, and other sites. This can be an all-day affair if you choose to take advantage of the picnic and recreational facilities. Keep in mind, however, that when Washington's men first appeared on the scene, it was completely wooded. Under his orders 900 huts were constructed and provided with firewood, and abatises and redoubts were built, which pretty well accounted for whole tracts of trees that stood where there are now open fields. The area immediately surrounding the park is mixed rural-suburban. Don't be surprised if you see visitors to the park taking riding instruction along its bridle path, flying model airplanes, or playing ball. This is a recreational area in many respects as well as a historic site.

The **Washington's Headquarters** building contains a number of furnishings and relics directly associated with his residence. There is a very large parking lot behind it, and in an adjoining building, a refreshment stand and rest rooms. Valley Forge State Park is too easily accessible, too well publicized and known not to attract hordes of visitors, especially during the summer months. I have been there during every season of the year and it has something different to offer each season, including a wonderful display of dogwood blossoms in the spring.

From Valley Forge, it is a simple matter to return either to the Pennsylvania Turnpike or to U.S. 30 and proceed east to Philadelphia to cover the Battle of Germantown, the capture of Forts Mifflin and Mercer, and the well-known sites in the city itself which are so intimately connected with the Revolution.

THE PHILADELPHIA SITES

Like Valley Forge Philadelphia is a national shrine, known as the "cradle of liberty"; as every schoolboy or schoolgirl knows, it was in this city that the Declaration of Independence was drawn up, ratified, and first announced to the world. In Philadelphia is **Independence National Historic Park** containing a number of buildings connected with the colonial period, both pre- and post-Revolution; many housed scenes directly connected with the Revolution. Included are Carpenters' Hall in which the First Continental Congress met in 1774, Independence Hall where the Second Continental Congress met and adopted the Declaration, Independence Square where the Declaration was first read publicly on July 8, 1776, the Liberty Bell and Christ Church burial ground where seven signers are buried, including Benjamin Franklin.

Also in Philadelphia are Betsy Ross's house in which she is supposed to have made the first American flag; a large number of homes dating from the colonial period, many in an excellent state of preservation and still lived in; a number of interesting and important museums; Germantown, the scene of the only American attempt to retake Philadelphia; the site of Fort Mifflin where a heroic stand was made against overwhelming British odds; and just across the Delaware, Fort Mercer in Red Bank, New Jersey, where the British lion had its Hessian paw stung.

As you might expect, urbanization (particularly urban redevelopment) has overtaken some of these sites, but though they have been squeezed and hemmed in and sometimes overshadowed, they have not been obliterated. In fact, old Philadelphia, the Philadelphia of colonial times, remains to a surprising extent.

At least two days, possibly three, should be devoted to covering the Philadelphia sites. There are a number of excellent hotels, motels, and motor inns in and around the city. There are several motels with parking garages off Market Street, not too far from the major site areas and the center of the city at Market and Broad streets. Since Philadelphia has an excellent bus system and a subway, you can save on parking fees and all the bother that goes with driving through big city traffic and looking for parking by leaving your car at a motel.

Most of the Philadelphia sites are within an area roughly bordered on the east and west by 12th Street and Delaware Avenue (along the river) and Race and South streets on the north and south. If you prefer to drive from place to place, there are parking garages and lots handy to most sites—there is a very large parking lot just two blocks from Independence Square at Chestnut and Third, in front of the U.S. Customhouse, which charged $0.50 for all-day parking from 9 A.M. to 6 P.M. when I was there—but be prepared for one-way streets all over the place, morning and evening rush-hour traffic, and restricted curbside parking.

A good place to begin is the Tourist Information Center at 16th and Arch streets, which also has a huge, underground parking lot. The center is amply supplied with all manner of street maps, pamphlets, and attendants who will help you lay out walking tours, rapid transit tours, driving tours, anything you like, and tell you exactly how to get any place in the city. Incidentally, you can walk from the Tourist Center to the historic sites and do them on foot. This is an admirable way to see Philadelphia as well as the sites, but the distance you cover in a day's meandering can be extensive, so be prepared with good walking shoes and well-exercised muscles. Phone booths in Philadelphia are handy points of reference no matter where you are; each has a city map posted on it with the historic sites clearly marked.

A good place to start your tour, oddly enough, is in a contemporary building, or rather at the top of it. The Penn Mutual Life Insurance Company building at Sixth and Walnut has an *observation deck* on the very top directly overlooking Independence Square and what Penn Mutual advertises as "the most historic square mile in America." The deck is open to the public, free, from April 1 through November 1, from 9 A.M. to 4 P.M. on weekdays and from 10 A.M. to 6 P.M. on weekends and holidays. Around the deck are a number of observation stations. Each one overlooks a section of the city and at each a recorded narration explains the view. An attendant will hand you a pamphlet which, page by page, directs your attention to the significant buildings as you walk from station to station. The narration also includes advertising messages for life insurance companies in general and Penn Mutual in particular, but being a captive audience in this case is worth it; the view gives you an excellent idea of where the sites are that you are likely to visit.

Independence Hall and Square is now part of Independence National Historic Park with a long, beautifully landscaped and terraced mall leading to it. It is in the midst of a recent urban renewal area. Some measure of the colonial appearance of the place has been preserved, however, because of the buildings themselves and the way in which they are grouped. Independence Hall, Carpenter Hall, the First Bank of the United States, New Hall, and Pemberton Hall are well preserved and whatever still needs doing to restore them to their colonial condition will probably be completed by the bicentennial. Behind Independence Hall is Independence Square which was set aside as a park during pre-Revolution times and has been maintained as such ever since.

Independence Hall itself will probably be your first stop. It contains the **Assembly Room** in which the Continental Congress met to pass on the Declaration of Independence. A Park Department guide gives a talk on the history of the room and describes the events that took place therein. The thirteen tables and chairs now there are not original to the room which was recently restored. The big chair behind the speaker's table on the dais, however, is the chair Washington sat on while he presided over the Constitutional Convention after the Revolution (the chair I described in the preface to this book); the silver inkstand on the table is the original, and was used by the delegates to sign the Declaration, the Articles of Confederation, and the Constitution; the bell and the candlesticks are replicas.

The long table to the left of the speaker's table was where Charles Thompson, the recording secretary, sat. Known as the Sam Adams of Philadelphia, he served as recording secretary for the Continental Congress from its first session in 1774 until its last in 1789, when the Constitution was signed and the new Congress took over. All the minutes of the Congress throughout that period were written in his hand.

After the British occupation of Philadelphia ended in June, 1778, Congress returned from York to take up residence in its old home, only to find a major cleanup was needed. The British had used the old State House as a barracks, a prison, and a hospital, and had left it in filthy condition.

In this building you may or may not see the **Liberty Bell**. It is there at this writing, but sometime during the next two years it will be moved into a building of its own two blocks east of Independence Hall. At present, a recording relates its history. Every time I have visited Independence Hall there has been a steady stream of visitors passing through the hall in which it stands and clustering around it. This is probably one of, if not the, most frequently visited spots in the country.

None of the other buildings adjacent to Independence Hall are connected with the Revolution, though that should not keep you from visiting them, particularly if this is your first visit to Philadelphia. **Carpenters' Hall**, where the first Continental Congress met in 1774, is about a block east. If you face the front of Independence Hall it is to your left, marked by white trim and steeple. A historical marker behind it identifies it as a hospital used by both the British and Americans and as a military storehouse by the Americans after they reoccupied the city in 1778. The hall is much as it was then, except that there was a fireplace at each end (there were, of course, no radiators) and the original floor was of wood. There are plans afoot to restore Carpenters' Hall to its original condition.

There is an interesting *museum* in a small, brick building to the right of Carpenters' Hall facing Chestnut Street, devoted to the history of the U.S. Marine Corps. It contains a number of fascinating dioramas and relics concerning naval and marine history and upstairs a wonderful cutaway model of the *Raleigh,* a thirty-two-gun American frigate, the first ship to carry the Stars and Stripes into action. To the left of Carpenters' Hall is the **Army-Navy Museum** which is devoted to the history of those two branches of service. Among the exhibits of particular interest is a diorama that depicts the fighting during the Battle of Saratoga; a full-size reconstruction that visitors walk through of a section of a gun deck of an early fighting ship of the line; an exhibit about John Paul Jones, the naval hero of the Revolution; and an illuminated map showing the major battles of the Revolution, including naval engagements. There is also an excellent exhibit using illuminated maps to explain the Yorktown campaign.

If by this time you're hungry for lunch and would like to get in another site at the same time as you're getting in some food, walk north to Market Street, then turn right to Second Street. Cross the Second Street intersection and look for Werner's Cafeteria and Delicatessen. On the side of the building, just before the entrance of what was once 48 High Street, is a *plaque* marking the site where the Declaration of Independence was first printed on July 5, 1776; the Constitution of the United States on September 19, 1787; Washington's Farewell Address on September 19, 1796; and America's first daily newspaper, September 21, 1784, in the print shop of Dunlap and Claypoole.

After lunch you will be in an excellent location to carry on your historical sightseeing. Turn left off Market Street up Second Street to **Christ Church** where many of the members of the Continental Congress worshipped and where some of the signers of the Declaration of Independence are buried. Here also is buried Major General Charles Lee, described on his tombstone as the "knight errant of liberty," that same Charles Lee who had the run-in with Washington at the Battle of Monmouth.

Inside the church are the pews of many of the leading figures of revolutionary times. Walking down the left side of the main aisle, you will find **Pew 56–58** in which General and Mrs. Washington worshipped. It is the fifth pew from the front on that side of the aisle, and it was voted by the vestrymen to the use of President John Adams in 1797. It was occupied by Lafayette on one occasion during his visit to the United States in 1824. Francis Hopkinson, a signer and secretary of the Continental Congress, worshipped in Pew 65 on the right side of the main aisle. Franklin worshipped in Pew 70. In the far left aisle in Pew 12 worshipped Elizabeth Ross, who at the behest of a congressional committee made the first American flag. In the burial area behind the church is buried Robert Morris, who signed the Declaration of Independence though he voted against it and was responsible more than any other person for financing Washington's armies and the war effort in general. Incidentally, Morris lost his fortune after the war and spent three years in prison for his debts in the old jail that stood where the Penn Mutual building is now.

Keep in mind that you are in the old part of Philadelphia. Most of the buildings are contemporary, but the streets by name and location are colonial and were well-known public thoroughfares during the Revolution.

Now walk on up Second Street away from Market Street to Arch Street and turn left until you see, on the right, a small, two-and-a-half-story, white frame house with a replica of the first flag flying outside. This is, of course, the **home of Betsy Ross.** The house is open from 9:30 A.M. to 5:15 P.M. daily. Behind the frame front is a small, colonial brick house with a small park to one side through which you will enter. The house is a restoration and the room in which the flag was made is duly noted. The walls, window sash, flooring, corner cupboard, and fireplace in this room are in their original state and so is most of the blue tiling around the fireplace.

There is an interesting exhibit on the ground floor of fire marks, iron emblems that residents of the city (and of some other cities) placed on the front of their homes to identify them as being under the protection of this or that fire company, which was supposed to come to the rescue should the need arise. In fact, as you walk through the old section of Philadelphia, notice the old colonial and early nineteenth-century buildings which still have their fire marks attached. You see them bolted to the bricks high above the street on the front facades.

When you leave the Betsy Ross house, turn to your right and continue along Arch Street to Third Street. On the opposite side of the street between Third and Fourth is the old Friends Meetinghouse. A historical marker at curbside informs us that the meetinghouse was erected in 1804, but the ground was first used as a burial ground in

1701. Now continue along Arch Street to **Christ Church burial ground** one block farther at Fifth. Here through an entrance between the high, iron posts, with a curbside marker pointing the way, you will find the burial place of Benjamin Franklin and his wife, Deborah. This is a fascinating old graveyard. Most of the graves and monuments are colonial. Here are buried other signers, including George Ross, Joseph Hughes, Francis Hopkinson (first native composer of songs and designer of the flag), and Benjamin Rush (the father of American psychiatry, and a physician general in the Continental Army). Special plaques mark their final resting place and you can spend a pleasant half hour wandering about finding them. The brick wall on Arch Street is original and was built in 1770.

Now turn off Arch Street to Market Street. About halfway between Third and Fourth streets, on the opposite side of Market Street, is a street sign for Oriana Street, the site of **Franklin's home.** Originally Oriana Street went under an archway in the row of buildings on that side of Market Street and Franklin's home was located beyond the arch.

When we were there early in 1971, the foundations of the house had been excavated. There was a plywood wall cutting off public access, but through sidewalk-superintendent viewing holes, I was able to see what is left of Oriana Street. An artist's rendering placed nearby by the Park Department showed that about where the fence stood was an archway leading into the street. I assume that by the bicentennial, this site will be open to the public and that, possibly, some reconstruction work will have taken place.

Walk down Market Street to Seventh Street, and stop along the way to take a look down the mall that extends between Fifth and Sixth streets from Race Street to Independence Hall. At Market Street you are about halfway down the mall. Down at the south end is Independence Hall, dwarfed by the modern building around it, a little bit of colonial America preserved in the midst of the rising pressures of urbanization.

Continue along Market Street to Seventh Street. Cross to the south side of Market Street; then turn and cross Seventh Street to a marker for the site where the house once stood in which Jefferson wrote the Declaration of Independence. I have a distinct recollection of visiting the house with my parents the first time I was in Philadelphia in 1927 and being shown, on the second floor, the room in which Jefferson drafted the great document.

Now walk down Seventh Street two blocks to Washington Square to visit the **Tomb of the Unknown Soldier of the Revolution.** According to tradition, many soldiers who died in the Revolution were buried here as were victims of the smallpox epidemic of 1793. A block and a half farther south brings you to Spruce Street. Turn right and walk a block and a half to a high brick wall between Eighth and Ninth streets. This is the **burial ground for Mikveh Israel**, the first Jewish congregation in Pennsylvania. Inside is buried Haym Salomon, who helped Robert Morris raise loans, both foreign and domestic, for the Patriots' cause. Unlike Morris, however, Salomon put his own personal fortune on the line.

There are a number of other sites either connected with the Revolution or with colonial times scattered at odd places throughout old Philadelphia. Off Arch Street between Second and First streets is **Elfreth's Alley,** set aside by a low brick wall. It is a bit of colonial Philadelphia which has been preserved intact and is now a national historic landmark. Every house along Elfreth's Alley dates from the eighteenth century, some from as early as 1724, and taken altogether they constitute the oldest continuously occupied residential street in the United States. Between these venerable facades run the old cobblestone street and the original brick sidewalks. Almost every house is still occupied. Some were not in the best repair when we were there, but there is an active program under the aegis of the Philadelphia Preservation Commission to preserve and, if necessary, restore the old landmark buildings.

Many of these houses feature inner courtyards which can be seen from the front and offer glimpses into delightful worlds of shrubs, flowers, and landscaped terraces. The two oldest houses on the street are numbers 120 and 122, which were built between 1724 and 1728. Number 126 is a *museum* which is open during the summer months. The original fire mark may be seen still attached to Number 114, high up on the front wall. Between 115 and 117 is an arched passageway which you may enter to see the courtyard behind firsthand. Elfreth's Alley gives you a real taste of colonial Philadelphia and should not be missed.

Still another interesting site is the inner courtyard of the **City Hall,** the huge building astride Market Street that sports a heroic statue of William Penn atop its dome. Archways lead in from either side so that, in effect, Market Street continues on, though only as a pedestrian walk. During the Revolution, this was a commons or drill ground on which militia and Continental Army units drilled, and in 1781 the French army camped here en route to Yorktown.

Society Hill is another preserved section of old Philadelphia you should visit. It is located between Pine and Spruce streets and between

First and Third streets. Here, too, the streets are lined with colonial-era homes all wonderfully preserved and lived in, many bearing identifying plaques giving the names of the original owners and the dates of their construction. At the corner of Second and Spruce streets is an old tavern called **Man Full of Trouble**, now a museum open on weekdays and Saturdays. At Pine and Third is **St. Peter's Church** where the Washingtons worshipped occasionally. In the churchyard are buried Benjamin Chew, whose house in Germantown was the center of heavy fighting during the Battle of Germantown; Stephen Decatur, the naval hero of the War of 1812; and the painter, Charles Willson Peale. Decatur's grave is marked by a Grecian column surmounted by a federal eagle.

At the corner of Second and Spruce streets is a restoration of the old *market building* that stood here in colonial times with its clock tower at one end and the colonnaded stall area down its length. You will see original market buildings like this in Boston and Charleston. They are all exactly alike and are copied after English market buildings, whose style of architecture goes back to medieval times. On the opposite side of the street is a row of modern shops built in a harmonizing style.

I have not mentioned many other ancient buildings, museums, and sites, which are all described in the literature you can pick up at the Tourist Center on Arch Stret. They include the Rodin Museum, the Philadelphia Zoo, the planetarium, the aquarium, etc. which you can visit according to your interests.

As you might expect, there are dozens of good restaurants in Philadelphia serving a wide variety of good foods. Don't miss Bookbinders, a big, bustling old restaurant, serving huge desserts. For a good directory of eating places, check Nancy Love's *Philadelphia Guide* magazine.

BATTLE OF GERMANTOWN

At the present time, Germantown is just another section of metropolitan Philadelphia about fifteen minutes by car from the center of the city. At the time of the Revolution, it was a small town five miles north of Philadelphia where many wealthy Philadelphians built summer homes to escape the heat and illness that usually afflicted the city during the warm months.

When the British occupied Philadelphia in September, 1777, they discovered that though they had the city, they might not be able to hold it. A series of forts along the Delaware River built by the rebels to control the water approaches to the city were yet to be captured. Until they were, supplying the British garrison was difficult; ships attempting to bring in supplies from the main British base in New York City were sure to come under devastating fire from the guns of the forts.

Howe set about subduing the Delaware forts by detaching several thousand men from his command and sending them into action along the mud flats and among the towns on both sides of the river. In addition, a sizeable number of men were needed to keep his line of communications and supplies open to Head of Elk, his only other means of contact with supportive forces. Philadelphia was held by a garrison under the command of Cornwallis; the main body of British troops, about 9,000, were camped in and around Germantown.

With the enemy so divided, Washington decided on a plan of attack to drive the British from Germantown. By October 3, Washington had moved his army from a site near Reading (where he had halted once he learned of Howe's march into Philadelphia) to within fifteen miles of Germantown. Calling upon other army units and the New Jersey militia for reinforcements, Washington built up his depleted strength to 8,000 Continental soldiers and 3,000 militiamen and decided to make his move.

The Continental Army would advance in four columns: two main columns, under Greene and Sullivan, aimed at the British right flank and center respectively, and two columns of militia advancing along the outer edges of the main attack. Howe was advised of the advance by a scout, but since he did not share Washington's confidence in American ability to mount an attack so soon after Brandywine, he did very little to prepare for it. As at Trenton and Princeton, the British again underestimated the Patriots' ability to bounce back after a defeat.

Philadelphia proper and Germantown are only a few miles apart, but the distance between eighteenth- and twentieth-century Germantown can only be measured in light-years. Two hundred years ago Germantown was a handful of homes; a few shops and artisans' quarters along Shippack Road, then Germantown's main street which corresponds to today's Germantown Avenue; and a few scattered country homes and farms to east and west. Today all that is part of a completely built-up area of streets and avenues lined with stores, apartment buildings, one-family homes cheek by jowl, low- and middle-income housing, expensive suburbs, and lots of traffic. As in Philadelphia, a substantial number of Germantown's eighteenth-century houses are still standing and some are even occupied. However, the farthest one can go toward recapitulating the battle is to visit those buildings and areas that mark the high points.

There is more than one way of getting from Philadelphia center to Germantown. For instance, you can take the Schuylkill Expressway west. Bear right on the Roosevelt Expressway at the sign for Route 1 north to

Trenton. Go off at the Broad Street exit; turn left onto 15th Street, then left again onto Courtland Street, which will lead you to Windrim Avenue. Turn left onto Windrim for a short distance to Germantown Avenue and turn right. Most of the sites you will visit are along Germantown Avenue.

An alternate route is to take Chestnut Street in downtown Philadelphia to Broad Street; turn north onto Broad Street and follow it to Germantown Avenue, which comes in at an angle from the left. Turn left onto Germantown Avenue and follow it out to the Germantown area.

Germantown Avenue is a busy, mixed business and residential street. Begin to look for the **Market Square Restoration** on the right side of the avenue soon after the intersection with Windrim Avenue. It is set off from the street by an iron picket fence. Beyond the fence is a large, open area in which the old jail, stocks, and town hall are located. A large, white sign facing the avenue announces the Market Square Restoration. A plaque at one end (the north end) of the square identifies it as the center of the British line. The right and left flanks extended out from here, the left flank along Schoolhouse Lane, which is the one-way street going off to the left from Germantown Avenue as you face north, and the right flank extending down Church Lane at the opposite end of the square. This is high ground and commands the approaches from the north along which the Americans came. From this point as you look up Germantown Avenue facing in the direction you followed to get here, you have the British-eye view of the battle; you are looking into the American advance.

There are parking meters along the street in front of Market Square; leave your car and cross the street to inspect the **Desher–Morris House.** This is the house in which Howe established his headquarters after the battle. The furniture belonged to the Morris family, who bought the house in 1834. President Washington rented the house during the summers of 1793 and 1794 to escape the heat and yellow fever of Philadelphia. During the second summer, his wife's grandchildren lived with them. Washington was a familiar figure to the residents of Germantown as he walked its streets and visited the local carpenter and blacksmith, both of whom were Continental Army veterans. He was frequently seen driving back and forth to Philadelphia attending to his duties as chief executive.

Visitors are allowed to walk into all the rooms, including the bedrooms in which George and Martha Washington slept. In Washington's room, hanging on the wall, is his framed life mask. In a child's room upstairs is a wonderful Noah's ark with carved wooden figures and an eighteenth-century kaleidoscope that still works. The house also exhibits Thomas Sully's portrait of Patrick Henry.

Before you move on from the Market Square area, where the British parked their artillery, you can trace the British left under the command of Knyphausen by marking its anchor point about a mile from Germantown Avenue along Schoolhouse Lane. At Market Square, Schoolhouse Lane is one-way going in the wrong direction. If you turn left, however, on the next street up and take that for several blocks to an avenue that takes you left, you will get back to Schoolhouse Lane at a point where it becomes two-way. Turn right onto Schoolhouse Lane. After driving through a suburban area and crossing a railroad track, the road winds around down a hill to Ridge Avenue and Schoolhouse Lane. This is about as far as the British left extended. Below this point is the Schuylkill River. The American farthest right column of militia halted its advance a little distance north or to the right of this point.

Take Schoolhouse Lane back to Germantown Avenue; turn left onto the avenue and take it to the intersection with Washington Lane. On the left side of the avenue you will see a fieldstone colonial cottage, the home of the Women's Club of Germantown. This is the old **Johnston House**, built in 1760 and located at the center of heavy fighting during the battle. The house is supposed to bear the scars of shot and shell, but though I walked all around and examined it carefully, I did not find a single mark I could definitely identify as that of a projectile. But I may not have known what to look for. I have since visited another colonial building that was the object of attack during the Revolution, and the marks left by the musket and rifle balls are unmistakable—long, slanting gouges into the wood usually ending in a definite, jagged hole. Perhaps when you view the Johnston House, you will be able to verify that the house does indeed bear such scars.

Like many of the old houses in Germantown, the Johnston House is not usually open to the public, but the Germantown Historical Society conducts a tour of historic houses in town each year in the spring.

On the opposite side of the avenue is the Concord Schoolhouse built in 1775. Just beside it is Upper Germantown Burying Ground in which fifty-three Revolutionary War soldiers are buried, including five unknown soldiers.

Continue up the avenue to Johnston Street and park at the curb. At the far end of a landscaped, tree-shaded area that takes in a full square block sits Cliveden, otherwise known as the **Chew House,** the home of Benjamin Chew whose grave you visited in St. Peter's graveyard in Philadelphia. Since the Chew House figured so prominently in the fighting and may, in fact, have been a turning point, this is as good a place as any to catch up on the story of the battle.

The night of October 3, Washington's men began the march to their jumping-off points. At dawn the next morning, Saturday, October 4, the battle opened as the American advance drove in the British outposts in Mount Airy, now a suburban area at the north end of Germantown Avenue. The Americans advanced through a dense fog across what were then open farmlands crisscrossed by rail fences. Greene was late getting into position and Sullivan diverted General Wayne's brigade toward the left (the British right) where Greene's men should have been to cover his flank. The British fell back, unable to see the advancing enemy clearly because of the fog. During this retreat Lieutenant Colonel Thomas Musgrave led a small detachment of men into the Chew House and converted it into a strong point. Unaware of this because of the fog, Sullivan and Wayne led their men past the house. Musgrave's men then opened fire and the Americans suddenly realized that a British force remained to their rear.

In the meantime, Greene had caught up with the rest of the army and, as planned, tried to turn the British right flank at a place called Lucken's Mill east of Chew House, then turned to advance on Market Square. Some of his brigades did so well that one commanded by General John Peter Gabriel Muhlenberg (another clergyman turned soldier) pushed through the British center and penetrated to the enemy's rear, only to be driven back by superior forces. While this was going on, the center column had been advancing steadily. Washington was about to give the order for the entire army to advance when the victory that seemed to be within his grasp suddenly eluded him. No one knows exactly why, but the rebel forces began to fall back. Most historians believe that in the fog and the confusion caused by the firing around the Chew House, two American brigades, perhaps under Wayne and General Adam Stephen, began to fire at each other, and the word spread through the ranks that the British had come up behind the advancing units and were attacking. The retreat became a panic-stricken rout; despite all efforts to stop it, the entire attack had to be called off and the American forces withdrawn. Cornwallis came up with fresh troops and Washington was forced to give up the attempt to take Germantown.

Chew House and the action around it are the subjects of a well-known painting which can be found in any illustrated history of the Revolution. The picture shows the house exactly as you see it today, a solid-looking, two-story, brick building with two front dormers and solid brick chimneys protruding from the roof. Until recently it was a private residence, but the house is now open to the public on a limited basis. You can get a good view of it up the driveway from Germantown Avenue. Notice that from this angle you are seeing the house as it is depicted in the battle scene. A brick wall sets off the property from the surrounding streets, but if you walk down Johnston Street to the farther end, at a point where the house is quite close to the wall, you can get a closeup look if you're tall enough to see over the wall. Since it was the target of small arms and cannon fire—one gun was set up just on the other side of Germantown Avenue—it undoubtedly bears scars of the occasion, though from the street I found them impossible to make out.

Opposite the main entrance to the Chew House, on the other side of Germantown Avenue, stands **Upsala**, a large colonial mansion built toward the end of the 1700s. During the battle the site was occupied by a smaller house. The Americans placed a cannon in front of it and blasted away at Chew House across the road. You can inspect the grounds around Upsala without hindrance and stand about where the gun stood on that early October day in 1777. Surprisingly there are no markers in front of either Upsala or the Chew House.

One block farther along Germantown Avenue you will come to Upsal Street. On one side of the intersection is a contemporary church. Across the intersection a short distance from the corner stands a building that looks as though it might have been a two-family house in colonial times. Twin flights of steps lead up to its doors from either side. This is the **Billmeyer House**, erected in 1727. During the battle Washington directed the fighting around Chew House from this point, according to the plaque in front of the house. In view of the circumstances of the battle and according to everything I have read, it is more likely that the commander in chief stood here and swore a blue streak, for Chew House was nothing but a diversion and holding or gaining it did not affect the British or American positions one way or the other. The plaque says that the house bears the marks of the battle and of the British attempts to burn it. The scars do show up on this house—those gouge marks in the wood which you can see as you walk around it. Remember that the church on the corner had not yet been built then, nor had any of the other homes along the avenue or on the side streets with the exception of Upsala, Chew House, and Billmeyer House. All around them were probably open fields, and undoubtedly a clear line of fire existed between the Billmeyer House and the Chew House.

American casualties in Germantown were about 670 killed and wounded. Fifty-three of the dead lay on the lawns around Chew House. Four hundred Americans were taken prisoner. The British lost 537 killed and wounded and fourteen taken prisoner, and remained in control of Germantown. Nevertheless, the rebels refused to accept the results as a defeat because they felt rightly or wrongly they had been so close to victory. The army's morale remained high; Washington was applauded for his boldness and aggressiveness; and some historians believe the action at Germantown influenced the French decision to ally themselves with the American cause almost as much as Burgoyne's surrender later that same month.

Holding Germantown was not that important to the British, however. Soon after the battle, Howe withdrew his forces and turned his attention to reducing the Delaware River forts; Germantown returned to American control. During the following actions against Fort Mifflin, Thomas Paine in Germantown is supposed to have heard the explosion of the British warship Augusta when she blew up on the Delaware River mud flats, and Washington is supposed to have watched the smoke rising from an engagement between American and British ships from the roof of the Chew House.

There is a delightful place to eat in Germantown, called Valley Green Inn, right along the path the American militia took. It is rather difficult to find, but if you have the time, ask directions and take a stab at it. It's on Springfield Avenue and Wissahickon Creek and it stands where an old inn stood in 1683. The present building was built in 1850 and the path the militia took is on the left.

FORT MIFFLIN

Having repulsed the rebels at Germantown, the British now moved against the river forts at Billingsport, Port Island (Fort Mifflin), and Red Bank, New Jersey (Fort Mercer). The action at Fort Mercer occurred during the siege of Fort Mifflin, but since Mercer was on the Jersey side of the Delaware, it is more convenient to cover the Fort Mifflin story before leaving Philadelphia for Mercer.

Go back onto the Schuylkill Expressway, Interstate 76, in the direction of Philadelphia and follow the signs for the airport. This will lead to Interstate 676. Leave 676 at the exit marked for the airport. This takes you back onto the streets of Philadelphia at about Fifth Street. Continue to follow the airport signs over the Penrose Avenue Bridge. From this point on there are some differences of opinion among the directions given on the various Fort Mifflin pamphlets. One pamphlet tells you to go off the Penrose Avenue Bridge at Airport Circle; go around the circle to Island Avenue South, and follow green directional signs to Old Fort Mifflin. Having followed other directions which led to a great deal of meandering, I advise you to try the Island Avenue South route. No matter which way you come, there is only one road leading up to the site, a two-lane blacktop road, not in the best condition by any means, that snakes its way through what can only be described as a wasteland.

We took the first right turn after crossing the bridge and we were out in the midst of river marshes which extended on both sides of the road. As we drove along, truck farms and auto wrecking yards appeared here and there. Soon after coming off the bridge we did see two signs for Fort Mifflin pointing in the direction we were going, but at a crucial point the signs petered out and we were on our own. The local farmers, many of whom spoke Italian and little English, had no clear idea of where the Fort was and it wasn't until we found a knowledgeable group of workers clustered around the entrance to one of the auto wrecking yards that we were finally straightened out.

The road wound gradually to the right, then passed an auto wrecking place on the left, then made a right turn and a left turn, and then followed a long straightaway or causeway with marshlands on either side. (A landmark to look for at this point is a new vehicular bridge on your left.) At the end of the causeway, the road curved to the right and we came to a fork in the road. We took the right fork and drove past tank farms and more marshland until quite suddenly there was an official army sign saying "U.S. Fort Mifflin" and an arrow indicating a left turn. The road leads to the present army installation, new Fort Mifflin to the left and the old Fort Mifflin to the right. There is a parking field just before the drawbridge over the outermoat to the fort entrance. Two or three hundred feet above our heads, planes with their landing gears down headed for one of the runways of the Philadelphia International Airport.

To Philadelphia history buffs, Fort Mifflin is the Alamo of the Revolution. They have some justification for their belief; here on this muddy stretch of ground a small garrison, never numbering more than 500 and usually numbering a lot less, stood up for forty days to everything the British army and fleet could bring to bear on them, which was considerable even in those days.

Originally the fort stood on an island called Port Island, which is sometimes confused with nearby Mud Island. At the time, Port Island was cut off from the mainland by a channel which led from the confluence of the Schuylkill and Delaware rivers, which is to your left as you face the fort's entrance, back into the Delaware off to your right in the direction of the airport. Over the years the channel has been filled in, as was a good part of the river near the bank between the confluence and the airport. If that channel were still open, it would be behind you. At present a railroad spur runs right over it.

The fort is open seven days a week from 10 A.M. until 4 P.M. Militia drills are demonstrated on Sundays and guided tours are conducted during the week. Admission is $1.00 for adults and $0.50 for children. It is administered for the Philadelphia Recreation Department by the Shackamaxon Society, Inc., a nonprofit organization of Philadelphia businessmen dedicated to projects that promote Philadelphia. There are usually a number of men and boys at the fort in colonial costumes and uniforms of their own making. All of them are history buffs and Fort Mifflin enthusiasts. Many put in most of their spare time carrying out restoration work, taking part in archaeological digs, and forming a mock detachment that stages drills and reenactments.

The cut stone and brick walls of the present fort were built on the foundations of the first fort begun by the British in 1773. When the Revolution broke out, the fort was still incomplete. The local committee of safety under Benjamin Franklin launched a campaign to finish the job. Major General Thomas Mifflin was put in charge of the work by General Washington. When the fort was finished it consisted of earthen embankments with outlying palisades and four timber blockhouses. Inside the fort were two long barracks buildings and a number of other structures that may have been bombproofs in which ammunition was stored. According to the diagram, the entire fort area extended less than a half mile along its longitudinal axis and less than an eighth of a mile across its width. An old eighteenth-century plan of the fort shows that it covered less than half of Port Island, most of which was a mud flat. Almost directly opposite, Fort Mercer was built in Red Bank, New Jersey, and a redoubt at Billingsport farther west. Between both banks of the river chains and chevaux-de-frise were stretched (obstacles made of tree trunks or wooden beams with long pointed protrusions fastened across their lengths) from fort to fort effectively blocking the passageway. Forts and chain together presented Howe's supply ships with a formidable series of obstacles he had to overcome if he was ever to properly supply and feed his Philadelphia garrison.

Under the direction of Captain John Montresor, a British army engineer and the very man who had designed the original fort, preparations for the attack began on the land side on what was then called Providence Island, now the area you crossed getting here from the Penrose Avenue Bridge. Montresor's job was to set up artillery locations for the planned bombardment of the fort. American rowing galleys did their best to disrupt the work, but though they chased the first work party away, the British returned in strength and finished the job. As the British continued during the next few days to establish more land batteries and place floating batteries on the river, the American galleys dueled with them, but to little avail. By October 11, the British were firing on the fort. Many of the British shells, however, fell into the mud around and in the fort where they sank and their fuses went out. Sporadic fighting raged around the British gun positions as the Americans sought to capture or destroy them while the British continued to shell the fort from the land. The fort was manned then by about 450 men. It mounted four guns in each of the blockhouses and a battery of ten eighteen-pounders. Always short of ammunition, it answered back as best it could.

By October 15, the British guns were firing every half hour and the American ships were forced to retire to the New Jersey side of the river. Red-hot cannonballs now began to fall inside the fort setting fire to the barracks. As the bombardment continued, reinforcements managed to sneak in at night and American commando units did what they could to cut British supply lines to the batteries, destroy bridges and dikes, and harass the enemy in general. On October 22, Fort Mercer was attacked and successfully drove off the attackers. By this time, British ships of the line were engaged in the bombardment. That night two of them, the *Augusta* and the *Merlin,* ran aground on the mud flats in the middle of the river. When they were discovered the next day, both forts opened up and set them afire. Both ships were abandoned by their crews, and the *Augusta* blew up.

Howe was furious over the delay in getting his supplies upriver and began referring to Fort Mifflin as "that cursed little mud fort." He was unrelenting in his efforts, however, and began to prepare for a mighty final bombardment. By early November, conditions inside the fort were grim. On November 7, of the 320 men inside the fort, only 115 were able to stand to their guns.

During the long weeks of siege, Washington had taken a personal interest in the fight and directed some of it. He enlisted the aid of some French engineers, the best engineers in the eighteenth century. At one point he replaced the commander of the fort, Lieutenant Colonel Samuel Smith, with such an engineer, the Baron d'Arendt, despite Smith's objections. D'Arendt became ill and had to be removed (reinforcements and removals were carried out at night in small boats that sneaked up and down the river under the guns of the British ships) and Smith resumed command. Another Frenchman who also helped storm Stony Point, the

Vicomte de Fleury, had the defenders increase the height of the walls, but to no avail.

On November 10 the final assault began. The British guns fired every half hour gradually reducing the barracks, the walls, and the blockhouses to rubble. The defenders, weakened by exposure to the damp and cold, did their best to rebuild the walls at night only to have them knocked to smithereens the next day by the British guns. Ammunition was so low that by the eleventh, Smith was rewarding his men with a tot of rum for every British cannonball they could retrieve. That same day, a cannonball knocked Smith unconscious and he had to be removed. Washington ordered the garrison to hold out "to the last extremity."

By November 13, three of the four blockhouses had been destroyed and half of the men could not answer the muster. On the fourteenth, the British put new floating batteries into operation which the fort's gunners managed to destroy, though there were only eleven cannon still shooting.

On the morning of the fifteenth, the British began an intensified bombardment, firing 1,000 shots every twenty minutes. Up to this point, their ships had been confined to the main channel of the Delaware, since the back channel was blocked by a chevaux-de-frise. Sometime that day or the night before, someone either by accident or intent let slip the chain and the obstacle dropped to the bottom. The frigate *Vigilant* and the sloop *Fury* entered the channel and began to fire at point-blank range at the fort while marines and sailors in the rigging dropped hand grenades and fired small arms deftly down into it, killing every man who rushed to man the guns. The entire west wall of the fort was demolished and by early afternoon, the fort was completely out of ammunition. The bombardment ended as night fell. Under cover of darkness, the defenders who were still able, forty of them, left the fort after setting fire to the ruins. They left the flag flying. The next day, Sunday morning, the British occupied the fort and found the ruins littered with bodies. The American dead in Fort Mifflin have been estimated at between 250 and 400. The siege cost the British seven dead. Fort Mercer had to be evacuated a week later and the first British supply ship reached Philadelphia on November 23.

The siege had been a matter of great embarrassment to the British: it had taken more than a month to reduce one poorly manned, undergunned, little fort. Furthermore, by the time the job was done and Howe could turn back to face Washington and the main rebel army, winter was setting in and prolonged campaigning was out of the question. With the Continental Army safe in camp on high ground at Valley Forge and Burgoyne's campaign a failure, there was nothing to do but sit out the winter comfortably in Philadelphia. Even that was to prove little comfort, however, for seven months later Howe was replaced by Clinton and the British army was evacuating Philadelphia and retiring to New York City and Staten Island.

Most of what you see today at the Fort Mifflin site, stone and brick walls, interior buildings, and ramparts, were added after the Revolution. The fort was rebuilt in 1798 on top of the foundations laid down by Montresor. These foundations show in places as do some of the original granite blocks. The fort was manned during the War of 1812, but saw no action. It was enlarged during the Civil War and used as a prison for captured Confederate soldiers who were kept in the damp bombproofs underground. The present outer fortifications date from the Civil War period. During World War I, it was used to store ammunition; an anti-aircraft battery was stationed in it during World War II, and it was again used for storage during the Korean conflict. Title to it passed from the federal government to the city of Philadelphia in 1962. The big, studded doors to the main entrance and to the sally ports were installed when the fort was rebuilt in 1798.

As you enter the fort, the Delaware River and Fort Mercer on the opposite bank are behind you; the mud flats where the fort's defenders retrieved spent British cannonballs were to your right and ahead beyond the fort in the direction of the airport runway. You can walk along the *ramparts* and into some of the buildings and down into the *bombproofs* in which you will find the frames of the tiered bunks on which the Confederate prisoners slept. Among the relics in the fort at the time we visited was a Revolutionary War cannon which had seen service at Brandy-wine. It was one of the guns the Americans managed to save only to lose it in the Schuylkill River as they retreated to Chester.

The remains of the gun mounts along the ramparts were installed during the Civil War. From the top of the ramparts you can see for yourself how close in the British ships came during the bombardment; the river's edge is only 150 feet away, perhaps less. On a clear day, the flagpole and ramparts of Fort Mercer can be seen distinctly on the New Jersey shore.

At the time of this writing, two soft drink machines in a small souvenir shop, also equipped with a coffee-maker, provide the only rations available to visitors. The present garrison, however, hopes to have a souvenir shop and refreshment center going outside the walls by the time of the bicentennial.

FORT MERCER

To get to Fort Mifflin's sister fort, Fort Mercer, retrace your route to Philadelphia across the Penrose Avenue Bridge along State Route 291. When it meets Interstate 676, go onto 676 and follow the signs for the Walt Whitman Bridge. Once over the bridge, take Route 130 south. Look for the exit signs to a town called National Park, and follow the signs along Hessian Avenue. As you come through the town you will see signs reading "Red Bank National Park, Fort Mercer Ahead"; the park is on the river. Turn off into a parking area on your right on a high bluff of ground overlooking a beach that extends along the river's edge. Along the bluff extending from the park entrance in the opposite direction are picnic tables and open, grassy recreation areas.

It was on this *bluff* that Fort Mercer was built. What remains of it is now part of a very pretty, well-kept park. At the entrance is an old house and a long shed containing important relics of the fort and its purpose. The ramparts are well marked and there are also several memorials to the men who fought and died here. Flights of steps lead down to the beach.

Looking across the river, it is not as easy to see Fort Mifflin from Fort Mercer as it is to see Mercer from Mifflin. You can see the airport where the planes are landing, but Mifflin does not stand out as well since it is on low ground.

As Howe prepared to sweep away the Delaware River obstacles, he sent a land force to attack the as yet unfinished redoubt at Billingsport west of Mercer which was abandoned when the force approached it from the rear. At the time Fort Mercer was just an earthwork, the remains of which you now see before you. Its armaments consisted of fourteen cannon. With its back protected by the high bluff above the river, its land side was protected by a ditch, part of which is still evident, and an abatis. It was manned by 400 Rhode Islanders under the command of Colonel Christopher Greene, who was a distant relative of General Nathanael Greene. Greene was a veteran of Arnold's march to Quebec. He had been captured in that ill-fated assault and had remained a prisoner until August, 1777.

On October 21, Colonel Carl Emil Kurt von Donop with 2,000

Hessians marched to Haddonfield, New Jersey, and camped there before moving on to attack Fort Mercer. Early on the morning of October 22, a Saturday, he approached the fort following the very road you drove along to reach the park. (You may have noticed it is called **Hessian Avenue.**) The fort was surrounded by cleared land, beyond which was a wooded area. Inside the fort, the defenders were principally occupied with keeping an eye on the ninety-four ships of the British fleet which were anchored in the Delaware. Across the river, Fort Mifflin was under attack from Howe's land batteries.

In Fort Mercer was a Frenchman, the Chevalier de Mauduit du Plessis, another of those ever present French engineers who had been sent to assist Greene. Du Plessis was worth his weight in gold. He suggested building an inner wall between the outer breastworks and the inner redoubt to reduce the size of the perimeter the Rhode Islanders had to defend. Greene accepted the suggestion and the new wall was finished by the time von Donop and company showed up.

The Hessians were discovered as they approached the fort. Greene withdrew his men from the outer works and concealed them behind the new wall under orders to stay out of sight. The Hessians were in position by about noon but did not attempt to move against the fort until late afternoon. They began by sending an officer under a flag to demand the fort's surrender under threat of a no-quarter attack. Greene refused and the attack began. The Hessians were divided into two columns which converged on the fort from the north and south simultaneously. Von Donop chose to lead the southern column.

When the attackers reached the outer breastworks, they found them abandoned. Believing the defenders had fled, the Hessians approached the inner wall across the ditch that lay between. As they prepared to climb the wall to take possession of the fort, Greene gave the word. Springing up from concealment, the Americans poured a sustained volley into the closely packed ranks of the men below. A small cannon partially concealed by a side abutment added a hail of grapeshot to the rain of musket balls. The Hessians went down in heaps, von Donop among them severely wounded in one leg. The attackers withdrew, regrouped, and attacked again only to be met by a second volley as deadly as the first as they attempted to move forward over the bodies of their fallen comrades.

By this time a number of American galleys on the river had rowed close enough to shore to add their fire to that of the garrison. The Hessians fell back in disorder leaving 400 dead and wounded at the bottom of the ditch. As they withdrew toward Haddonfield along Hessian Road they were hurried on their way by the galleys which continued to bombard them from the river. One hundred of the wounded Hessians and an additional twenty were made prisoners. Von Donop was found among the fallen by Du Plessis and carried into the fort. The next day he was taken to the Whitall home, the little colonial house near the park entrance, where he died three days later. The fort's defenders lost about fourteen killed and twenty-three wounded.

There are guns mounted at various points in the park, none of them original to the site. As you inspect the fort's remains, follow a path that leads along the top of the **breastwork**, which I take to be the remains of the inner redoubt. A sign in the ditch asks visitors to stay up on the path. I assume the original breastworks were much higher and have been worn down by erosion over the years. I also suspect that some part of them must have been leveled or otherwise destroyed. The *memorial column* commemorates the fort and its defense. According to the inscription on the column, the Hessians lost almost 600 men, including thirty-six officers, a figure that might include those who were taken prisoner, as well as the dead and wounded. The statue at the top is that of Greene.

North is roughly upstream, south downriver, the direction from which von Donop led his column, probably from a point somewhere near the **Whitall House.** Tradition has it that the lady of the house refused to leave when the battle was imminent, but remained seated in her living room working away at her spinning wheel until a cannonball crashed through an upper wall. She prudently picked up her work and brought it down to the basement where she continued until the battle was over. The house then became a hospital for the wounded, both Americans and Hessians, and she is supposed to have attended to both with equal tenderness although she scolded the Hessians for intruding on the peace and security of the American people. Take a walk along the beach and look back up at the fort on the bluff to see how formidable an obstacle it was to attack from the water with its breastworks raised to proper height, necessitating the overland approach. Don't forget that the chevaux-de-frise that extended across the river from Mercer to Mifflin made it impossible for the British ships to get close enough to reduce both forts.

When Mifflin finally fell, its survivors rowed across the river to Mercer. As another 2,000 British began to march on the fort, however, Greene abandoned it during the night of November 20–21. Greene, who was rewarded by Congress with a sword, went on to command a regiment of black troops from Rhode Island, led his men in a spirited action during the Battle of Rhode Island as you shall see, and continued to serve until he was killed at Croton River in Westchester County, New York, by a Tory band on May 14, 1781, just before the Continental Army began its march to Yorktown.

Von Donop was buried near the fort but the site of the grave has been lost. He was supposed to have said as he lay dying, "It is finishing a noble career early [he was thirty-seven] but I die a victim of my ambition and of the avarice of my sovereign," but the statement is unlikely. The Whitall House is a small museum which is open to the public on week-ends from 2 to 4 P.M. and on July 4.

Inside the long shed are the remains of one of the *chevaux-de-frise* that extended across the river between the two forts. It was brought up out of the river in 1936 after having been immersed for about 170 years. This particular structure utilized 296 pine logs which were supplied by a number of local farmers, including Mr. Whitall who lived in the nearby house. Each section was about sixty-five feet long and twenty inches square with two to four heavy timbers, each tipped or sheathed in iron, extending outward at an angle of about forty-five degrees. The entire obstacle was lined with 30,000 feet of two-inch plank. It was floated out across the river and then sunk by using stone cribs to weight it down and held by anchors so that the points of the protruding timbers lay about four feet below the low-water mark. The logs on exhibit are estimated to be about 300 years old. Each of them is about thirty feet long and attached to them are portions of the chain that held them together. Also on exhibit are boxes of grapeshot picked up around the ditch that sur-rounds the old breastworks.

This is a lovely spot for a picnic lunch with lots of picnic tables available along the bluff overlooking the beach. There is parking both at the fort and at the picnic grounds. Rest rooms are available. I cannot vouch for refreshments. The beach may be open for bathing during the summer months if anyone cares to take his or her chances swimming in the Delaware River.

V.

SULLIVAN'S
CAMPAIGN AGAINST
THE IROQUOIS

While the big battles and campaigns were being fought in the main arenas of the Revolution, the frontiers in western New York and Pennsylvania continued to be the scene of sideshow activities that were as important in their way. On their outcome depended the shape of future relations between the new republic crowded along the Atlantic seaboard and the native populations of western lands into which settlers were already beginning to push. Also at stake was future control of what was then called the Northwest Territory, the lands bordering the Great Lakes which are now the states of Illinois, Michigan, Wisconsin, Indiana, and part of Minnesota. Beyond those immediate questions, emerging from the violent contacts between the Indians and the settlers in the border areas was a pattern of action and reaction, to be repeated over and over again from New York to the Mississippi and beyond, of Indian tribes trying to protect their homelands from white encroachment; making alliances with either the young country to the east or with its enemies, whichever party seemed to offer the best terms; and invariably losing no matter which group of white contenders for the land won.

By 1779, Indian and Tory raiders based in Canada and the Iroquois lands in what is now western New York, prompted Washington to mount an offensive designed to destroy the Indians' ability to wage war against the border settlements. George Rogers Clark was operating against the British in the Northwest. Major General John Sullivan was placed in command in the east. He was fresh from a fiasco at Newport, Rhode Island (which you covered during your tour of the New England sites in Volume I) during which he had insulted and argued with the French naval commander d'Estaing and in general done his inadvertent best to cause the French to repent of their alliance with the colonies. Sullivan was to base his expedition in Easton, Pennsylvania; lead it north through the Wyoming Valley, recently the scene of a massacre; and at Tioga Point meet a column under Brigadier General James Clinton (who had taken part in the defense of Forts Montgomery and Clinton), which was to come south from the Mohawk Valley. At the same time Colonel Daniel Brodhead was to lead an expedition east along the valley of the Allegheny from Pittsburgh, destroying Indian villages along the way and meeting with Sullivan at the Indian village of Genessee (near modern Geneseo) for a joint attack on Fort Niagara, fountainhead for much of the British-inspired Indian activity in both states.

Sullivan shilly-shallied in Pennsylvania for the longest time, before he finally got started, and then moved at a snail's pace. He and Clinton did meet at Tioga Point, now the Pennsylvania town of Athens, and the combined force proceeded from there. Brodhead did all he was supposed to, but stopped about fifty miles short of meeting up with Clinton and Sullivan, forcing them to give up the idea of attacking Niagara.

That's getting a little ahead of the story, however. You can cover this campaign in two stages by following Sullivan's route through eastern Pennsylvania to the New York border, then picking it up near Elmira for the Battle of Newton, and then continuing on with Sullivan and Clinton to their farthest penetration into Iroquois territory.

SULLIVAN'S MARCH

The route Sullivan followed with his army and many of the places they camped have been remembered and marked by the Pennsylvania Historical and Museum Commission. Many of these sites, however, are located along the Susquehanna River. I traced the route and found the sites a scant two weeks before Hurricane Agnes and her attendant low pressure phenomena caused the Susquehanna to overflow her banks in June, 1972, in the worst floods ever recorded in this country. A newspaper reporter wrote that it was like a loose string being pulled taut. The Susquehanna, swollen by days of relentless rain, straightened herself out all along her sinuous length, filling the narrow gorge through which she flows with a flood of water from hillside to hillside, and undoubtedly inundating all the Sullivan March sites along her banks. What remains of historical markers, Esther's Rock, the Battle of Wyoming site, and all the other landmarks I found I do not know. What follows is a record of what

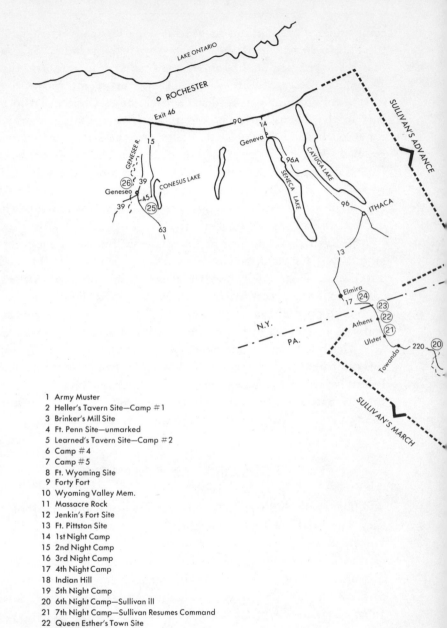

1 Army Muster
2 Heller's Tavern Site—Camp #1
3 Brinker's Mill Site
4 Ft. Penn Site—unmarked
5 Learned's Tavern Site—Camp #2
6 Camp #4
7 Camp #5
8 Ft. Wyoming Site
9 Forty Fort
10 Wyoming Valley Mem.
11 Massacre Rock
12 Jenkin's Fort Site
13 Ft. Pittston Site
14 1st Night Camp
15 2nd Night Camp
16 3rd Night Camp
17 4th Night Camp
18 Indian Hill
19 5th Night Camp
20 6th Night Camp—Sullivan ill
21 7th Night Camp—Sullivan Resumes Command
22 Queen Esther's Town Site
23 Ft. Sullivan Site—Tioga Pt.
24 Newtown Battlefield
25 Ambush Site
26 Boyd-Parker Mem.—Little Beard's Town Site

SULLIVAN'S MARCH

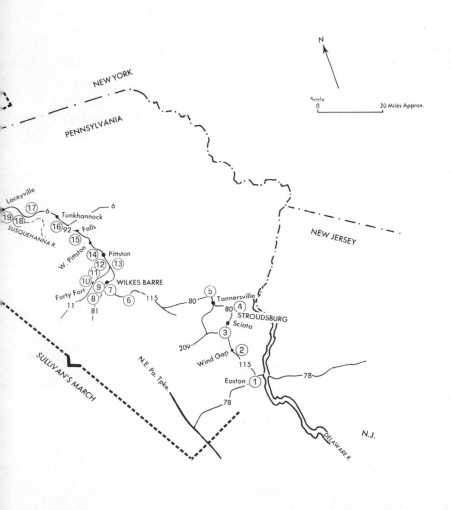

I found before the flooding. Undoubtedly the sites will be marked again by the state historical society, but you must expect some discrepancy between my descriptions and what you will see when you follow Sullivan's army.

The trail starts in Easton just across the Delaware River from the New Jersey town of Phillipsburg. Coming north from the Philadelphia area, take the northbound branch of the Pennsylvania Turnpike to Interstate 78, then 78 east to Easton. If you come from the north, take the Jersey Turnpike south to Interstate 287 (one exit south of the Garden State Parkway interchange). Take 287 to Interstate 78, and 78 (or Route 22) west to Phillipsburg and then across the river to Easton where Sullivan organized his march. The march began on Friday, June 18, 1779, north of Easton at a spot along the Delaware River just off Pennsylvania Road 115. Take 78-22 through the town to 115 and turn north. A marker is at the spot and since you are near the river, you should become aware that part of Sullivan's expedition moved up the river on bateaux.

Route 115 in Easton is also called, for part of its length, the **Sullivan Trail.** Two historical markers have been placed in the vicinity of the army's campgrounds. The first appears on the right side of the road where a triangular plot of ground divides 115 from a street going off to the right called Old Sullivan Trail. This marker is the first of a series of highly distinctive markers, the Sullivan Expedition markers, placed many years ago along the entire trail from Easton up to Geneseo. Each consisted of a bronze plaque showing a map of the routes of the American armies and the sites of the engagements fought. They are mounted on tall, rounded pillars of granite. I still found a number of them along the route; others have either been replaced by newer markers or partially vandalized.

We followed **Old Sullivan Trail,** which may be what is left in this area of the original road, just to see where it led and found that it described a semicircle for several blocks along a hillside covered with streets lined with comfortable suburban homes before leading back to Route 115. A barrier at the north end of the street prevented me from actually getting onto 115 and I had to turn around and go back. Back on 115 you may miss a second marker partially obscured by trees, opposite a Mobil gas station, that cites the preparations for the march.

The army gathered here from May 7 until it left on June 18, by which time Sullivan had collected about 2,500 men, 120 boats, and an assortment of some 2,000 pack horses and cattle, with enough provisions to see the army through the entire campaign. Because of the size of the expedition, however, and the accumulation of supplies that went along with it, it was almost two months before Tioga Point was reached and the army was in position to launch its drive into enemy territory.

Before you set off to follow the line of march, let me caution you that recent highway construction in this part of Pennsylvania has caused some confusion that current highway maps do not entirely clear up. Certain roads like state routes 115 and 209, for example, have been replaced by newer, faster roads. Some sections of the old roads have not been absorbed in the new construction, but remain intact with the old road signs still in place. In every case the newer highways bypass the historic sites you are interested in. In so far as it was humanly possible, I have traced out a route that will take you through this maze with a minimum of backtracking and fumbling. Keep in mind, however, that when in doubt and confronted with a choice, follow the old road.

Take 115 north out of Easton to 512, which joins 115 a little south of the town of Wind Gap. Keep your eyes open for the old and new markers for the army's camp on its first night out of Easton. They both mark the site of **Heller's Tavern** where the army was gung ho; the next morning it was up at 4 A.M. and on its way over the mountains. Heller's Tavern has long since disappeared, but there is a newer establishment nearby, a contemporary bar in an old frame farmhouse. It is hardly colonial in appearance, but at least it keeps up the ancient character of the neighborhood.

Continue north along 115 through the town of Wind Gap and leave it for the new Route 115, a faster road, until you come to Route 209, marked Business 209. Make a sharp left onto 209 and take it south (paralleling part of the road you just drove along and going back generally in the direction from which you came) into the town of Sciota. You will find the second site on the right side of the road. When we visited the spot, we found a new marker here for Learned's Tavern, which should have been in Tannersville, farther north, the site of the end of the second day's march. If it is still there, ignore the Learned Tavern marker. Instead, push aside the branches of a large spruce tree behind it and uncover another of the old expedition markers which marks the site correctly of **Brinker's Mill**, a storehouse and advance post for the expedition. There is a contemporary one-family home nearby and a pond just off the road which may be the remains of the old millpond.

Now go back to Business 209; take it north to 115, and take 115 north to Interstate 80. We went into Stroudsburg looking for the site of Fort Penn, to which some of the survivors of the Wyoming Massacre fled in 1778, but were unable to find the marker that is supposed to be on the site. Take 1-80 west to Exit 45 to Route 715 toward Route 611, which takes you into Tannersville. Less than a half a mile along 611, look on the right for the Coral Reef Hotel which sports a Polynesian facade. Alongside this refugee from a Hollywood South Seas set is a brook and a small, wooden bridge on Old Mill Road. Close to the bridge right on the road is another of the old Sullivan Expedition markers on the site of **Learned's Tavern.** Described as the last house on the frontier, here the army stopped to rest at the end of the second day's march on June 19, 1779, sixteen miles from Easton. Learned's Tavern does not seem to exist any longer, but again, as in Wind Gap, the character of the neighborhood is kept up by a contemporary version, in this case the Coral Reef.

Go back along 611 onto 715 and back onto Interstate 80 west to the exit for Route 115 north. Take 115, which goes onto and over a series of wooded ridges. That this is the route the army followed will be verified within about fourteen miles by keystone-shaped signs which identify the road as **Sullivan's Trail–Wyoming Mountain.** Fifteen miles from 1-80, you will see on your left the marker for the army's fourth night's camp. Sullivan's men reached this point after marching twenty miles from Learned's Tavern through what was then virgin wilderness. If you miss this site, continue on to an entrance to the Pennsylvania Turnpike, then turn around and head back in the direction from which you came. In exactly one mile, you will see the fourth night's marker on your right at the side of the road.

Continue along 115 north toward Wilkes-Barre. Shortly after you pass the turnpike entrance at the top of the mountain, the road starts to descend quite steeply and signs will appear for runaway-truck stoppers, sections of dirt road branching off 115 at regular intervals. Each of these truck stoppers goes up an incline guaranteed to stop runaway trucks, I assume. As you come down this grade, look for the point where 115 reaches an entrance onto Interstate 81. Near that point was where the army stopped to *camp* on its fifth night out. There was a marker here at one time, 6.3 miles southeast of Wilkes-Barre, according to the directory of Pennsylvania historical markers, but it was probably removed during the construction of the interstate. The actual camping site was a short distance west of the interstate entrance, to your left. Obviously the army hadn't made much progress from its last campsite. Washington complained about this lack of speed, but Sullivan replied that the army had to carry all its own provisions, hence could not move any faster.

Continuing north along 115, you will come to Route 309. Turn left onto 309; pass through a railroad underpass, and you will be on East Market Street as you enter Wilkes-Barre. Wilkes-Barre was almost completely inundated during the flood of June, 1972, but since the site you are look-ing for is located in the heart of town, you should have no trouble find-ing it. Follow East Market Street to the Public Square, a large, round area in the heart of the business district into which all the town's main streets lead. In the center of the square is a park and on the farther side was a historical marker for the site of the **Wilkes-Barre Fort**, also known as Fort Wyoming, which was surrendered in 1778 to the British along with the other forts in the valley. Sullivan and his army marched into Fort Wyoming on Wednesday, June 23, 1779, before continuing through the rest of the Wyoming Valley.

Leave Public Square via Market Street (on the opposite side of the square from East Market) and take it via a bridge over the Susquehanna to U.S. 11, which is also Wyoming Avenue. Turn right onto Wyoming Avenue for a short drive to the town of Forty Fort. It won't seem as though you are going from one town to another, for you will drive through one continuous urban area. At the corner of Wyoming Avenue and Wesley Street stands an imposing building surmounted by a steeple and weather vane, graced by a row of six Georgian pillars along the Wyoming Avenue side. This is the Forty Fort Borough Building. Opposite it on the other side is the Forty Fort Cemetery. At the corner of Wesley and Wyoming, in the middle of a small, grass plot is a marker on the site of **Forty Fort**, which was named after forty Connecticut settlers who settled this immediate area in 1769.

You are now in the area of the Wyoming Valley Massacre, one of the two events—the other was the Cherry Valley Massacre—that brought about the Sullivan Expedition. We will go into the full details of the massacre at the next site. It was to Forty Fort that many of the survivors of the Battle of Wyoming fled after the American surrender on July 3, 1778, but Forty Fort itself was surrendered the next day.

Continue along Wyoming Avenue through a residential area. A park-like area will appear on your right with a *monument* set off the road on a grassy slope, surrounded by an iron, picket fence with an entrance flanked on either side by two old cannon. Huge locusts shade this memo-rial to the 300 men under Colonel Zebulon Butler and Colonel Nathan Denison who stood up against a combined force of 1,100 Tories and Indi-ans under the command of Major John Butler.

BATTLE OF WYOMING

What happened here in the Wyoming Valley was another of those instances which characterized the American Revolution as, in a very real sense, the first of its civil wars. For many years settlement of the valley had been contested by Connecticut and Pennsylvania with the Connecticut faction winning out. In fact, by 1774 the Connecticut General Assembly had formed the settlement into the township of Westmoreland. Three to four thousand people lived along this stretch of the Susquehanna, many of them Tories. When the war broke out, both Whigs and Tories built forts to protect themselves. Among the fortifications were Fort Wintermoot, named for a prominent Tory family, and about ten rebel forts which included Forts Jenkins and Wyoming and Forty Fort. Numbers of Tories were arrested by their Whig neighbors and not a few were imprisoned for their allegiance to the crown. When Major John Butler marched into the valley July, 1778, at the head of about 400 Tories and 500 Iroquois, he was joined by about 200 Tories eager to get some of their own back.

Many of the men of the Wyoming Valley who supported the rebel cause had marched off to join the Continental Army. Colonel Zebulon Butler (no relative of John Butler) and Colonel Denison managed to muster about 360 militia. Other valley men elected to stay on at one or the other of the forts where they felt they could best protect their families. Despite the obvious disparagement in size between the two forces, on Friday, July 3, 1778, Butler and Denison led their untrained men out toward the enemy. An attempt at surprise failed, but nevertheless they opened an attack, only to become enveloped by the vastly superior Tories and Indians who swept around their flanks and demoralized them.

During the rout and massacre of men, women, and children that followed up and down the valley, Zebulon Butler escaped with his wife while Denison led the survivors to Forty Fort. The next day he accepted John Butler's terms of surrender, by which the inhabitants of the valley agreed to lay down their arms for the duration of the war, destroy their fortifications, and desist from persecuting their Tory neighbors. According to some accounts, Butler's Indians got out of hand and started after the Forty Fort people as they tried to get away through the swamps and woods along the river. Tales of atrocities, including the torture and burning to death of many of the rebels, spread throughout the colonies. Other accounts say that John Butler did his best to keep his Iroquois from harming any but those who had actively resisted. Still others say that the surrender terms were lived up to, but that the Wyoming Valley Tories who had joined Butler insisted on taking revenge for the treatment they had received at the hands of the Whigs.

After the battle, the rebel dead were buried in a mass grave on the battle site. According to the inscription on the fieldstone obelisk on the site, it was erected over the "bones of the slain." That same inscription cites this as being near the actual battle site. There is nothing there now to remind us of the bloody events that took place up and down present Wyoming Avenue and throughout the surrounding area as urbanization has overtaken the pine woods, swamps, and cleared fields. About 300 of the Patriots died; the enemy lost only three killed and a few wounded. More than 1,000 homes were destroyed, and a large quantity of livestock was carried off by Butler who withdrew from here to Tioga Point (Athens) and then to Niagara. The names listed on the monument as buried here amount to about 165. The two guns that stand guard are of Civil War vintage, having once been part of the defenses of New York harbor where they were mounted in the casements of Fort Hancock at Sandy Hook.

Continue north along Wyoming Avenue to Eighth Street; make a right and proceed four blocks to Susquehanna Avenue. Turn left onto the avenue and within a half block you will find the **Bloody Rock.** Along this shady, residential street on the right opposite the Wyoming Progressive Club, look for an iron, picket fence enclosing a small area between the sidewalk and the curb. Inside, protruding through the soil, is the top of a large rock covered by an iron grating, presumably to ward off the chisels of souvenir hunters. According to the marker here, after the Battle of Wyoming more than fourteen rebel captives were murdered on this rock by "a vengeful Indian woman" who brained them with a maul. An older marker puts the blame on Queen Esther. She was the granddaughter of a French woman who was taken captive by the Iroquois during her teens. Esther married a Seneca chief and is supposed to have taken part in the Battle of Wyoming. One account of the atrocity says that sixteen rebels were killed on the rock and that Esther used a knife and tomahawk and that nine others were killed nearby. This is local, popular legend at the bottom of which, somewhere, lies a kernel of truth. Benson J. Lossing, a historian who visited the rock in 1848, described it as being at least eighteen inches above the ground and containing what may be rose quartz; its reddish color, he writes, was thought at the time of his visit to be bloodstains.

Continue along Susquehanna Avenue for another half block to Seventh Street; turn left onto Seventh, and take it back to Wyoming Avenue. Turn right onto Wyoming (which is also Route 11); take it into West Pittston to a wide, circular plaza with roads going off in several directions and a bridge at the east end which leads into

Pittston. If you can, pull off to one side somewhere, perhaps before you enter the plaza, and cross to what looks like a private home set off from the road by an expanse of lawn on the lefthand side of the bridge as you would face it to cross the river. Here on the lawn, set off by a hedge, is a marker for **Jenkins Fort**, the stockaded home of John Jenkins. Built in 1776 by Connecticut settlers as one of the rebel forts along the Susquehanna, it was surrendered to Butler's force on July 1, 1778, and was then burned.

Now cross the bridge into Pittston. As you come off the bridge on the Pittston side, turn left onto Pittston Avenue and follow it several blocks as it parallels the river on your left to an intersection with Parsonage Street. There at the intersection, set off on a knoll on the grounds of an abandoned public school building, are two markers, one of them an old Sullivan Expedition marker. The newer marker explains that this is the site of **Fort Pittston** which was built in 1722 by Connecticut proprietors and was surrendered to the British in 1778. It was partially destroyed by Butler's men and restored in 1780, from which time it guarded the valley until the end of the Revolution. The old marker says that it marks the southern side of the fort in which 400 fugitives gathered in June and July, 1778, seeking refuge from the Tories and Indians. In command were Captain Jeremiah Blanchard and Lieutenant Timothy Keyes. The fort obviously stood on high ground overlooking the river as do the markers. If this was the site of the southern side, then the rest of the fort occupied the ground between the markers and the river, an area now containing a lumberyard on the opposite side of Pittston Avenue. Parsonage Street is a solid line of houses cheek by jowl; Pittston Avenue is completely built up and the city of Pittston has overtaken the old fort.

Go back along Pittston Avenue to Jenkins Fort Bridge, and return to the plaza on the other side of the river. From the plaza, take Route 92 north; clocking one mile as you drive with the river immediately to your right, look on your right for the marker of the site of the Sullivan Expedition's first *camp* after leaving Wilkes-Barre. The campsite was on the opposite side the river. You have just passed under a girder bridge before reaching the markers, and as you look across the river you may see what I saw before the June, 1972, floods: a tree-shaded bank with what looks like a beach along the water and a river road clearly visible above the riverbank.

Continue north along 92, following the Susequehanna below you to the right, as the road dips and rises along the low bluffs that edge the stream until you see one of the old granite markers on your left at the side of the road. It is followed shortly by a new marker for the site of the army's second-night camp. This *campsite* was also on the opposite bank of the river. If you pass these markers without seeing them, you will realize your mistake when you reach an iron girder bridge which takes 92 across the Susquehanna into the hamlet of Falls. Turn around and clock 2.6 miles back to the markers.

Assuming that you have kept your eyes peeled and have not missed the sites, continue north along 92 until you reach the bridge; cross the river; go through Falls, and continue on 92 until it meets U.S. 6. Take 6 west into Tunkannock on East Tioga Street which you follow right through the town. One block beyond the traffic light in the center of town on the left side of the street are two markers for the army's *campsite* on Tuesday, August 3, 1779, the third night out of Fort Wyoming. The actual site was down the hill to your left along the north bank of the Susquehanna River.

Continue west on 6 until you see a blue sign for the village of Black Walnut on the right. About a tenth of a mile farther, you will see a road going off to the right. Make a sharp turn onto that road. A short distance up the road stands a farm building on the right with two silos and a marker for the camp made on August 4, 1779. The *campsite* was on the lowland probably below this spot toward the river which you can see through the trees. Finding this site took a little doing. The marker directory gave it a location on U.S. 6 and U.S. 309. Actually the old U.S. 6 is this bit of road you are now on, and has been supplanted by the newer U.S. 6, the road on which you have been traveling.

Since the old U.S. 6 dead-ends to the east you will have to turn around and go back the way you came to get back on U.S. 6 west. You will go through the hamlet of Skinner's Eddy, pass three exits for Laceyville, and then come to a marker for *Indian Hill* on the right side of the road. According to this marker, the hill to the southeast was where on Tuesday, September 29, 1778, a battle took place between a militia force led by Colonel Thomas Hartley and some Indians. Just two days before, Hartley had burned out Queen Esther's town which was located near present-day Athens. This is an echo of the Wyoming Valley Massacre, for Hartley was avenging Bloody Rock. You can expect to pick up other echoes of that event as you travel on through Pennsylvania. To find the hill, remember that you have been traveling west by a little north. The hill, therefore, will be to your left behind your left shoulder.

As you continue driving along 6, you will enjoy the constantly unfolding view off to your left front, as you parallel the Susquehanna winding its way through the wooded hills that are the principal features of this part of the state. In 3.5 miles you will see on the left side of the road one of the old Sullivan Expedition markers and a newer marker for the *camp* of August 5–7 which was located just to the west. There is a Tastee–Freeze stand just beyond the markers. In about eight miles beyond the town of Wyalusing, you will reach the site of the *camp* of August 8–9. At this point, Sullivan became ill and handed over command of the army temporarily to Lieutenant Colonel Daniel Whiting. The actual campsite was closer to the river on the lowland to your left.

Continue on U.S. 6 but be careful; now you are back on the old U.S. 6, a two-lane winding road hugging the side of a hill with cliffs to your right and a beautiful view of the Susquehanna Valley to your left. In the town of Towanda, shortly after crossing a bridge over the river, you will almost immediately come to a junction with U.S. 220 at a traffic light. Turn right onto U.S. 220 north/U.S. 6 west. A bit farther, U.S. 220N will go off to the right. Follow it and notice the markers along the way for various Indian trails which the tribes followed when they hunted or went on the warpath. All around you are what were wooded hills in frontier days but today are covered with cleared farmlands.

Four miles along 220 takes you to the town of Ulster; 1.6 miles from the blinker light in town is the site of the army *camp* of August 9–10, the seventh and last overnight stop for Sullivan's men before they reached Tioga Point. At this camp Sullivan, his health restored, resumed command of the army. The river is now on your right. The camp was on the lowlands between this spot and the riverbank on what are called the Sheshequin Flats, now plowed farmland.

Continue on 220 to the town-limit signs for Athens. Shortly after, on the right side of the road, you will see a marker for **Queen Esther's town,** which was located below you on the flatlands near the river. The terrain has obviously been disturbed by the railroad line that has run through the site for many years. This is the town that was burned by Colonel Hartley, who fought the battle on Indian Hill back along U.S. 6 just west of Laceyville.

You may have noticed just before you reached the Queen Esther marker what seemed to be another and newer U.S. 220 going off to the right with a sign for Athens pointing in that direction. Road conditions may be a little different when you come through, for that new road is probably going to be a 220-bypass which will take traffic around the town. You should follow the old road to the Indian village site and the other Athens markers.

As you come into Athens (or Tioga Point), you will cross a bridge. Notice to your right a marker for the *carrying path* along which Indians carried their canoes as they came down the Chemung River to get to the Susquehanna; both rivers come together near here. One of the old Sullivan Expedition markers stands nearby on your left.

Coming off the bridge, you will reach Tioga Street onto which you should make a left. Park at the two markers on the right for **Fort Sullivan.** One is the state marker which tells you that General Sullivan built a fort here on August 18, 1779, which, with the camp formed by the army around the fort, became the base for the campaign into the Iroquois territory. The other, a bronze plaque mounted on a granite boulder behind a fire hydrant, tells us that the army, 5,000 strong, was made up of four brigades from New York, New Jersey, Pennsylvania, and New Hampshire as well as Proctor's artillery and Parr's riflemen. The fort itself, garrisoned by 250 New Jersey soldiers under the command of Colonel Israel Shrieve, consisted of four blockhouses, curtain walls, and an abatis.

Directly behind the markers is a large, rectangular, grassy area shaded by big, old trees with private homes on either side. It seemed to me to be a park. I strolled down its length looking for some evidence of the old fort until I reached the far end where the ground fell away into a tangled, swampy area. The fort and the camp stood on a peninsula, what you are standing on now, formed by the two rivers. The site is perfectly level and shows no trace of what stood here two hundred years ago. Tioga Point Museum is close by, but it was closed at the time of our visit and we could not pursue the subject any further.

Now walk a short distance back to the bridge and continue beyond it until you see at curbside a bronze plaque on a granite block which reads "Here within the confines of Fort Sullivan were buried August 14, 1779, several soldiers killed the previous day in a skirmish at Chemung, as attested by Solomon Colada, soldier in the ranks, who returned to live in Athens the rest of his life. The statement was corroborated by finding skeletons previous to 1839."

The memorial is of more than passing interest; it gives us some idea of the dimensions of Fort Sullivan, since it marks a spot that was "within the confines of the fort." We now know that the area encompassed by the fort included the land between the fort markers and this point. Since the river is just across the street, the fort must have extended back away from it. Since it had four blockhouses, that suggests a four-sided structure, perhaps with the blockhouses at each corner. A visit to the Tioga Point Museum will probably give you a more exact picture of the appearance of Fort Sullivan, its exact dimensions, and the site on which it stood. It was here at Tioga Point that Clinton and his men joined Sullivan before the combined force went on to its confrontation with the Indians at Newtown.

We covered Sullivan's Pennsylvania route in a day and a half. It should not take you more than two days, or a day and a half if you want to push a little.

NEWTOWN BATTLEFIELD

Leaving Athens, take Route 220 north and cross the New York–Pennsylvania border. Take 220 to State Route 17 west. You are now heading for the modern city of Elmira. The Chemung River is on your left just the other side of the road, but at the foot of a hill and therefore out of sight. The farmlands you can see beyond that and ahead to your left front are in the Chemung Valley. You are now on the edge of the heartland of the Iroquois Confederation. The area around you was the home of the Seneca Indians.

Look for a motel set back off Route 17 on your right called The Red Jacket. It is named for a Seneca chief who led his tribe against the American rebels, but later supported the new republic during the War of 1812. Some distance beyond the motel, you will see a tall, white stone shaft on the top of a high hill, a *memorial* to Sullivan and his expedition. The Red Jacket Motel is on the site of the Battle of Newtown. Most of the fighting, however, raged over the lands on the other side of Route 17, in what are now private farms along the river flats, and west and north of the motel as far as the foot of Sullivan Hill on which the monument stands.

As Sullivan advanced up the Susquehanna, John Butler had kept an eye on him, trying to determine what he was up to. Once Sullivan reached Tioga Point, his thrust was clear: he was headed straight for the heart of the Confederation and possibly on to Fort Niagara. Word sent north for reinforcements brought Walter Butler south to help his son. With 250 Tories and 800 Iroquois, the Butlers prepared to put up some sort of resistance. The Indians, seeing their villages and farmlands threatened, insisted on making a stand at once and chose the Newtown site for an ambush on what was actually the border of their territory.

For a bird's-eye view of the area for a start, continue west along Route 17 past the Red Jacket for two or three miles, stopping to notice a Sullivan Expedition bronze marker on a granite boulder and then a state historical marker identifying the approximate site of the Indian town of **Newtown.** Both markers are on your right just off the road.

Keep your eyes open for the sign "Newtown Battlefield Reservation" with an arrow indicating a right turn off Route 17. The turnoff will take you to a road which goes to the top of **Sullivan Hill.** Richard and I walked to the top on a cold, clear, winter day because the road was too icy to attempt the drive. It was a beautiful one-mile hike with the view gradually opening out on our right and deer bounding over the wooded slopes on our left.

The entire hill is part of a state park whose crowning glory is the **Sullivan Monument** at the top. The hill is 1,507 feet above sea level and 600 feet above the floor of the valley, and it includes campsites, cabins, picnic pavilion and shelters, a ball field, a playground for small children, horseshoes, softball fields, and volleyball courts, and nature trails. There are ample parking facilities, many picnic tables and barbecue pits, and altogether it is a delightful place for a picnic, an hour, or an afternoon of relaxation.

The memorial shaft is fifty-nine feet high and stands at the highest point on the hill, overlooking the Chemung Valley. With your back to the monument and the valley spread out below you, you are facing south toward Pennsylvania. The combined forces of Clinton and Sullivan came over the hills on the horizon and across the broad fields immediately before you which were woods at the time. To your left a line of trees marks the river, which skirts the near side of the valley, just beyond Route 17 below you, and continues off to your right. Along that line of trees is about where the enemy force of about 1,000 Tories and Indians under the Butlers and Joseph Brant, attempted to ambush the Americans from a fortified position. At the foot of the hill directly below you and therefore too close for you to see, is the site of some hand-to-hand fighting which took place before the Indians, demoralized by the artillery fire, broke and fled to the north.

Leaving the park, return to Route 17; turn left and follow it back until you see a sign on your right indicating a turnoff to Wellsburg. As you were driving along this stretch of road, you must have noticed just beyond the road on your right a low, wooded ridge. As you turn off on the road to Wellsburg, the ridge, which is still on your right, ends abruptly opposite a white, frame farmhouse, looking as though a giant knife had sliced it open at just that spot. A marker identifies the *ridge* as the left flank of the Tory-Indian position, a concealed breastwork which was detected by Sullivan's advance scouts. Sullivan's artillery opened fire from a position beyond the breastwork and off toward the river beyond the fields. Part of his force came across the field toward this point—the breastworks began down near the river, extended up this way and across the line now marked by Route 17—turned this flank, and drove the enemy west and north back across present Route 17, across the site where the motel stands and to the foot of Sullivan Hill. A town dump at the east end of the ridge should not deter you. A path leads up to the top of the ridge and you can walk along its length and explore it to your heart's content. There was too much snow about when I visited the site to determine if anything was left of the breastworks, and I cannot say whether the low, long mound that lies at the south foot of the ridge was the work of human hands of long ago.

Continuing a little farther east along 17, you will come to a parking area off the road and another of the bronze Sullivan Expedition markers. A paved footpath leads from the parking area up a fairly steep, lightly wooded hill from which you can look down at the river, the river flats, the remains of an old railroad bed and the fields beyond. You are at about the spot, I believe, where the American attack began the movement that turned the Tory-Indian flank. Looking down to your right along the river flats, you can see the area across which the Americans advanced. Somewhere off on what are now fields to your right is where Sullivan's artillery blasted away at the breastwork on the ridge. Both this site and the Wellsburg road turnoff are within easy walking distance of the Red Jacket Motel.

That is about as much of the battlefield as you can see at the time of this writing. Most of it, as you have surely surmised, is on private land. There are plans, however, for extending the interpretative aspects of the area in time for the bicentennial.

Though the casualties suffered by both sides were comparatively insignificant—Sullivan's army won the victory at the cost of four casualties, and the Indians and Tories lost about eleven people, including one woman —the results were significant. The Indians were thrown back in confusion and terror, leaving the way open for Sullivan's men to advance into the heart of the Iroquois country.

SULLIVAN'S ADVANCE

From Newtown battlefield, take 17 west into Elmira; turn off onto Route 13 toward Ithaca; then take Route 96 north to look for signs of Sullivan's route. A marker appears just south of Trumansburg about thirteen miles north of Ithaca; a short distance beyond Trumansburg, another indicates the site where one of Sullivan's officers saw Lake Cayuga. For further evidence of Sullivan's exploits and those of his men, however, you will have to use modern highway facilities to get you to the action, unless you care to spend most of a day meandering across the hills and valleys of the Finger Lakes country, a delightful prospect but only if you have the time to spare.

Continue on 96 and 96A to Geneva; then take Route 14 north to the New York State Thruway. Take the thruway west to Exit 46 (the second Rochester exit) to find what is misnamed on state road maps and in the New York State Historic Trust booklet of historic sites the Sullivan Monument. Actually it is a monument to some of his men, but not to him.

You are now in the Genesee River country at the farthest western point of Sullivan's advance toward Fort Niagara. Its capture was to have climaxed the campaign; but when Brodhead did not appear, Sullivan destroyed as many Indian villages as possible, including orchards and croplands, before returning the way he had come.

From Exit 46, take U.S. 15 south to Millville and continue south along State Route 256. Lake Conesus will be visible on your left as 256 hugs the west shore of the lake. When the south end of the lake becomes visible off to your left front, watch for a road going off to the right marked County Road 45. The very next road to your right is David Grey Hill Road. This road can be a real fooler, as the signpost at the road junction is on your left. If you miss it, you will come to a road going off to the left called Decola Shores Road at a clearly marked intersection, signifying you have gone too far. Incidentally, if you're interested in exploring American history beyond the Revolution, there is a cemetery a few miles farther on the right where Captain Daniel Shays, the leader of Shays' Rebellion in 1786 and 1787, is buried.

Back to the Revolution. Turn right onto David Grey Hill Road, a steep and rather rough road which I can vouch is not cleared of snow during the winter by the county. At the top of the hill, a farm appears just to the right, and a two-story country home to the left off in the woods. A dirt path leads off the road to the left where a wooden fence sets off a small park established by the county park commission. At the right of this little park, which boasts a picnic pavilion with long picnic tables, is an old, farm-equipment shed just beyond a hurricane fence. A gate in the fence takes you onto a path down into a little ravine, across an ancient, winding brook, then up a grassy slope at the top of which is a tall, granite *monument* surrounded by a wooden fence breached by a gate.

The memorial marks the spot where a twenty-six-man patrol, sent out by Sullivan under the command of Lieutenant Thomas Boyd, was ambushed by a party of Tories and Indians under the command of Walter Butler. Twenty-two men were killed and buried near this spot. Two or three escaped, and Lieutenant Boyd and Sergeant Michael Parker were captured. The names of the fallen scouts are engraved on the monument. Just beyond the monument is another, higher hill which marks the approximate spot where the ambushers lay in wait. At the present time this is all open pasture or cropland, but two hundred years ago it was wooded terrain. At the time the ambush took place, Sullivan and his main force were a day's march east of Genesee.

Returning to Route 256, retrace your route to the north for a short distance to County Road 45, which will now be on your left, and turn onto it. Do not be confused by the fact that it is also called Willard Gray Hillard Hill Road or that subsequently it becomes Daniel Morris Road and other things besides. You are now in the backcountry of Livingston County or, to put it more picturesquely, the country of the Genesee River, which you will cross shortly. All around you are rolling farmlands, mostly pasture lands; this is horse and cattle country where frisky colts race and buck about in the spring and herds of saddle and racing ponies sheltered from the sun under the trees stretch their necks over the road-side fences. County Road 45 takes two or three right-angle turns as it goes through Hunts Corner and then Hampton Corners where it meets State Route 63. Turn right, or north, onto 63 for a short distance to the intersection with Route 39 which comes in from the left. Turn left onto 39; follow it over a bridge that crosses the Genesee River.

Shortly after the bridge, watch for a historical marker on the left. It sits on the side of the road just inside a small, rail fence-enclosed park. This is **Boyd-Parker Memorial.** In it is a granite boulder with two plaques. The marker says that this is where Lieutenant Boyd and Sergeant Parker were tortured by their captors and killed. A huge, old oak, easily more than 150 years old, may be the "torture tree" mentioned on the marker. There are a few picnic tables about. One of the plaques is another Sullivan Route bronze marker; the other, however, identifies the park as part of the site where the Indian village, Little Beard's town, stood. The day after the scouts' capture and death, Sullivan reached the area, found their bodies, and destroyed the village. This site was the high-water mark of his expedition.

What was accomplished by this expedition? Although only one small battle was fought at a loss of less than a dozen men, the results far outweighed the cost.

Fort Niagara was not captured and the Iroquois did return the following year to raid the settlements again, but their power as a league was broken. Sullivan had destroyed their farms and orchards so thoroughly that the tribes were forced to move to Fort Niagara where they lived on British charity for the rest of that year and most of the next. The Confederation never recovered from this blow. Through Sullivan's campaign, the western part of the state was fully opened to the wave of settlers who rolled over it during the years that immediately followed.

Though revolutionary allies of the British, the Iroquois tribes sided with the Americans during the War of 1812 and resisted Joseph Brant's efforts to build a great Indian state in the Northwest Territory. The Six Nations of the confederacy eventually wore themselves out trying to dominate the Algonquin Indians, and all their lands were taken over by rapacious white settlers who took brutal advantage of their weakened state.

You have had a taste of frontier warfare during the Revolution in this book. Now it is time to turn south to trace the opening events of the Revolution there and its final battles.

BIBLIOGRAPHY

GENERAL

ADAMS, JAMES TRUSLOW, ed. *Atlas of American History*. 2d rev. ed. New York, 1943.

———. *Dictionary of American History*. 5 vols. 2d ed., rev. New York, 1942.

The American Heritage Book of the Revolution. The Editors of American Heritage. New York, 1958.

American Heritage Pictorial Atlas of United States History. The Editors of American Heritage. New York, 1966.

BEARD, CHARLES A. and MARY R. *A Basic History of the United States*. New York, 1944.

BOATNER, MARK M., III. *Encyclopedia of the American Revolution*. New York, 1966.

CARRINGTON, HENRY B. *Battles of the American Revolution*. New York, 1877.

CHASTELLUX, MARQUIS DE. *Travels in North America* . . . Translated and Edited by Howard C. Rice, Jr. 2 vols. Chapel Hill, N.C., 1963.

COMMAGER, HENRY STEELE and MORRIS, RICHARD B., eds. *The Spirit of 'Seventy-six* . . . 2 vols. Indianapolis and New York, 1958.

DUPUY, R. ERNEST and TREVOR N. *The Compact History of the Revolutionary War*. New York, 1963.

FLEXNER, JAMES T. *George Washington: The Forge of Experience* (1732–1775). Boston, 1965.

———. *George Washington in the American Revolution* (1775–1783). Boston, 1967.

FORD, COREY. *A Peculiar Service*. Boston, 1965.

FREEMAN, DOUGLAS S., et al. *George Washington: A Biography*. 7 vols. New York, 1948–57.

GREENE, EVARTS B. *The Revolutionary Generation 1763–1790*. New York, 1943.

HICKS, JOHN D. *The Federal Union*. Boston and New York, 1937.

HIGGINBOTHAM, DON. *The War of American Independence*. New York, 1971.

HUNT, GAILLARD. *Fragments of Revolutionary History*. Brooklyn, N.Y., 1892.

LANCASTER, BRUCE. *From Lexington to Liberty*. Garden City, N.Y., 1955.

LOSSING, BENSON J. *The Pictorial Field Book of the American Revolution*. 2 vols. New York, 1850–52.

MILLER, JOHN C. *Origins of the American Revolution*. Boston, 1943.

MONTROSS, LYNN. *Rag, Tag and Bobtail* . . . New York, 1952.

NATIONAL PARK SERVICE. *National Register of Historic Places*. Washington, D.C., 1969.

SARLES, FRANK B., JR. and SHEDD, CHARLES E. *Colonials and Patriots*. Vol. 6. National Survey of Historic Sites and Buildings. Washington, D.C., 1964.

SCHEER, GEORGE F. and RANKIN, HUGH F. *Rebels and Redcoats*. Cleveland and New York, 1957.

TALLMADGE, BENJAMIN. *Memoir of* . . . Boston, 1876.

TREVELYAN, GEORGE M. *History of England*. New York, 1953.

TUNIS, EDWIN. *Colonial Living*. New York, 1957.

VAN DOREN, CARL. *Secret History of the American Revolution*. New York, 1941.

WARD, CHRISTOPHER. *The War of the Revolution*. Edited by John R. Alden. 2 vols. New York, 1952.

WASHINGTON, GEORGE. *Affectionately Yours, George Washington*. Edited by Thomas J. Fleming. New York, 1967.

THE MIDDLE COLONIES: NEW JERSEY AND PENNSYLVANIA

ANDRÉ, JOHN. *Major André's Journal* . . . Tarrytown, N.Y., 1930.

CHIDSEY, DONALD BARR. *July 4, 1776*. New York, 1958.

———. *Valley Forge*. New York, 1959

COBB, GENEVIEVE C. *Rockingham*. Princeton, N.J., 1958.

FAST, HOWARD. *The Crossing*. New York, 1971.

HUTTON, ANN HAWKES. *George Washington Crossed Here*. Philadelphia, 1966.

MARTIN, JOSEPH PLUMB. *A Soldier of Morristown*. Arno Press Eyewitness of the American Revolution Series. New York, 1962.

PIERCE, ARTHUR D. *Smuggler's Woods* . . . New Brunswick, N.J., 1960.

ROSENTHAL, BARON DE. (Major John Rose). "Journal of a Volunteer Expedition to Sandusky," *Pennsylvania Magazine of History and Biography*. Philadelphia, 1894.

SENTER, ISAAC. *The Journal of* . . . Philadelphia, 1846.

TOWNSEND, JOSEPH. *Some Account of* . . . *the Battle of Brandywine* . . . New York, 1846.

INDEX

Adams, John, 123
Albany, N.Y., 87
Alexander, Gen. William, Lord Stirling, 20, 54, 68, 98, 99, 102, 107
Algonquin Indians, 161
Alloway Creek, 80, 81–82
Amboy (Perth Amboy), N.J., 38, 43
André, Maj. John, 112
Archaeological sites
  at Fort Lee, 12–13
  at Fort Mifflin, 134
  at Monmouth Battlefield (authorized), 64
Arnold, Gen. Benedict, 61, 138
Arthur Kill, 52, 53, 56
Assunpink Creek, 23, 29, 31–33, 37
Athens (Tioga Point), Pa., 143, 151, 154–156
Atlantic City, N.J., 77
Augusta, 132, 135

Baltimore, Md., 61, 87
Basking Ridge, N.J., 15–16, 43, 61
Battlefield Farm (Brandywine), 107
Baylor's Massacre, 12, 112
Bear Tavern (N.J.), 25, 26
Berrien, John, 40
Berrien, Widow, 40–41
Billmeyer House (Germantown, Pa.), 131
Birmingham Friends Meetinghouse, 105–106
  cemetery next to, 105, 106
Birmingham Meetinghouse (Pa.), 97, 98–99, 100, 103
  Lafayette's Monument at, 108
Birmingham Meeting Road, 100–101, 105, 106, 107, 108, 109

Black Watch, 69, 112
Blanchard, Capt. Jeremiah, 152
Bloody Rock (Wilkes-Barre), 151, 153
Boatner, Mark, 82
Bordentown, N.J., 23, 27
Boston, Mass., 126
Boudinot, Elias, 41
Bowen, Ezekiel, 112
Boyd, Lt. Thomas, 160
Braddock, Gen. Edward, 62
Brandywine (Creek), 88, 89, 92, 93, 95, 97, 99–100, 111
Brandywine, Battle of, 6, 55, 76, 77, 88–110
  casualties of, 109
  route of British in, 89–96
Brandywine battlefield
  Anvil (Welch's) Tavern in, 89, 90–91
  Birmingham Meetinghouse in, see Birmingham Meetinghouse
  Chadd's Ford in, see Chadd's Ford
  Jeffries Ford in, 100
  Osborne's Hill in, 102, 104–105, 107
  Sconneltown in, 97, 101
  Strode's Mill in, 102
  Trimble's Ford in 99
  Warren Tavern in, 110
Brandywine Battlefield Park, 93, 94–95, 109
Brandywine River Museum, 93
Brant, Joseph, 157, 166
Briar Hill, N.J., 60, 65
Bridgeton, N.J., 77
  Potter's Tavern in, 77–78
Brodhead, Col. Daniel, 143, 159
Bucks County, History of, 26

Bucks County, Pa., 16, 17, 19, 26
Bucks County Canal, 21
Bucks County Historical Tourist Commission, 26
Bucks County Playhouse, 26
Burgoyne, Gen. John, 61, 62, 87, 137
Burr, Aaron, 69
Butler, Maj. John, 149, 150, 151, 156
Butler, Walter, 156, 160
Butler, Col. Zebulon, 149, 150

Cadwalader, Col. John, 23, 27, 30, 31, 37
Caldwell, Hannah Ogden, 56
Caldwell, Rev. James, 54, 56, 57–58
Caldwell Parsonage Museum (Union, N.J.), 56
Calvinists, 6
Cannonball House (Union, N.J.), 56–57
Cape May, N.J., 77
Carlisle, Earl of, 61
Carlisle Commission, 61, 112
Carpenters' Hall (Philadelphia), 119, 121–122
Carter, James, 104
Chadd, John, 96
Chadd, John, House, 92, 95, 96
Chadd's Ford (Pa.), 87, 88, 89, 90, 91–92, 98, 100, 101, 103, 107
Chadd's Ford village, Pa., 97
  Brandywine Battlefield Park in, 93, 94
  Brandywine River Museum in, 93
  Chadd's Ford Inn in, 94
  Lafayette House in, 94
  Washington's Headquarters in, 94, 95
Chambly, Fort, 46
Charleston, S.C., 87, 126
Chastellux, Chevalier de, 45
Chemung River and Valley, 155, 156, 157
Cherry Valley Massacre, 149
Chester, Pa., 97, 109, 137
Chester County, Pa., 89, 92–93, 108, 114
Chevaux-de-frise, 140–141
Chew, Benjamin, 126, 129
Chew House (Germantown, Pa.), 129, 132
  painting of, 130–131
Cheyney, Thomas, 95, 98, 101
Christiana Creek, 87
Cincinnati, Society of, 46
Civil War, 137, 151
Clark, George Rogers, 142
Clark, Thomas, House, 36, 38
Clinton, Gen. Sir Henry, 10, 52–53, 57, 61, 62–63, 64–65, 68, 69, 70, 72, 75, 137
Clinton, Gen. James, 143, 156, 157
Closter's Landing, N.J., 10, 11
Cobb, Genevieve C., 41

Cohansey River, 79
Coldstream Guards, 69
Connecticut, Wyoming Valley and, 150
Connecticut Farms (Union), N.J., 52, 54
  burning of, 52, 57
  Caldwell Parsonage Museum in, 56
  Cannonball House in, 56–57
  route to, 54–55
Connecticut Farms Presbyterian Church, 55–56
Constitution, Fort (see also Lee, Fort), 9
Constitution, U.S., 121
Constitutional Convention, 121
Continental Army, 3, 125, 150
  at Battles of Trenton, 30–31
  Delaware crossings of, 6, 14, 15, 30, 32, 33
  improvement of, 61
  at Monmouth, 59–60, 61–72 passim
  Morristown encampments of, 6, 43–52
  Pennsylvania encampment of, 16–21
  Valley Forge encampment of, 116–118, 136–137
Continental Congress, 3, 6, 30, 40, 51, 55, 76, 115, 121
  First, 119, 121
  Second, 119, 121
  Washington and, 14, 22, 39, 41, 44, 72
Continental money, 22
Conway Cabal, 20
Cooch's Bridge (Del.), 85–87, 90
Cooper, James Fenimore, 93
Corbin, Margaret ("Captain Molly"), 70–71
Cornwallis, Lord Charles, 3, 6, 15, 23, 30, 31–32, 35, 37, 38, 65, 66, 87, 89, 97, 98, 99, 103, 130
  Jersey landing of, 9–14
Coryell's Ferry (Lambertville, N.J.), 26, 61
Craig House (Freehold, N.J.), 71
Cranbury, N.J., 63
Crisis, The (Paine), 22
Cumberland County Historical Society, 78

Daily, Darius, 83
Daily, Denis, 83
D'Arendt, Baron, 135
Davis, Amos, 103–104
Davis, Daniel, 104
Dayton, Gen. Elias, 55–56, 57
Decatur, Stephen, 126
Declaration of Independence, 35, 78, 119, 121, 122, 123, 124
Delaware, 83
Delaware and Raritan Canal, 21

Delaware River and Valley, 3, 17, 30, 61, 74, 76, 79, 132–141, 146
Delaware River crossing, 6, 14, 15, 30, 32, 33, 38
  reenactment of, 25
Delaware River forts, 6, 115, 126–127, 132–141
  chevaux-de-frise between, 140–141
Denison, Col. Nathan, 149, 150
Desher-Morris House (Germantown, Pa.), 128
d'Estaing, Admiral Charles Hector Theodat, Comte, 142–143
Dickinson, Philemon, 28
Dilworthtown (Dilworth), Pa., 97, 109
  Dilworth Inn in, 109
Dunlap, William, 42–43
Du Plessis, Chevalier de Mauduit, 139, 140
Durham boats, 17, 18, 19, 23, 25
Dutch landowners, 74

Eakins, Thomas, 29
Easton, Pa., 17, 143, 146
  Sullivan Trail in, 146
Edgewater, N.J., 12
Elizabeth, N.J., 52, 53
  cannon in, 53–54
  First Presbyterian Church in, 54
Elizabethtown, N.J., 52, 53, 54, 56, 74, 75
Elizabethtown Point, N.J., 58
Elkton, Md., 87
Elmira, N.Y., 143, 156, 159
Encyclopedia of the American Revolution (Boatner), 82
Englishtown, N.J., 59, 63, 64, 67, 68
  Village Inn in, 71–72
Esther, Queen, 151, 153, 154
Ewing, Gen. James, 23, 27, 29, 30, 31

Fallen Timbers, Battle of, 115
Fauntleroy, Capt. Henry, 60
Ferguson, Capt. Patrick, 77, 109–110
Ferguson's Rifles, 91
Ferry Inn (Pennsylvania encampment), 16–17
First Bank of the United States (Philadelphia), 120
Fithian House (Roadstown, N.J.), 79
Flag (Stars and Stripes), 87
  Betsy Ross and, 119, 123
Flag Museum, 24, 25
Fleury, Vicomte Louis de, 135–136
Ford, Col. Jacob, Jr., 45
Ford Mansion (Morristown, N.J.), 44–46
Ford, Widow, 45
Fort Lee, N.J. (see also Lee, Fort), 12

Forty Fort, 149
Forty Fort, Pa., 149, 150
France, French alliance, 61, 62, 63, 125, 142–143
Franklin, Benjamin, 115, 119, 123, 124, 134
Franklin, Deborah, 124
Franklin's home (Philadelphia), 124
Freehold, N.J. (Monmouth Courthouse), 59, 60, 63, 64, 65
  Craig House at, 71
  museum in, 65, 66, 70, 71
French and Indian War, 62

Gates, Gen. Horatio, 22
Geneseo, N.Y., 143, 146
Genessee (Indian village), 143
George III, King, 10
Germans, in Pennsylvania, 6
German soldiers (see also Hessians), 11, 27
Germantown, Battle of, 55, 112, 115, 118, 126–132
  action in, 129–131
  casualties in, 131
Germantown, Pa., 6, 110, 126, 127
  Billmeyer House in, 131
  Chew House in, 129, 130–131, 132
  Desher-Morris House in, 128
  directions to, 127–128
  Johnston House in, 129
  Market Square Restoration in, 128
  Upsala in, 131
  Valley Green Inn (restaurant) in, 132
Germantown Historical Society, 129
Gilpin, Gideon and Sarah, 94, 96
Glover, Col. John, 23
Great Valley Road, 98, 100
Greene, Col. Christopher, 138, 140
Greene, Fort, 118
Greene, Gen. Nathanael, 12, 25, 37, 53, 57, 60, 61, 68, 71, 98, 99, 108, 117, 127, 130, 138
Greenwich, N.J., 78
  Cohansey Wharf in, 79
  monument in, 78
  museum in, 78
Greenwich Historical Society, 78
Grey, Gen. Charles ("No-flint"), 112

Hackensack, N.J., 74
Hackensack River, 12, 14
Haddonfield, N.J., 139
Hamilton, Alexander, 39, 69, 115
Hancock, Fort, 151
Hancock, Judge William, 81

Hancock's Bridge, N.J., 80–83
  Hancock House in, 81, 82–83
  massacre at, 82–83
  Shourd House in, 83
Hand, Col. Edward, 31
Harlem Heights, Battle of, 69
Hartley, Col. Thomas, 153, 154
Hasbrouck House (Newburgh, N.Y.), 41, 49
Hays, John, 70
Hays, Mrs. John, see Pitcher, Molly
Head of Elk, Md., 87, 103, 127
Heath, Gen. William, 9
Henry, Patrick, 128
Hermitage, The (Trenton, N.J.), 28
Hessian Hill, 88–89
Hessians, 11, 22, 52, 55, 57, 68, 87, 119, 138–141
  at Battle of Brandywine, 88–89, 91, 92, 103, 104, 105, 109
  at Battle of Trenton, 23, 27, 28, 29, 30, 32, 33, 38, 72
Hewitt, Mrs. Mary T., 81, 82, 83
Holmes, Col. Asher, 80
Hopkinson, Francis, 123, 124
Howe, Gen. Sir William, 6, 9, 15, 16, 23, 30, 33, 38, 61, 62, 75, 111, 127, 132, 135, 136, 138
  and Battle of Brandywine, 89, 93, 95, 97, 99, 100, 102, 104, 110
  Philadelphia campaign of (1777–78), 85–141
Huddy, Joseph, 60
Hudson Highlands, 9, 62–63
Hudson River and Valley, 6, 7, 53, 87
Hughes, Joseph, 124

Independence Hall and Square (Philadelphia), 119, 120–121
  Assembly Room at, 121
Indians (see also Tory-Indian forces), 76, 92, 150, 151, 156, 160–161
  in border settlements, 142
Indian trails, 154
Irish immigrants, 74
Iroquois Confederation, 156, 160–161
Iroquois Indians, 55
  Battle of Wyoming and, 150, 151
  Sullivan's campaign against, 142–161

Jägers, 11, 28, 69, 72
Jeffers, Emmet, 101
Jefferson, Thomas, 115, 124
Jeffries Ford, 100

Jenkins, Fort, 150, 152
Jenkins, John, 152
Jockey Hollow Cemetery, 50
Jockey Hollow site (Morristown, N.J.), 47–52
  army hospital at, 49–50
  Grande Parade at, 51
  Pennsylvania Line mutiny at, 48, 51
  Sugar Loaf Hill at, 49
  Wick House at, 48–49
Johnson, Rut, 24
Johnston House (Germantown, Pa.), 129
Jones, John Paul, 122
Jones, Samuel, 104

Kennett Meetinghouse (Kennett Square, Pa.), 88, 91
Kennett Meetinghouse, Old (Kennett Square, Pa.), 88, 90, 91
Kennett Square, Pa., 88, 90, 91, 99
Keyes, Lt. Timothy, 152
King of Prussia, Pa., 116
King's Mountain, 77
Kip's Bay (Manhattan Island), 10, 69
Knox, Gen. Henry, 49
Knyphausen, Baron von, 6, 27, 29, 32, 52, 53, 54, 56, 57, 61, 64–65, 87, 88, 89, 91, 92, 97, 98, 105, 115–116, 129

Lafayette, George Washington, 94
Lafayette, Marquis de, 45, 62, 63, 64, 93, 94, 97, 107, 108–109, 115, 123
Lafayette House (Chadd's Ford village, Pa.), 94
Lambertville, N.J., 26, 61
Lee, Gen. Charles, 9, 14, 15, 20, 61, 122
  background and character of, 62
  at Battle of Monmouth, 62, 63, 64, 65, 66–67, 68, 71–72
  capture of, 15–16, 61
Lee, Fort (Fort Constitution), 15, 70
  capture of, 6, 10, 11, 12
  planned restoration of, 13–14
  site of, 12–13
Leutze, Emanuel, 18
Liberty bell (Bridgeton, N.J.), 78
Liberty Bell (Philadelphia), 119, 121
Liberty Trails (Pa.), 90
Lincoln, Gen. Benjamin, 53
Little Egg Harbor (Tuckerton, N.J.), 76, 77
Livingston, William, 54
Long Island, Battle of, 20, 69, 89
Longwood Gardens, 99, 100
Loring, Mrs. Joshua, 15

Lossing, Benson J., 151
Love, Nancy, 126
Ludwig, Molly ("Molly Pitcher"), 70–71

McKee City, N.J., 77
McKonkey, Samuel, 16, 23, 24
McKonkey Ferry, 16, 23–24
McKonkey Ferry House, 23–25
Madison, James, 115
Malta Island (Delaware River), 18, 23
Manhattan Island (see also New York City), 9
Martin, Joseph Plumb, 49, 52, 75
Mawhood, Col. Charles, 35, 36–37, 38, 39, 80, 81
Maxwell, Gen. William ("Scotch Willie"), 55, 87, 88, 90, 91, 92, 98, 109
Meetinghouse Road, 97, 107
Mercer, Fort, 118, 119, 135, 137, 138–141
    directions to, 138
    Hessian attack on, 138–140
    memorial column at, 140
    Whitall House at, 140, 141
Mercer, Gen. Hugh, 35–36, 37
Mercer County, N.J., 16
Merlin, 135
Mifflin, Fort, 118, 119, 132–138, 140
    bombproofs and ramparts of, 137
    casualties at, 136
    design and construction of, 134
    directions to, 132–133
    history of, 137
    siege of, 132, 134–137
Mifflin, Gen. Thomas, 117, 134
Mincock Island, 76, 77
Miralles, Don Juan de, 45
Mohawk Valley, 143
Monckton, Lt. Col. Henry, 60, 66, 69, 70
Monmouth, Battle of, 6, 7, 55, 59–73, 110, 112
    casualties of, 72
    scope of, 61–62, 64
    significance of, 72–73
Monmouth battlefield, 75
    Battle Orchard at, 67–68, 70, 71
    Comb's Hill at, 60, 68, 71
    Craig House at, 71
    development of, 63–64
    directions to, 59
    Lee's line in, 66, 68
    "Molly Pitcher's Spring" at, 59, 70
    Tennent Church and battlefield overlook at, 59, 60, 69, 70, 71
    Tennent parsonage at, 60, 67–68, 70, 71, 72
    Washington-Lee meeting (marker) on, 67
Monmouth Battlefield State Park, 63–64
    plans for development of, 64
Monmouth Battle Monument, 65
Monmouth County, N.J., 75
Monmouth County Historical Society, 65, 66
Monmouth Courthouse (Freehold), N.J., 60, 63, 64, 65, 70
Monroe, James, 20, 29
Montgomery, Gen. Richard, 53
Montresor, Capt. John, 134, 137
Moore, Benjamin, 21
Moore, Capt. James, 21
Morris, Robert, 123, 125
Morris Plains, N.J., 52
Morristown, N.J. (see also Jockey Hollow site), 6, 39, 43–52, 53, 57, 74
    Ford mansion in, 44–45
    Fort Nonsense in, 46–47
    Knox's artillery camp at, 51
    museum in, 45, 46
    restoration of, 49–51
Morristown National Historic Park, 44
Mount Vernon, 41–42, 45
Muhlenberg, Fort, 116, 118
Muhlenberg, Gen. John Peter Gabriel, 130
Mullica River, 75, 76
Museums
    in Chadd's Ford village, 93
    in Connecticut Farms (Union), N.J., 56
    at Delaware Crossing site, 24–25
    at Fort Mercer, 141
    in Freehold, N.J., 65, 66, 70, 71
    in Greenwich, N.J., 78
    in Hancock's Bridge, N.J., 82–83
    in Morristown, N.J., 45, 46
    in Philadelphia, 122, 125, 126
    in Tioga Point (Athens, Pa.), 155, 156
    in Trenton, N.J. (Old Barracks), 32
Musgrave, Lt. Col. Thomas, 130
Mystic Island (N.J.), 77

National Park Service, 44, 45
Naval forces
    American, 122, 132, 135, 139–140
    British, 75, 79, 132, 135–136, 137, 139
Newark, N.J., 14, 23
New Brunswick, N.J., 14, 23, 30, 31, 38, 39, 43, 52, 63
Newburgh, N.Y., 41
New England states, 9, 53, 142
New Hall (Philadelphia), 120

New Hope, Pa., 26
New Jersey
  campaign of 1776-77 in, 9-58
  ocean counties of, 74-84
  settlement and growth of, 3-6, 75
  strategic significance of, 3
New Jersey militia, 15-16, 61-62, 87, 127
New Jersey State Department of Conservation
    and Economic Development, 64
Newtown Battlefield, 156-161
  Boyd-Parker Memorial in, 160-161
  Sullivan Hill and Mounment in, 157
New Windsor, N.Y., 49
New York City, 15, 23, 59-60, 62, 63, 85,
    151
Niagara, Fort, 143, 151, 156, 161
Nonsense, Fort (Morristown, N.J.), 46-47
North Castle (Armonk), N.Y., 14, 62, 67
Northwest Territory, 142, 161

Ocean counties (N.J.), 74-84
Old Sullivan Trail (Pa.), 146
Old Tappan, N.J., 112
Osborne's Hill (Brandywine battlefield), 102,
    103, 104-105, 107

Paine, Thomas, 22, 132
Palisades Interstate Park Commission, 13
Palisades Park, Cornwallis's headquarters at,
    10-11
Paoli, Pa., 110-115, 116
  Wayne House at, 113-115
Paoli massacre, 111-112, 113
Paoli Memorial Grounds, 111
Parker, Sgt. Michael, 160
Peale, Charles Willson, 39, 126
Pemberton Hall (Philadelphia), 120
Penn, Fort, 147
Penn, William, 92, 125
Pennington, N.J., 23
Pennington Road, 25, 26, 27-28
Pennsylvania
  size and significance of, 6
  Sullivan's March in, 143-156
Pennsylvania encampment (see also Washing-
    ton Crossing State Park, Pa.), 16-21
  Bowman Hill and Tower at, 19, 21
  Durham boat at, 17, 18
  Ferry Inn at, 16-17
  Memorial Building at, 17-18
  Pidcock's gristmill at, 20
  Thompson-Neely House at, 19-20, 21
Pennsylvania Historical and Museum Commis-
    sion, 143

Pennsylvania Line, mutiny of, 48, 51
Pennsylvania Line encampment, 49
Perth Amboy, N.J., 38, 43
Philadelphia, Pa., 15, 17, 22, 30, 41, 45, 51,
    59, 75, 110, 112, 136
  accommodations and transportation in, 119-
    120
  Army-Navy Museum in, 122
  Betsy Ross's House in, 119, 123
  British occupation of, 6, 61, 74, 115, 126,
    137
  and campaign of 1777-78, 6, 85-141
  as center of campaigns, 3, 6
  Carpenters' Hall in, 119, 121-122
  Christ Church in, 122-123
  Christ Church burial ground in, 123, 124
  City Hall in, 125
  Elfreth's Alley in, 125
  Franklin's Home in, 124
  Germantown sites in, see Germantown, Pa.
  Independence Hall and Square in, 119, 120-
    121
  Independence National Historic Park in,
    119, 120
  Liberty Bell in, 119, 121
  Man Full of Trouble tavern in, 126
  Mikveh Israel burial ground in, 125
  old Friends Meetinghouse in, 123
  restaurants in, 126
  St. Peter's Church and graveyard in, 126,
    129
  Society Hill in, 125-126
  Tomb of the Unknown Soldier of the Rev-
    olution in, 125
  Tourist Information Center in, 120, 126
Philadelphia Associators, 22
Philadelphia Guide magazine, 126
Philadelphia Preservation Commission, 125
Phillipsburg, N.J., 146
Picnic and recreation facilities
  at Chadd's Ford, Pa., 94
  at Fort Mercer, 141
  at Jockey Hollow (Morristown, N.J.), 51
  at Palisades Shore Trail, 10, 12
  at Valley Forge, 24, 117
  at Washington Crossing State Park (N.J.
    and Pa.), 14, 20, 21
Pidcock, John, 19-20
Pierce, Jacob, 91
Pitcher, Molly, 70-71
Pittsburgh, Pa., 143
Pittston, Fort, 152
Pittston, Pa., 151-152
Plain Dealer, 77

Pompton, N.J., 53, 57
Pompton Lakes, N.J., Jersey Line mutiny at,
    51–52
Port Island (*see also* Mifflin, Fort), 132, 133,
    134
Potter's Tavern (Bridgeton, N.J.), 77–78
Prescott, Gen. Richard, 61
Princeton, Battle of, 6, 32, 33–39, 57, 74, 127
Princeton, N.J., 14, 23, 30, 31, 51, 63
    Clark House in, 36
    Mercer Heights in, 34, 35, 36
    Mercer Oak in, 34, 36
    Nassau Hall in, 36, 38–39
    Quaker Meetinghouse in, 35
    Rockingham site near, 40–43
Princeton Battlefield Monument, 34
Princeton University, 34, 39
Privateers, 76
Proctor, Col. Thomas, 109
Providence Island, 134
Pulaski, Count Casimir, 76–77, 107
Pulaski Legion, 76–77
Pyle, Howard, 93
Pyle's Ford, 93, 95

Rall, Col. Johann, 27, 29, 30
Ramapo Hills, 43
Reading, Pa., 115, 127
Recreation facilities, *see* picnic and recreation
    facilities
Red Bank, N.J. (*see also* Mercer, Fort), 119,
    132, 134
Rhode Island, Battle of, 140
Ring, Benjamin, 95, 96
Ringwood, N.J., 43
Roadstown, N.J., 79
Rochambeau, Comte de, 45
Roche Fontaine, Capt. Bichet de, 48
Rockingham, 40–43
Rockingham—Washington's Headquarters
    (Cobb), 41
Ross, Elizabeth (Betsy), 119, 123
Ross, George, 124
Rush, Benjamin, 124

St. Clair, Gen. Arthur, 33, 48
St. John, Oliver, 25
St. Lawrence River, 53
Salem, N.J., 81, 84
Salem County Historical Society, 84
Salem Historical Association, 81
Salomon, Haym, 125
Sanderson, Christian, 95
Sanderson House, 96

Sandy Hook, N.J., 63, 70, 151
Sandy Hollow, Pa., 97, 108–109
Saratoga, Battle of, 61, 63, 110, 122
Saratoga battlefield, 49
Sconneltown, Pa., 97, 101
Scottish immigrants, 74
Seneca Indians, 156
Shackamaxon Society, Inc., 134
Shaw's Bridge, 100
Shays, Capt. Daniel, 159
Shippen Mansion (Kennett Square, Pa.), 89
Ships, *see* Naval forces
Shourd, Thomas, House (Hancock's Bridge,
    N.J.), 83
Shrieve, Col. Israel, 155
Simcoe's Rangers, 65, 77, 80, 81–82
Smith, Lt. Col. Samuel, 135, 136
Soldier at Morristown, A (Martin), 52
Springfield, N.J., raid on, 6, 52–58, 87
Staten Island, N.Y., 52–53, 54, 63, 74, 87
Stephen, Gen. Adam, 98, 99, 102, 107
Steuben, Gen. (Baron) von, 61, 69, 117
Stevenson, R. L., 93
Stockton, Richard, 35, 40
Stony Brook, N.J., 34, 35
Stony Point, N.Y., 54, 112, 135
Strode's Mill, 102
Stroud, Richard, 103
Sullivan, Fort, 155–156
Sullivan, Gen. John, 7, 16, 22, 25, 29, 30, 32,
    39, 55, 95, 98, 102, 107, 127, 130
    campaign against Iroquois of, 142–161
Sullivan's March, 143–156
Sullivan's March, route of
    Brinker's Mill on, 147
    campsites on, 152–153, 154
    Fort Wyoming on, 149
    Heller's Tavern on, 147
    Learned's Tavern on, 147, 148
Sullivan's Trail-Wyoming Mountain, 148
Sullivan's Way, 26, 27
Sullivan Trail, 146
Sullivan Trail, Old, 146
Sully, Thomas, 128
Susquehanna River, 7, 150, 152–153, 155, 156
    flooding of, 143–146
Sutton, Ann Hawkes, 15

Taylor, John G., 107
Tea Burners Farm, 79
Tennent, N.J., 59, 60, 65, 67, 69
Thatcher, Dr. James, 49
Thompson, Charles, 121

Thompson-Neely House (Washington Crossing State Park), 19–20, 21
Ticonderoga, Fort, 43, 87
Tilton, Dr. James, 50
Tioga Point (Athens), Pa., 143, 147, 151, 154–156
Tories, Tory sentiment, 141
  in New Jersey, 6, 27, 33, 56, 74, 80
  in Pennsylvania, 6, 33, 150
Tory-Indian forces, 142, 149, 150, 157–158
Townsend, Joseph, 101, 102–103, 104–106
Townsend, William, 101, 103
Treaty of Paris, 39
Trent, William, 33
Trent, William, House, 33
Trenton, Battles of, 6, 25–33, 74, 127
  First, 26–31
  Second (Assunpink Creek), 31–33
Trenton, N.J., 14, 15, 17, 21, 25, 52
  accommodations in, 26
  Battle Monument in, 25, 28–29
  Hessian surrender site in, 30
  Old Barracks in, 29, 32–33
  routes taken to, 25–26, 27–28
  St. Michael's Church in, 29
  traffic and parking in, 28
  Trent House in, 33
  Washington's stand at, site of, 31
Trimble's Ford, 99
Trois Rivières, Canada, 55
Tuckerton (Little Egg Harbor), N.J., 76, 77

Union, N.J., see Connecticut Farms
Unknown soldier, first, 20
Unknown Soldier of the Revolution, Tomb of (Philadelphia), 124–125
Upsala (Germantown, Pa.), 131
Urbanization, historic sites affected by, 7, 27, 75, 119, 127, 151

Valley Forge, 7, 55, 60, 61, 74, 82, 115–118, 137
  directions to, 116
  Washington's Headquarters at, 118
  winter visit to, 24, 116–117
Valley Forge State Park, 116–118
  Visitor's Center and tour road at, 117–118
van Merckel, Peter, 39
Vigilant, 136
Virginia, 6, 77
von Donop, Col. Carl Emil Kurt, 138–139, 140, 141

Ware, Joseph, 83
War of 1812, 137, 156, 161

Washington, Fort, 70
  fall of, 9, 27
Washington, George, 35, 37, 46, 53, 54, 57, 76, 85, 111, 115, 122, 126, 135, 136, 142, 148
  and Battle of Brandywine, 90, 94, 98, 102, 107, 108, 109–110
  and Battle of Germantown, 127, 128, 129, 130, 132
  and Battle of Monmouth, 61–63, 64, 66–67, 68, 70, 71–72
  and Battles of Trenton, 29, 33
  Congress and, see Continental Congress
  Delaware River crossing of, 3, 6, 15, 18, 21–26, 33
  at Delaware River encampment, 2, 6, 15
  portrayals of, 17, 18, 39, 95
  reputation and fame of, 3, 42–43
  at Valley Forge, 116, 117, 118
Washington, Martha, 41–42, 46, 117, 122, 126, 128
Washington, Capt. William, 20, 29
Washington Crossing State Park (N.J.), 21
  Bear Tavern in, 25, 26
  Continental Lane in, 25
  Flag Museum in, 24, 25
  McKonkey Ferry House in, 23–25
Washington Crossing State Park (Pa.), 14
  Bowman Hill and Tower in, 19
  burial spot at, 20–21
  Durham boat at, 17, 18
  General Sullivan Pavilion in, 20
  Memorial Building in, 17–18
  Pidcock gristmill in, 20
  Thompson-Neely House, 19–20
Washington Crossing the Delaware (Leutze), 18
Washington Grove (N.J.), 21–22
Washington's birthday, special events on, 25
Washington's Farewell Address, 122
Watchung Mountains, 14, 43, 57
Wayne, Anthony, 113
Wayne, Gen. Anthony ("Mad Anthony"), 48, 51, 64, 68, 69, 80, 82, 107, 109, 130
  and Paoli, Pa., 111–115
Wayne, Polly, 114
Wayne family, 113–114
Wayne House (Paoli, Pa.), 113–115
Westchester County, N.Y., 9, 141
West Point, N.Y., 53, 71
Whigs, 33, 150
Whitall House (Fort Mercer), 140, 141
White Clay Creek, 87
White Horse, Pa., 110

White Plains, Battle of, 9
Whiting, Lt. Col. Daniel, 154
Wick, Henry, 48
Wick, Henry, House (Morristown, N.J.), 48–
    49
Wick, Tempe, 48–49
Wilkes-Barre, Pa., 148–152
  Battle of Wyoming at, sites of, 149–151
  Bloody Rock in, 151
Wilkes-Barre Fort, *see* Wyoming, Fort
Williamsburg, Va., 78
Wilmington, Del., 87, 101, 110

Wilson, Capt. William, 60, 66, 69–70
Wind Gap, Pa., 147, 148
Wintermoot, Fort, 150
World Wars I and II, 137
Wyeth, Andrew, 93
Wyeth, James, 93
Wyeth, N. C., 93
Wyoming, Battle and Massacre of, 143, 147,
    149–151, 153

York, Pa., 115, 121
Yorktown, Battle of, 3, 10, 110, 122, 141